When students become engaged with subject matter and are given opportunities to think and interpret, they retain more knowledge and understand it more deeply. The Architecture of Learning *is a welcome book at this time in our development of mind, brain, and education connections. This book provides neuro*-logical *and teacher-friendly guidance for designing instruction that aligns with current research in how the brain learns.*

Judy Willis, M.D., M.Ed.
Board-certified Neurologist and Middle School Teacher
Author of *Research-Based Strategies to Ignite Student Learning*

This is a fascinating book presenting a unique approach integrating teaching theory with the latest findings in neuroscience. It provides a compelling argument for how children learn and how best to teach them. It gives teachers and professionals a structure or architecture to help guide practice. The book is very well written using analogies and real-life examples to illustrate the theory. I found it clear, easy to read and yet thought-provoking. I would thoroughly recommend this book to teachers and other professionals involved in education.

Dr. Jonathan Reed
Clinical Psychologist/Neuropsychologist
Recolo Ltd. (UK)
Editor, *Child Neuropsychology* published by Wiley Blackwell

Dr. Washburn masterfully unfolds the Architecture of Learning Blueprint to reveal an instructional design which has the potential to transform both classroom and individual learning experiences. He has included vivid illustrations and real-life scenarios that bring clarity and a deeper understanding of the Architecture of Learning structure. The five strands of learning presented in The Architecture of Learning *facilitate thinking beyond classroom experiences into life situations. The foundation of a rich experience followed by comprehension, elaboration, and application of that experience enables students to build relevant connections as the lessons progress. Additionally,* The Architecture of Learning *provides tools that equip learners to integrate knowledge in other situations. Dr. Washburn's discussion of assessments identifies best practices in evaluating students. He emphasizes the necessity to match student assessment with classroom instruction. I am convinced that teachers who implement Dr. Washburn's Architecture of Learning Blueprints will provide their students with experiences that foster critical thinking, facilitate discovery, and form lifelong learners.*

Dr. Karen L. Upton, Principal
Norfolk Christian Lower School
Norfolk, VA

The Architecture of Learning *offers a useful, practical framework for developing instruction. It is an enjoyable read, written clearly with lively, memorable examples.*

Tommi Himberg
Finnish Centre of Excellence in Interdisciplinary Music Research
Department of Music, University of Jyväskylä
Finland

Kevin Washburn offers life-changing insights from both theory and practice through his applied architectural principles. A lifetime of study and application gives Kevin an urgent, yet practical message for those interested in transformational approaches that work for our era. This book will change the way you think, learn and assess, with intelligence-fair results.

Ellen Weber, Ph.D.
MITA International Brain Center Director
Pittsford, NY

Teachers enter classrooms with a toolbox full of instructional strategies. These "tools of the trade" are often haphazardly and ineffectively used when there is not a clear plan for instruction or a clear understanding of the process of learning. The Architecture of Learning instructional design allows teachers the opportunity to effectively put their "tools" to work to become master craftsmen of teaching as they design instruction that builds learning. Teachers trained to use this research-based instructional model learn to become draftsmen (of instructional blueprints), architects (of instructional design and concepts), builders (of learning) and inspectors (as they assess learning, provide feedback for improvement, and look for the essential elements of the learning process). We have used this model of instruction at our school for several years and can truly say that the Architecture of Learning instructional design has improved classroom teaching and, more importantly, has produced long-lasting learning that endures beyond the final exam!

Tasha Holliday, Assistant Head of School
First Presbyterian Day School
Jackson, MS

Like architecture, learning is not attained by happenstance, but is a matter of design. Great design arranges and utilizes necessary elements to meet the needs of the environment and achieve its purpose. Like an architect, Kevin provides a blueprint that shows us how to carefully build the bricks of learning (experience, comprehension, elaboration, application, and intention) into a master plan that constructs meaningful learning. Architecture of Learning *offers a blueprint for us to become masterful designers of learning.*

Rob Jacobs
Blogger, Education Innovation

THE ARCHITECTURE OF LEARNING

Designing Instruction for the Learning Brain

KEVIN D. WASHBURN

Kelley,
Teach. You are
changing lives!
Kevin D. Washburn
10-21-2011

Clerestory press

The Architecture of Learning:
Designing Instruction for the Learning Brain

Published in the United States by Clerestory Press
A division of Clerestory Learning/Make Way for Books, LLC
Pelham, AL
www.clerestorylearning.com

Publisher Cataloging-In-Publication Data

Washburn, Kevin David.
The Architecture of learning : designing instruction for the learning brain / Kevin D. Washburn.
p. cm.
ISBN 9780984345908
Includes bibliographical references and index.
1. Teaching. 2. Learning, Psychology of. 3. Instructional systems—Design. 4. Teachers—Training of. 5. Education—Study and teaching.
I. Title.
LB1060 W37 2010
370.15—dc22 2009941976

Book Design Julia Washburn
Index AfterWords Editorial Services
Proofreading Rich Klin
Cover Images
©iStockphoto.com/ktsimage
©iStockphoto.com/ImageMediaGroup
Back Cover Portrait Barry C. Altmark Photography

Printed in the United States of America on acid-free paper

FIRST EDITION

1 2 3 4 5 6 7 8 9 10 CPC 15 14 13 12 11 10

For Julia, my beautiful wife, whose insights are always valuable and whose faith never wavers.

ACKNOWLEDGMENTS

To friends who have proven authentic and provided the courage to press on: David and Marjorie Calvanico, colleagues, friends, insightful editors, and great dinner companions; Michael and Daniele Evans and Doug and Patti Moore, true friendship's reference points; Dr. Alan and Joan Graustein, for refusing to allow me to collect dust; Mary Lou Sharpee, the epitome of colleague and friend; Rita Hoffman, who provided insights into Architecture of Learning's potential depth; Kim Franklin of Trinity Western University—thanks for igniting my thinking about narrative; Dr. Judy Willis, a source of optimism, advice, and encouragement just when it was needed.

To my teachers, all of them, from W. A. Olmstead Elementary School in Harpursville, NY through the graduate faculties of various institutions, who taught me more than the content of their lessons; Dr. Arden Post of Calvin College, a teacher, a mentor, an inspiration, and one who taught and modeled that being professional means never ceasing to grow.

To all the educators to whom I have had the privilege of presenting Architecture of Learning—thanks for your questions, your insights, and your work with the model.

To my family, especially my parents, whose personal sacrifices provided opportunities to learn, and my in-laws, who encourage my efforts and listen to my ramblings.

To Mr. John Paine, editor extraordinaire, who helped me see from a reader's perspective, guided my head and hand through the revision process, and encouraged me to pursue publication.

To Kurt Andersen, whose radio program *Studio 360* provides a relevant and intriguing morsel every week, and Dr. Ginger Campbell, whose *Brain Science Podcast* is a continuous stream of valuable information.

Finally, to Susan Morris, Dr. Azalia Moore, and in loving memory of Dr. Rebecca Carwile, for believing I had something worth sharing.

CONTENTS

THE ARCHITECTURE OF LEARNING

THE FOUNDATION

Defining *Teacher* and *Designing* Instruction

He greeted us at the classroom door—a tall, thin man with graying sideburns, bright eyes framed by dark-rimmed glasses, and a different colored sweater vest for each day of the week. His teaching led my ten-year-old mind through exciting worlds—outer space, amphibians, the water cycle, and the human digestive system. "What makes food travel *down* the esophagus," he asked, "while we sit *up* at the table?" Having just finished a unit on the Earth, we suggested that gravity pulls food *down* the esophagus while we sit *up* and eat. That seemed reasonable enough. After all, he had taught us the properties of gravity.

The next day he cleared a space at the front of the classroom. He reminded us of our gravity proposition and then called up a student. Placing a carpet sample on the floor, he asked the student to use the classroom wall for support while performing a headstand. On the floor he then placed a glass of water with an angled straw sticking out of the top and asked the student to take a drink. The student sucked on the straw, and we waited for the water to dribble out of his nose. But to our surprise, our fellow student swallowed that water! "Muscles in the esophagus push food downward to the stomach," our teacher explained. "Gravity does not pull food into the stomach."

He could have skipped the headstanding student and straw demonstration and just told us this fact. Yet he was prompting us to think in order to produce lasting learning. He designed an effective *teaching* lesson because he understood *learning.*

In contrast, a high school math teacher of mine, who also owned a large sweater vest collection, would leap from topic to topic, presenting disjointed concepts and skills like pieces collected from different jigsaw puzzles. Many of us frequently failed his tests, which we retook and corrected repeatedly until we "learned" the material. Though he knew his content, his teaching was ineffective because he did not understand the process of learning.

The term *teacher* implies learning. Dictionaries define *teacher* as an individual who causes another *to learn* something. If students do not learn, the teacher has been whistling in the wind.

Recent news headlines blazon the shortcomings of standardized test results. They accuse teachers of neglecting specific groups of students and announce state government takeovers of "failing" schools. What drives such accusations? *A lack of learning.* The public expects teachers to produce learning.

To be effective, a teacher must align instructional methods with learning's cognitive processes, the brain's ways of constructing understanding and forming memories. Although "teachable moments" do occur spontaneously, a good teacher provides *consistently* effective instruction. Learning is produced through deliberate instructional design.

Instructional design differs from *lesson planning,* the term we traditionally use to describe a teacher's pre-instruction preparation. Though *planning* implies forethought, *design* reaches beyond the standard plan. Designers communicate by *intentionally* combining elements. For example, technology writer Robin Williams claims graphic designers use four "interconnected" elements to convey ideas: proximity, alignment, repetition, and contrast.[1] Similarly, teachers combine four elements to design instruction: an understanding of students, a knowledge of learning, an awareness of subject matter types, and a sequence of classroom activities that mirrors how the brain processes new data. Combining these elements requires more than traditional lesson planning; it requires instructional *design*.

You have probably had teachers who planned lessons but failed to design instruction. In my undergraduate days, I had a professor who carried a large three-ring notebook. When he opened that notebook and set it down on a lectern, class began. He "taught" by reading his notebook aloud while we tried to reproduce his treasured tome in our own notebooks. I cannot recall a single concept or skill I learned in that class. Even if "planned," lessons read from lecterns limit learning because they fail to engage essential learning processes.

Contrast this with an effective learning experience. During those same college days I enjoyed a master teacher in an educational psychology course. This professor came to class with carefully crafted instruction, a distinct New Jersey accent, and enough energy to engage our attention. Group work, discussions, lectures, textbook reading—she *designed* every activity to optimize learning.

Such contrasting experiences illustrate an important principle: *the quality of a teacher's instructional design often determines the quality of a teacher's instruction*. Research confirms this: "Many breakdowns in student learning may be a function of poor classroom curriculum design," suggests Robert J. Marzano in *What Works in Schools*. "...the expert teacher has acquired a wide array of instructional strategies along with the knowledge of when these strategies might be the most useful."[2] Informed instructional design produces effective teaching.

Designing instruction yields two outcomes that improve teaching. First, it deepens the teacher's mastery of the material. By crafting a design, he identifies connections between the subject matter and personal experiences. These connections deepen his own understanding of the subject matter to be taught. Researchers Bransford, Brown, and Cocking stress the importance of this: "Expert teachers know the structure of their disciplines, and this knowledge provides them with cognitive roadmaps that guide the assignments they give students, the assessments they use to gauge students' progress, and the questions they ask in the give and take of classroom life. In short, their knowledge of the discipline and their knowledge of pedagogy interact."[3]

Second, designing instruction engages a teacher in selecting effective methods and putting them in a logical sequence. "It is perhaps self-evident," explains Marzano, "that more effective teachers use more effective instructional strategies."[4] Effective teachers produce learning that endures. Educators Diane Halpern and Milton Hakel explain that effective instruction is needed because as teachers, "we are teaching for some time in the future when the knowledge and skills that are learned in our classes are tested in contexts that we cannot know and with assessments that we cannot design. We need to provide an education that lasts a lifetime, which means thinking beyond the end of the semester, and let the learning principles for long-term retention and flexible recall guide our teaching practices."[5]

Teachers like my elementary science teacher understand learning. Understanding learning improves instructional design. Improved instructional design generates better teaching. Understanding *learning* produces effective *teaching*.

An Author's Note

I have been a teacher for more than twenty years, and I write from this perspective. My interest in neurocognitive research is a by-product of my passion for enabling learning. I find learning, memory, creativity, and critical thinking especially intriguing topics, and I hope my findings in these areas have been accurately translated into tools for my colleagues.

Instruction can produce learning that lasts beyond the school year, learning that enriches the learner's life. Students depend on teachers to possess the ability to teach what they know effectively. Hopefully, this book will enable all of us to *design* better instruction so we teach with greater effectiveness. I know my understanding of learning and ability to design instruction have benefitted from writing it.

Chapter 1

BUILDING BLOCKS

Understanding How Students Learn

"All of the following words contain two vowels," the puzzle-meister explained. While driving to church, I usually listen to the Sunday morning puzzle. "Simply drop one of the vowels to form a new word," he continued. "Then replace the dropped vowel and drop the word's other vowel to form another new word. For example, from *feast* you can form *fest* and *fast*. Ready?" I multitask, listening, thinking, driving and occasionally shouting answers. "The first word is *wheat*."

"*What* and *whet*," I shout. Too bad radio is a one-way audio experience.

Imagine you're a passenger in my car on this particular Sunday morning. What words would you form from *found*? Remember, drop one vowel to form the first word. Then replace it and drop the other vowel to form the second word. (Answers: *fund* and *fond*.) *Heard*? (*herd* and *hard*.) *Bloat*? (*blat* and *blot*.) What a difference one letter can make!

I find the alphabet fascinating. Letters form the visual building blocks of words, and different combinations create different words. Altering a single letter can dramatically change meaning.

Like words, the process of learning contains building blocks that when arranged in various combinations foster different types of learning.

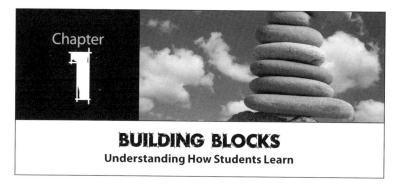

Learning's Building Blocks

Five processes, or building blocks, interact to produce learning:

- **Experience**
- **Comprehension**
- **Elaboration**
- **Application**
- **Intention**

Through *experience,* your brain gains raw sensory data. During *comprehension,* the brain sorts, labels, and organizes the raw sensory data. Through *elaboration,* the brain examines the organized data for patterns, recalls relevant prior experiences, and blends the new data with your experiences to construct understanding. During *application* the brain practices using the new skill knowledge. Finally, through *intention,* the brain uses the new understanding or skills in widened contexts.

Experience

We have heard the adage all our lives: "Experience is the best teacher." By itself, though, experience is not learning. It does, however, play an essential role in learning: it provides sensory data to the brain. As an individual interacts with the environment, her nervous system relays data upward to her brain's sensory registers. This data represents learning's raw material.

The problem is, too much data in too little time overwhelms the brain. It registers a rapid flow of data, but the flood prevents the additional mental activity required for learning.

Let's take a simple example. I enjoy roller coasters. Nothing makes me laugh like racing over looping tracks in connected cars with constantly changing stimuli bombarding my senses. "Wow, that was awesome!" I exclaim as the ride ends and I walk down the exit ramp. Friends who chose to "sit this one out" begin to inquire: "What made it awesome? How is this ride better than the one on the other side of the park?" Though I try, I cannot detail the ride's sequence of thrills. At best, I might remember a few features ("The loop twisted upside-down!") and an overall feeling ("It felt like I was floating!"), but the coaster's details came too fast for my brain to do more than register their existence within the passing moment. My memory-forming processes had no time to engage.

Data floods of a similar nature occur in school. When I taught in a departmentalized middle school, I saw what I called the "seventh-period shutdown." Students came to the day's final class period looking like they had ridden six different forty-five-minute roller coasters. Each one, operated by a different teacher, bombarded them with new information, and the rising data flood overwhelmed their brains' capacities to process it. I knew they would go home at night, sit down to dinner, and face the age-old question: "So, what did you learn in school today?" They would give the inevitable answer: "Nothing."

Imagine all that incoming data as an assortment of loose change. Did you ever own one of those banks that sorts coins? Experience resembles dropping loose change into such a bank. If the bank had an exit hole that coins fell through before reaching the sorting section, the coins would be like experiences that the brain didn't process. Data not processed is short-lived. Visual data lasts "only about a fifth of a second,"[1] and auditory data exhibits a similarly short life span.[2]

To learn, the brain must do more with the coins. "We often talk of knowledge as though it could be divorced from thinking, as though it could be gathered up by one person and given to another in the form of a collection of sentences to remember," explains critical thinking expert Richard Paul. "When we talk in this way we forget that knowledge, by its very nature, depends on thought. Knowledge is produced by thought, analyzed by thought, comprehended by thought, organized, evaluated, maintained, and transformed by thought. Knowledge exists, properly speaking, only in minds that have comprehended it and constructed it through thought."[3] Learning requires mental activity. Raw experience *by itself* is not the best teacher.

If the brain grabs the coins and keeps them from a rapid exit, it can begin identifying and sorting the coins. It can begin constructing long-term memory. As **FIGURE 1.1** shows, working memory, the brain's systems that maintain "information in short-term store for the purpose of executing a task-specific goal," is the gateway to long-term storage.[4] Working memory holds the "coins" as the brain comprehends them.

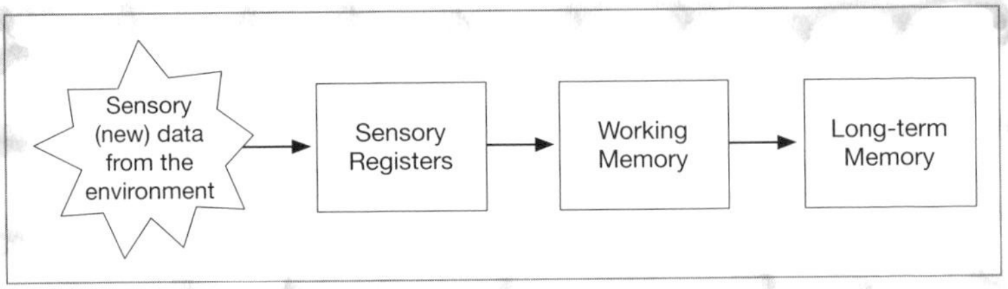

FIGURE 1.1 From Environmental Stimuli to Long-term Memory

Comprehension

In the back of her closet, my mother kept a metal tin with a rose-covered lid that once held chocolates. She converted it to contain her extensive button collection. Some buttons had been pulled from childhood coats, others had their original display cards, and still others my mother discovered in parking lots and stairwells.

I loved sorting those buttons. I sorted them by size, shape, or color. I sorted them by the number of holes they had. I sorted them according to the type of clothing to which I imagined they belonged. I could classify those buttons in endless ways.

Imagine my mother's collected buttons as incoming sensory data. During the comprehension stage, the brain assigns labels (e.g., "red," "large," "square") and organizes data much as I sorted those buttons. In *This Is Your Brain on Music*, neuroscientist Daniel J. Levitin describes such processing as *feature extraction*: "The brain extracts basic, low-level features from the music, using specialized neural networks that decompose the signal into information about pitch, timbre, spatial location, loudness, reverberant environment, tone durations, and the onset times for different notes (and for different components of tones)."[5] In other words, the brain engages in comprehension, initially sorting music's components much like I sorted buttons.

But how does the brain label and sort nonmusical data? The primary tool that aids comprehension is language. We often talk to ourselves (at least *inside* our heads) when grasping new material. We use language both as a guide and as content for thinking. Researcher Diane Halpern describes thought and language as possessing "mutual influence," stating, "We use language not only to convey our thoughts, but also to mold and shape them."[6] Obviously not all thinking is language-based. But when we initially comprehend—label and sort—new data, we think with language.

Test this idea for yourself. Deliberately think through the information on experience detailed in the previous section. As you review **FIGURE 1.1**, you will likely initiate a mental monologue. If asked to portray your understanding in a visual form, you would likely develop a verbal explanation while creating the graphic. The process of creating the graphic could, in turn, spark additional ideas that you would initially process via words.

In fact, the actual words used for processing affect thinking. Experts Richard Paul and Linda Elder claim that a "command of distinctions" between terms shapes the content and quality of thought.[7] A lack of terminology limits processing, and a lack of additional processing via working memory prevents the new data from being learned.

Consider the experience of self-confessed vocabularian Ammon Shea. Wanting to delay the sadness of reading a book's last page, Shea decided to read one of the longest books available, the complete *Oxford English Dictionary*. Within its nearly 22,000 pages, Shea discovered words associated with known experiences for which he lacked terminology. For example, the scent that steams from pavement just as it starts to rain, he discovered, has a name: *petrichor*. Similarly, he discovered that having yellow teeth similar to those of some rodents makes one *xanthodontous*. Learning new terms such as these increased Shea's thinking about the associated experiences and concepts.[8] Knowing terms associated with a concept improves comprehension.

If repeated enough, comprehension can lead to low-level learning. For example, to merely memorize the Gettysburg Address, I would focus on restating the right words in their correct order. I can accomplish this by sequencing Lincoln's phrases and rehearsing them until I can restate the entire speech. Such material entails merely semantic memory—"thoughts that require only memorization, but no decision making, logical analysis, or reasoning."[9]

If I want to *understand* the Gettysburg Address—if I want

to grasp the *meaning* of Lincoln's words—so I can use it in the future, I must engage memory processes beyond comprehension. To build true understanding you must use "perceptual thought." That is thinking that overlays the new data with known experience and blends the two to produce meaning.[10] Your working memory must engage in elaboration.

Elaboration

First, let's take a technical look at how working memory functions. It comprises four interacting components. The *central executive* functions as a "limited capacity attentional control system," directing focus and concentration. The *phonological loop* holds and rehearses verbal and auditory-based information. The *visuo-spatial sketchpad* functions like the phonological loop, only with visually based information. The *episodic buffer* constructs "integrated representations" from new and recalled data.[11]

While the phonological loop and visuo-spatial sketchpad aid comprehension, the episodic buffer goes a step further and empowers elaboration. The episodic buffer overlays patterns formed from newly organized sensory data with long-term experiences to construct understanding (**FIGURE 1.2**). Researchers Fauconnier and Turner's term *conceptual blending* aptly describes episodic buffer activity.[12] The brain receives and sorts sensory data causing patterns to emerge. The patterns direct the brain to search its long-term memory stores for previous experiences that illustrate similar patterns. Daniel J. Levitin describes such processing as *feature integration*: "The frontal lobes access our hippocampus and regions in the interior of the temporal lobe and ask if there is anything in our memory banks that can help to understand this signal," explains Levitin. "Have I [experienced] this particular pattern before? If so, when? What does it mean?"[13] Once recalled, the previous experience provides a reference point for further thinking about the newly received data. According to Fauconnier and Turner, understanding develops as a person recognizes relevant connections between the reference point and the new data, and "blends" these ideas.[14] The blend builds the new understanding.

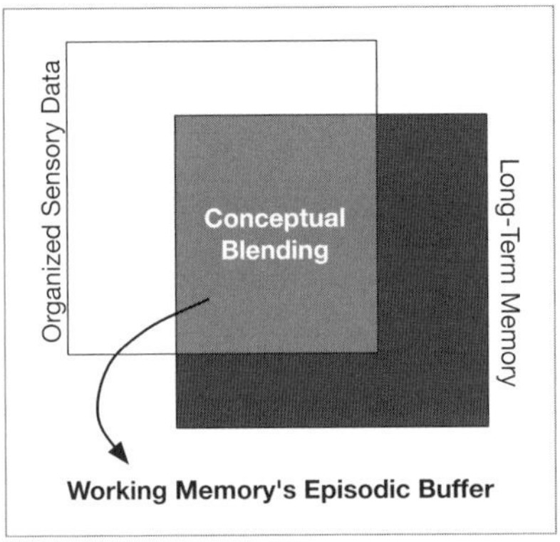

FIGURE 1.2 New and Recalled Data Blends in the Episodic Buffer

As a child, I loved finger painting. My elementary art teacher would walk around the classroom giving each of us a single-colored dollop of paint. We'd dig in, spreading it across our papers in beautifully abstract arrays. Then she'd sweep by again, this time giving each of us a different-colored dollop. Now the fun really began! We'd press our fingers into the new paint and blend it with the old paint. As the new and the old blended, different colors would emerge. We could still see the two distinct dollops represented in our artwork, but we could also see blending that created a color that possessed characteristics of both dollops, but was also different.

Through elaboration, the brain examines comprehended (i.e., labeled and sorted) data to identify patterns, uses the patterns it recognizes to recall relevant instances from long-term memory, and overlays or blends the new data with known experience. You mix the old dollop (previous experience) and a new dollop (new data) to create a new concept.

Film montage provides another useful analogy for conceptual blending. In *Three Uses of the Knife*, David Mamet explains:

> Originally the term [*montage*] meant the juxtaposition of two disparate and uninflected images in order to create in the mind of the viewer a third idea, which would advance the plot. (A man who's walking down the street turns his head and reaches tentatively in his pocket; shot of store window with a sign that says SALE; the viewer thinks, "Oh, that man would like to buy something.") The first idea juxtaposed with the second idea makes the viewer—us—create the third idea.[15]

During elaboration, the mind merges incoming data (Image 1) with prior experience (Image 2) to construct understanding and meaning (the "third idea").

FIGURE 1.3 shows the relationship between working memory, conceptual blending, and three of learning's five building blocks: experience, comprehension, and elaboration. Experience provides new data, establishing the first component for conceptual blending. Comprehension sorts, labels, and organizes the new data. Patterns emerge and trigger recall of relevant past experiences. The past experience provides a reference point, the second component for conceptual blending. Elaboration continues as working memory systems blend the new data and the reference point to construct understanding of the new data. When sufficiently processed, new data has a greater potential to reach long-term storage and, therefore, to be recalled and used.

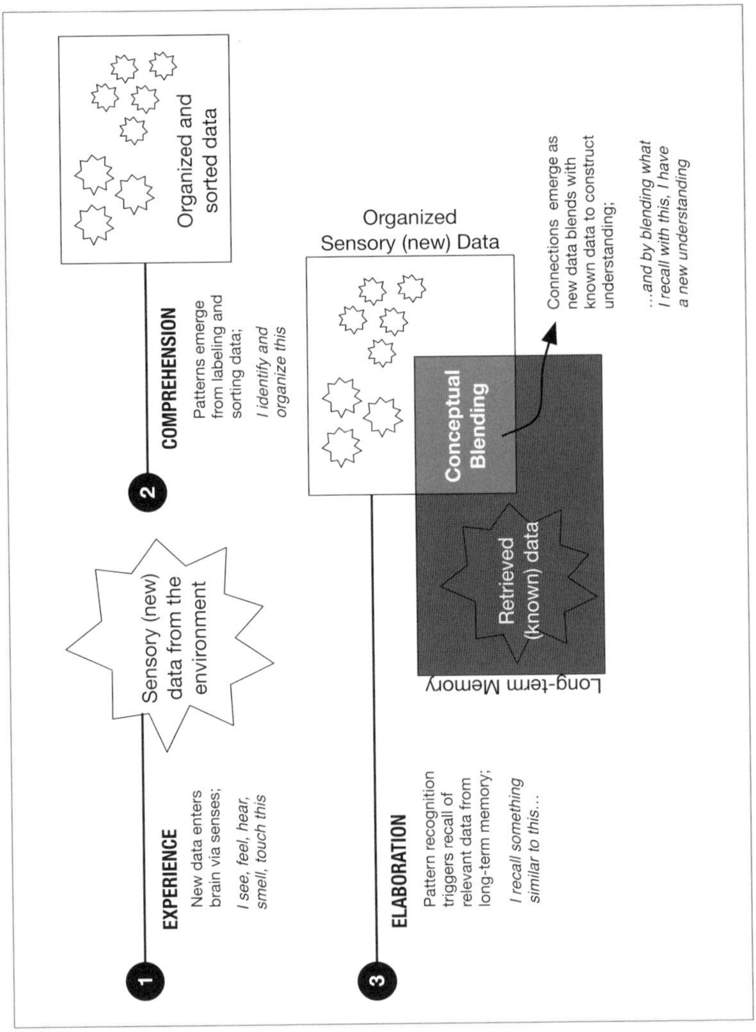

FIGURE 1.3 Overlay of Working Memory, Conceptual Blending, and Learning Processes

I recently saw an ad campaign that illustrates these relationships. The television commercial opens with individuals enthusiastically singing "Old MacDonald" at the top of their lungs. Some sing operatically, some with a country twang, and some with a rhythm-and-blues flavor. All the while they are washing their hands. As the song's final notes fade, an announcer explains that healthy hand-washing takes at least twenty seconds (new data), and that twenty seconds is about the length of time it takes to sing one verse of "Old MacDonald" (retrieved data provides a reference point). As the new idea of healthy hand-washing's time factor blends with the known idea of singing "Old MacDonald," the viewer understands how long to keep washing.

If we could eavesdrop on a viewer's brain as it processes the advertisement, we might hear the following (**FIGURE 1.4**): "Boy, these people sing 'Old MacDonald' with gusto! Why are they washing their hands while they do it? Hmm, healthy hand-washing takes a certain amount of time. I need to wash my hands for at least twenty seconds. What have I experienced that lasts about twenty seconds? 'Old MacDonald'? Oh, okay, if I sing 'Old MacDonald,' it takes about twenty seconds. So, when I wash my hands I can sing a verse of 'Old MacDonald' to know how long to spend in the soap and water. I get it!"

I have only seen this advertisement once, but ever since I have been singing "Old MacDonald" in my head each time I wash my hands. *Elaboration makes material memorable and meaningful.*

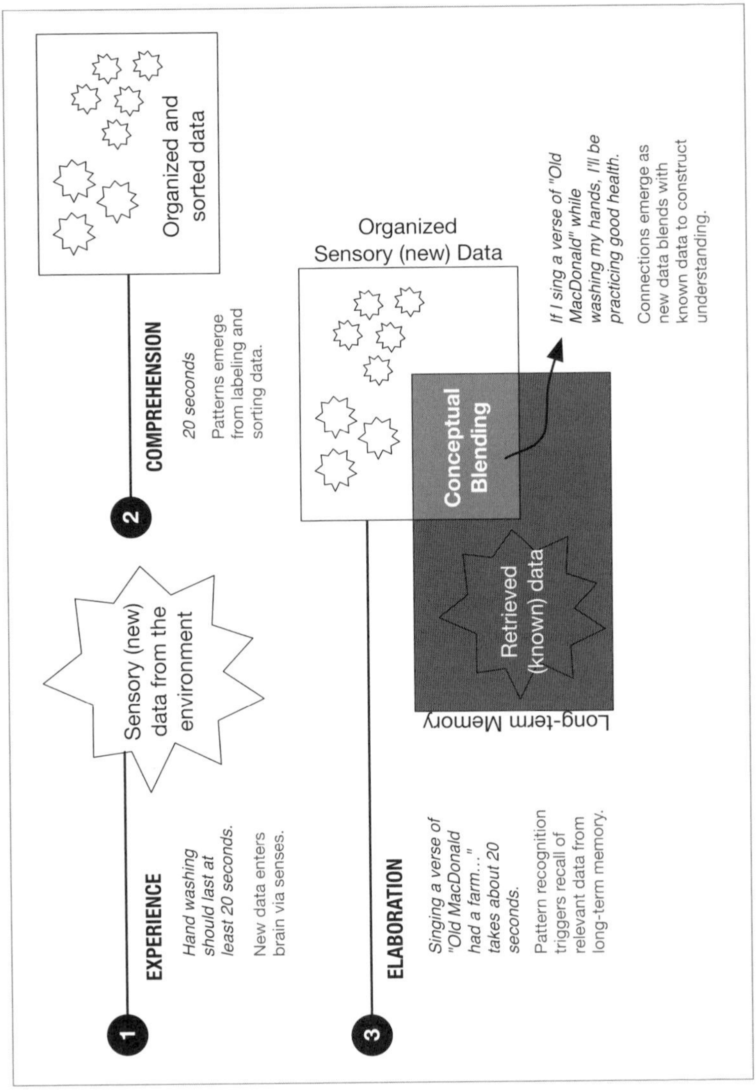

FIGURE 1.4 Hand-washing Commercial Processed to Construct Understanding

While mental monologues aid comprehension, nonverbal thought often aids elaboration. Psychologist Steven Pinker claims, "To think is to grasp a metaphor."[16] He then offers an example that illustrates the relationship between elaboration, nonverbal thought, and understanding: The Declaration of Independence opens with, "When, in the course of human events, it becomes necessary for one people to dissolve the political bonds which have connected them with another, and to assume among the powers of the earth, the separate and equal station to which the laws of nature and of nature's God entitle them, a decent respect to the opinions of mankind requires that they should declare the causes which impel them to the separation." Pinker explains how the blending that occurs during elaboration enables even children to construct understanding of the Declaration's lofty concepts:

> Children may not understand political alliances or intellectual argumentation, but they certainly understand rubber bands [as a reference point for political bonds] and fistfights [as a reference point for intellectual argumentation]. Conceptual metaphors point to an obvious way in which people could learn to reason about new, abstract concepts. They would notice, or have pointed out to them, a parallel between a physical realm they already understand and a conceptual realm they don't yet understand. This would explain not only how children learn difficult ideas as they grow up but how people of any age learn them in school or from expository prose. Analogies such as THE ATOM IS A SOLAR SYSTEM or AN ANTIBODY IS A LOCK FOR A KEY would be more than pedagogical devices; they would be the mechanism that the mind uses to understand otherwise inaccessible concepts.[17]

Increasing the variety of ways the brain processes information (e.g., both verbal and nonverbal) increases connections between new and known information.[18] Learners deepen their understanding of new information by representing it in varied forms. Howard Gardner's multiple intelligences (**TABLE 1.1**) offer one index of representational variety.[19]

INTELLIGENCE TYPE	IDEA REPRESENTATION
linguistic	ideas represented in spoken or written language
logical-mathematical	ideas represented numerically or in an analysis of "what has happened, and what may happen, under various scenarios" (p. 32)
musical	ideas represented through hearing or producing music
spatial	ideas represented in spatial organizations (e.g., flowcharts, concept maps)
bodily-kinesthetic	ideas represented through physical stances and movement
naturalist	ideas represented in taxonomies of natural elements
interpersonal	ideas represented in characterizations, exploring individual's distinctives, motivations, and needs
intrapersonal	ideas represented in self-awareness elements, such as "feelings, goals, fears, strengths, and weaknesses" (p. 39)
existential	ideas represented in "the biggest questions," such as those found in "religious, artistic, philosophical, and mythic" systems of thought (p. 41)

TABLE 1.1 Howard Gardner's Multiple Intelligences

To prevent "newly learned material from slipping away, it needs to enter the network of the brain's wiring," explains neurologist and educator Judy Willis. "Students can retain the new information by activating their previously learned knowledge that relates to the new material...Effective teaching uses strategies to help students recognize patterns and then make the connections required to process the new working memories so they can travel into the brain's long-term storage areas."[20] To engage such thinking, a teacher can challenge students to represent new concepts in different forms. For example:

- How would the phases of the American Revolution sound musically?
- How would a model of the human ear look if constructed from students' bodies?
- How could a mathematical process be represented in a cartoon?

Note what such tasks require of the learner. Significant connections between the new material (e.g., a mathematical process) and a nonverbal reference point (e.g., a cartoon) must be explored. For example, in representing phases of the American Revolution musically, the learner's thinking may include answering the following questions:

1. What are the phases of the American Revolution?
2. What are each phase's defining characteristics?
3. How can the defining characteristics be represented musically? What connections do I see/hear between the phase and musical expression?

The resulting connections, which stem from the student's life experience, create a conceptual network that gives him greater flexibility in thinking. More connections increase such flexibility and widen the contexts in which the new understanding may be useful. For example, in the network structure illustrated in **FIGURE 1.5**, a series of connections that link musical symbols with increasing tension and ongoing sibling conflict may enable the individual to represent the conflict with musical symbols. Representing the conflict in this symbolic form may spark new solutions. The individual may then be able to approach the conflict in ways that lessen tension or even promote a calm outcome. "How can I move the conflict from its current *forte* state," the student may think, "into a state of less fury—into a *mezzo-piano* state?" The connections enable flexible thinking that influence responses.

Transforming the resulting representation back to words for explanation causes the process to start all over again. With each recurrence, understanding deepens, and deeper understanding produces learning that lasts.

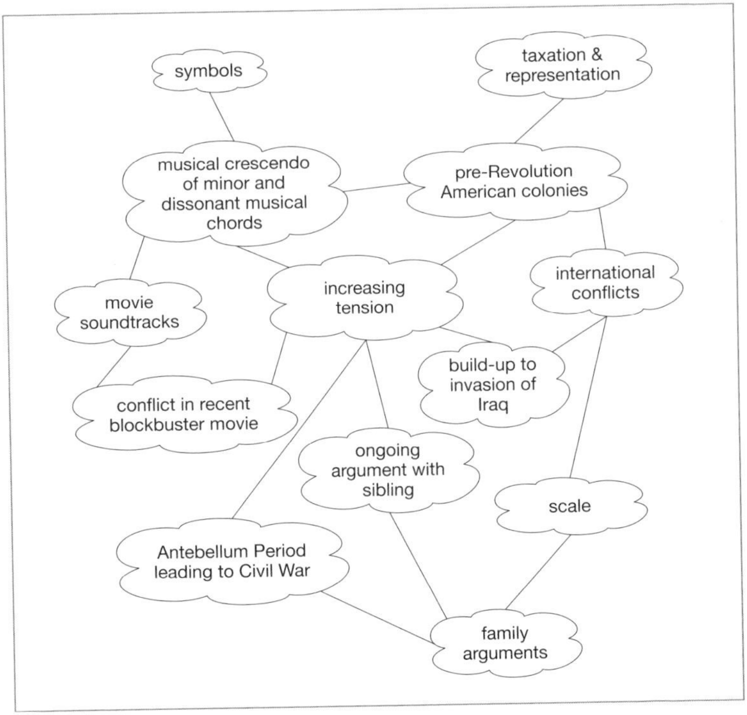

FIGURE 1.5 Example of a Partial Conceptual Network

Lasting learning can dramatically change a person's perspective. In *The Return of the Prodigal Son,* the late Yale Divinity School professor Henri Nouwen relates the following anecdote: "A seemingly insignificant encounter with a poster presenting a detail of Rembrandt's *The Return of the Prodigal Son* set in motion a long spiritual adventure that brought me to a new understanding of my vocation and offered me strength to live it. At the heart of this adventure is a seventeenth-century painting and its artist, a first-century parable and its author, and a twentieth-century person in search of life's meaning."[21] What was the network of connections that enabled Nouwen's conceptual blending? A seventeenth-century painting and its artist, and a first-century parable and its author linked to a twentieth-century person. From these came significant results: a new understanding of his vocation and the strength to live it. Elaboration leads to learning that is lasting, influential, and occasionally life-changing.

Application and Intention

Learning's final two building blocks lead to active responses. Application, often called practice, allows a student to show her understanding *within an instructional setting.* For example, recall your experience of learning how to change a car's flat tire. If you repeated the steps after watching a teacher demonstrate the process, you engaged in application. As you practiced, your teacher stood nearby and offered suggestions, such as "Don't forget to loosen the lug nuts before jacking up the car," and feedback—"That should be high enough."

While practicing a skill is essential for mastery, moving to the application stage too quickly is a common mistake. Traditional math textbooks often illustrate this rushed pace. The left page features a brief explanation and a few examples (experience), and the right page presents multiple practice exercises (application). Students are expected to perform the skill without going through the comprehension or elaboration stages.

Some teachers in other disciplines proceed similarly. For example, I once observed a middle school English class learning how to revise written drafts. The teacher defined *revising* for the students ("Revising means we reread our writing to make improvements") and then told the students to go do it. He moved directly from explanation to application, never suggesting a how-to process or engaging the students in thinking that would enable them to devise a practical approach to revising. Such instruction skips the processes (comprehension and elaboration) that foster understanding.

The teacher should have identified a specific target for revision, such as using active rather than passive voice. For example, writing *Congress will pass the bill tomorrow* rather than *The bill will be passed by Congress tomorrow*. Then he could explain and demonstrate specific steps for making these revisions, such as: read the text sentence by sentence, identify any written in passive voice, and revise those sentences by making the subject perform an action.

Then students could record the steps on index cards and place them in sequence, as if creating a flowchart. The pattern illustrated by the steps—review, identify, and improve—could be related to experiences from the students' lives, such as learning how to swing a bat: Revising for active voice is like learning how to swing a bat. In both you review what you've done, identify what you're doing wrong, and then make changes that improve the outcome. Sorting the index cards and connecting with past experiences help students understand they are using a process with specific steps that lead to better results. With a focus, the steps to address that focus, and an understanding based on their past experiences, the students are ready to practice. The teacher could provide paragraphs that the students revise as he stays nearby to offer review and redirection as needed. By leading students through experience, comprehension, elaboration, and application, the teacher equips students to use what they've learned with more independence and in wider contexts. He prepares them for learning's intention stage.

A person uses intention when applying a new understanding or skill in a novel context, such as a scenario that takes place *outside the classroom*. Intention occurs in the "real world" when a similar incident prompts recall of understood concepts or relevant skills. For example, changing a truly flat tire, perhaps at an interstate rest area, or revising a manuscript for active voice, represents intention. The learner applies the skill outside of its instructional context.

Intention also empowers critical thinking. For example, imagine a student who, in tenth-grade social studies, constructs a firm understanding of America's antebellum period leading up to the Civil War. As an adult, she reads about the cycle of conflict and compromise taking place in a country divided by racial or religious identity. Using the antebellum period as a reference point, she thinks, "This cycle cannot go on endlessly. Every compromise dissatisfies a large segment of the population. Either the sides have to reach a final point of compromise or increased conflict seems likely." Understanding this issue from the antebellum period enables her to make predictions. Depending on the circumstances, she may even be able to advise or take beneficial action in the case.

Unfortunately, intention rarely occurs. According to educator Eric Jensen, we see an "abysmal failure of students to transfer learning from school subjects to real life."[22] What contributes to a student's ability to use knowledge in widened or varied contexts? "The first factor that influences successful transfer is degree of mastery of the original subject," conclude Bransford, Brown, and Cocking. "Without an adequate level of initial learning, transfer cannot be expected. This point seems obvious, but it is often overlooked…Transfer is affected by the degree to which people learn *with understanding* rather than merely memorize sets of facts or follow a fixed set of procedures [italics added]."[23] If a teacher fails to engage students in comprehension and elaboration, the pattern recognition necessary for intention is less likely to develop. "It is important to be realistic about the amount of time it takes to learn complex subject matter," explain Bransford, Brown, and Cocking. "Much of this time involves the development of pattern recognition skills that support the identification of meaningful patterns of knowledge plus knowledge of their implications for future outcomes."[24] Teachers who design instruction with all of learning's stages produce learning that converts raw data into transferable knowledge.

Imagine a young adult with an interest in architecture. While in college, the budding architect sits in classes where knowledgeable professors present new, raw data. Returning to the dorm at the end of the day, he reviews the notes from the day's classes and sorts the material, grouping and connecting ideas. This labeling and sorting causes patterns to emerge, which triggers recall of his summer job at a construction site: "Oh, cantilevers support that stairwell, just like the beams used in building that loft back in

July." As the past experience and the new data blend, the budding architect's brain constructs understandings—insights erupt as new blends with known. Later, the student plans and builds a scale model of a building. During the process, the college professor offers suggestions and guidance, such as "Have you thought about a weight-bearing wall or other supporting option?" The student practices architectural principles by applying them within the classroom. Graduation arrives, and the newly educated architect travels to Europe. While there, certain buildings catch his eye, and soon he designs and oversees construction of original buildings inspired by those seen on the trip. The understanding constructed while in college empowers intention as the architect applies it in new and widened contexts.

Questions

1. In your own words, define each of learning's building blocks: experience, comprehension, elaboration, application, and intention.

2. What relationship does working memory have to learning?

3. The author used letters and words to illustrate how building blocks in varying combinations produce different results. Identify a different illustration of this concept and explain it as a metaphor for learning.

4. In your experience as a student, what stages of learning are teachers most likely to neglect? What is lost when these stages are missing?

Chapter 2

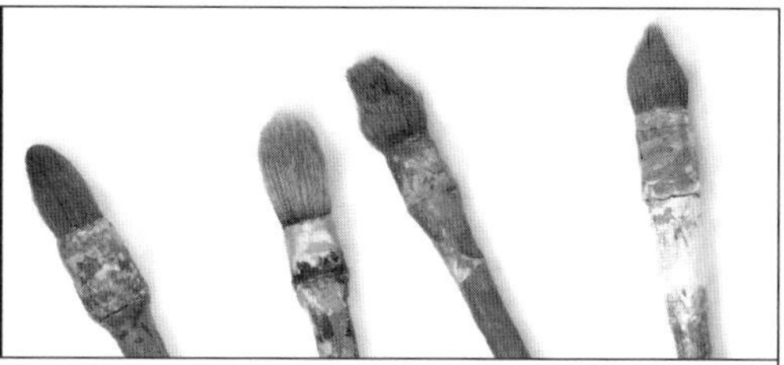

POWER TOOLS

Learning's Four Core Processes

Imagine four artists, each capable of producing a beautiful work, but there is a catch. Each can create a work of art only when all the others contribute their talents. Artist A can produce stunning results, but only when Artists B, C, and D contribute their talents to the effort. Likewise for Artists B, C, and D. These complementary artists have attempted working alone or with one or two others, but quickly discovered optimal results depended on a four-way interaction.

The core processes in learning reflect the complementary nature of this artist consortium. The five processes previously introduced—experience, comprehension, elaboration, application, and intention—interact to produce learning. The latter two, however, share underlying thought patterns that generate action. Application is employed *within the instructional setting*, while intention occurs *outside the instructional setting*. This leaves four cognitively distinct processes: experience, comprehension, elaboration, and application/intention. For efficiency, *application/intention* will be referred to simply as *application*.

Experience: Transforming Raw Data into Reference Points

Take a moment to recall a childhood experience. It might be the first time you stood at the end of a diving board. Maybe you won a spelling bee in fifth grade. Or you came in second because of one stupid word.

How many times throughout your life have you remembered that experience? Perhaps you frequently retell it to entertain others, consider it as you make important decisions, or recognize its influence on your perspectives.

All of these reasons to recall characterize one of my childhood memories. I grew up in a house with a large lawn that sloped dramatically. My father loved to mow the lawn, singing at the top of his lungs while maneuvering our yellow riding mower over hilly terrain. When I was old enough, he taught me to drive the mower and set me loose. (The singing, apparently, was optional.) On one side of the mower, a foot pedal controlled the clutch while the foot pedal on the other side controlled the brake. The previous spring, my father and older brother had proudly planted three apple trees in the backyard. While mowing, I suddenly found one of those trees directly in front of me. Panicking, I slammed my foot onto the wrong pedal, the clutch, freeing the mower to roll forward. On the slope, the mower gained speed, rolled over the tree, and sliced clean through its thin trunk. I thought my dad would kick me off the mower and never let me go near it again. But he laughed hysterically. "You should have seen your face!" he called across the yard. "Don't worry," he assured me, "that tree wasn't healthy anyway. Now we don't have to look out at a sick tree." He stopped and pointed down at the mower. "Do you know which side has the brake?" I nodded sheepishly. "Okay, keep going," he encouraged.

How many times have I thought of this incident? Too many to count. But if I never thought about that experience after it happened—if I did not consider its elements, how they fit together, the patterns they formed, and shared the results with others—my mental repertoire would lack this reference point. Through repeated recall, I have engaged learning's core processes. I know the individual elements (dad, lawn mower, clutch, brake, sloped yard, apple tree) and how they connect (sequentially, cause and effect): comprehension. Those relationships reveal patterns—clutches free while brakes restrain, and mistakes, if treated properly, aid in learning: elaboration. By retelling the experience, I'm putting all that knowledge and understanding to use: application. I frequently share this story with students to help put their minds at ease about learning a new topic. "Mistakes will be made," I explain. "We will make them, treat them lightheartedly, and then figure out where to find the brake."

Can you trace your processing of a childhood experience similarly? What are the parts and how do they connect (comprehension)? What pattern does the experience illustrate (elaboration)? Can you retell the experience (application)? If so, that experience provides a reference point for thinking about related experiences or ideas. We can think of this processing as *a sequence of thinking that focuses on the initial experience* (**FIGURE 2.1**).

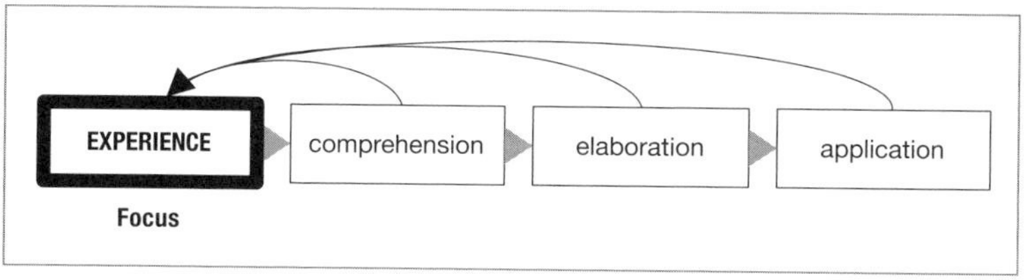

FIGURE 2.1 Core Processes Transforming Experience to Reference Point

Comprehension: Transforming Data into Knowledge

During the comprehension stage, the core processes identify and organize the knowledge gained during the experience, but that knowledge does not equal understanding or ability, as my high school basketball experience illustrates.

My coach was a patient man. I played basketball to be part of the team, not because I had any talent for the game. I had an understanding of defense, but I couldn't shoot. I remember my coach repeatedly working with me on my jump shot. I can still recite the steps involved:

1. Stand with your shoulders squarely facing the basket.
2. With your feet about shoulder-width apart, bend your knees while holding the ball just below your chin.
3. Hold the ball with your hand "cupped," with only your fingertips touching the ball. Use your other hand to balance the ball in that position.
4. Jump, bringing your feet together and launching the ball upward and forward, and giving the ball a backward spin as you release it.
5. Follow through, flipping your wrist so that your fingers point toward the basket.

Even though I never mastered the skill, I *know the steps* I had to practice. How did these facts become part of my knowledge cache?

My basketball coach explained and demonstrated each step in isolation and then as a connected motion. In other words, he gave my brain the raw data for shooting a jump shot. *As we sort and label the steps ourselves*, we rehearse the facts and their relationships. We begin to construct *knowledge*. At this point, the knowing is confined to restating the facts and organizing them correctly. My coach asked me to restate the steps in their correct order. He asked me to engage in comprehension, labeling and sequencing the steps with my own words. I then moved on to the next step: elaboration. I remember thinking that a jump shot was somewhat like batting in baseball, a skill I could do. Both involved bent knees at the beginning, featured full body movement, and required follow-through. By relating the two skills, I gained confidence in sequencing a jump shot's steps. Application then deepens knowledge by initiating recall of the facts and their relationships. Every time we worked on the jump shot, my coach would have me retell how it was done before actually trying it.

We can think of this process as *a sequence of thinking that focuses on comprehending important details of new data* (**FIGURE 2.2**). Experience provides the new data that will be used to construct new knowledge. Comprehension provides the content and structure of the developing knowledge. Elaboration emphasizes the organization component of comprehension by relating similar previous experiences. Application engages the brain in recall of the labeled and sorted data.

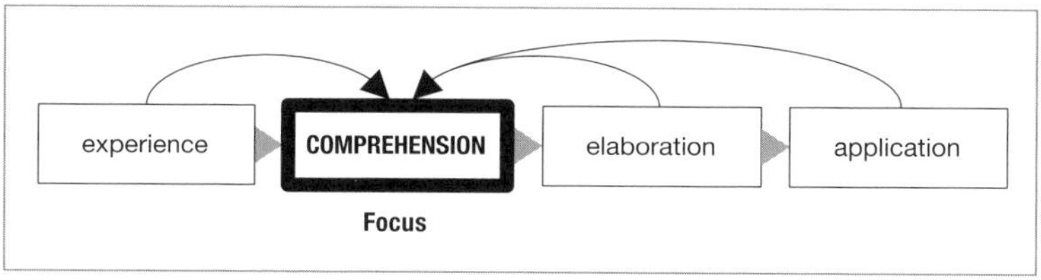

FIGURE 2.2 Core Processes Transforming Data to Knowledge

Learning that does not proceed beyond comprehension prevents additional proficiency. For example, imagine a student in a high school algebra class who can recite the following: "To combine like terms, first identify sets of like terms for one side of an equation. Second, add the coefficients. Then simplify that side of the equation. Finally, repeat for the other side of the equation." This student has labeled and sorted the data, but that does not equal understanding the concept of "like terms" nor the actual practice of combining them. Let's say he has to simplify the equation $3x + 8 + x = 30 - x + 11$. By doing the steps, he will reach: $4x + 8 = 41 - x$. If the teacher rushes ahead into a new algebraic concept, the student's knowledge of combining like terms will remain inert. He still needs sufficient processing to construct an understanding of like terms and practice to transform his understanding into using the new concept effectively.

Elaboration: Transforming Knowledge into Understanding

When the focus shifts to elaboration, the core processes interact to construct understanding. Elaboration makes the connections that generate *aha*'s. We have all seen the light go on in our students' eyes. How can we make that process deliberate?

Remember non-electronic encyclopedia, those sets of books that seemed to hold the world's collected knowledge? We were fortunate to have a set in my childhood home. They were pine green and cream-colored volumes with gold foil lettering on their spines. For me, the best pages in the entire set were the special acetate pages that showed the human skeletal system. Each partially transparent page could be laid on top of another. When you turned one acetate page, the body's muscles fell into place, overlaying the skeletal system so you could see both. Flip another page, and the cardiovascular system appeared. Layer upon layer, you could build the human body from the inside out simply by turning pages. Connections could be seen, relationships identified, and interactions recognized. In the precomputer age, it was technological magic!

Those acetate pages revealed how elements of the human body fit together, the patterns formed by muscle, blood, and bone, and they deepened the reader's understanding of how the body's structure and organization enabled its functions, such as movement and respiration.

We can think of this process as *a sequence of thinking that focuses on constructing understanding* (**FIGURE 2.3**). To continue the illustration, elaboration forms acetate pages out of new sensory data and past experience, allowing us to overlay and blend one with the other to discover connections. These discoveries weave organized facts into coherent understanding.

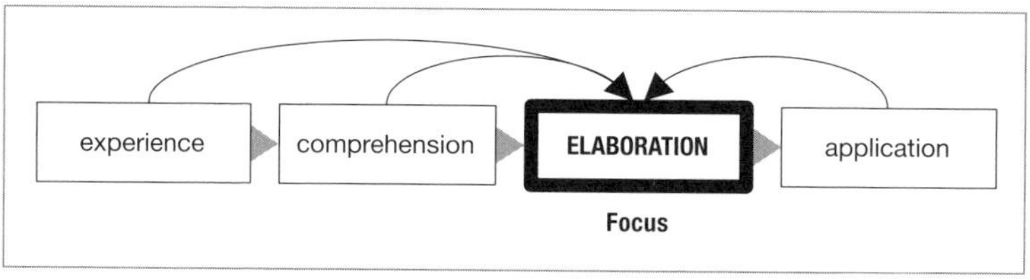

FIGURE 2.3 Core Processes Transforming Knowledge to Understanding

Newly gained knowledge, stemming from the comprehension stage, can be regarded as the first acetate page in the encyclopedia. Then the learner examines the second acetate page, noting the defining attributes of each. Elaboration blends both inputs to identify similarities, differences, and relationships between the new and the known; one acetate page overlays the other. The elements labeled and sorted during comprehension reveal their connections, and blending the new and known enables the brain to construct understanding of the new data.

Learning that does not proceed to elaboration and does not recognize patterns fails to make the connections that build understanding. For example, Miss Snyder takes her students on a special trip to the school cafeteria, where they follow the cafeteria manager to a room filled with stainless steel and conveyor belts. As they stand beside the industrial dishwasher, Miss Snyder explains that after they eat, their cafeteria trays are put through the dishwasher and then restacked for other students to use. The trays, explains Miss Snyder, make a big circle, moving into a student's hands, holding food while the student eats, being washed and returned to the tray pile by the cafeteria entrance, and then being used again by another student. The tray changes somewhat with each step—sometimes being clean and empty, sometimes full of food, and sometimes empty and dirty—but remains a cafeteria tray throughout. The students stand silent, riveted by these inner workings of the school's gastronomic center.

Back in the classroom, Miss Snyder begins explaining the water cycle's steps and sequence. She then asks, "Can you think of something we've seen that is similar to the water cycle?" Surprisingly, the students lack a response. They do not see what Miss Snyder desperately wants them to: like the cafeteria trays, water moves through a cycle, changing forms but always remaining water. To Miss Snyder, this relationship is clear and even helpful in understanding the water cycle, but the students struggle to recognize it and give an answer. How could they miss what she so clearly recognizes?

Connecting new sensory data and prior knowledge requires more than putting the two within cognitive reach of each other. The students did not understand the pattern illustrated by the cafeteria's inner workings, and without an understanding of the intended reference point, they were unable to blend it with the new instructional material. The students' awe never became an "Aha!"

During the elaboration phase, experience provides two inputs: one comprising newly organized sensory data (from comprehension) and one comprising relevant prior experiences pulled from long-term memory. Comprehension examines the two inputs independently, establishing the critical or defining elements of each. Elaboration, the focus process, overlays the two inputs to discover connections and construct understanding. Application then uses the understanding to construct an explanation, and in so doing, often fosters additional elaboration.

Application: Transforming Knowledge into Utility

During the application stage, the core processes interact to develop an expression of understanding or to enable the mastering of new skills. Our "Oh, I get it!" inevitably leads to an explanation of what it is we understand. As we think through our understanding, we often discover new ways to blend the new and the known, continuing to construct deeper understanding of the new material.

These expressions often take the form of similes. "Oh, the earth's structure—its core, mantle, and crust—is like an apple!" This use of figurative language makes sense given how elaboration functions. Two previously unrelated elements blend to construct new understanding.

Howard Gardner suggests that this blending, this search for connection, originates in childhood, which implies a natural inclination for constructing understanding through elaboration. As we age, Gardner suggests, our tendency to verbalize similes diminishes, but the tendency to think about and appreciate comparisons remains.[1] James E. Zull suggests such thinking connects the conceptual and the physical to promote understanding: "We cannot understand anything unless we create internal *neuronal networks that reflect some set of physical relationships that accurately map the relationships* in the concept" [italics added].[2]

Some material leads to a different form of application. Once a student knows the steps and understands the concepts that make up a new skill, she needs to try using the skill to achieve a result. Application provides the practice that constructs proficiency.

Unfortunately for my proficiency as a pianist, I grew up in an era of cool television and film theme songs. Who would want to practice four octaves of the B-major scale when they could play the theme from *Hill Street Blues*? As a result, I never mastered the fingering for scales.

My wife is an outstanding pianist and great teacher. When I became her student, she didn't want me to learn new theme songs; she wanted me to learn the scales first. She set the music in front of me, and I immediately started to try playing the notes. "Wait!" she said. "Let's take a minute to look at this scale. What key are you playing in? Look at the right-hand score. What finger plays the first note? Between what two notes does your thumb cross underneath to allow you to smoothly finish the scale?" All these questions! She wanted me to think before I actually played the notes. She continued, "Does the fingering for this scale match the fingering for any scales you know?" Now she wanted me to put the new data together with previous knowledge. Once I recognized the fingering pattern as being similar to a previously mastered scale, she had me try the scale for the first time. Even though I would need practice to develop accuracy and efficiency, I played the scale much better on the first attempt than I would have without her thought-prompting questions.

Practicing new learning develops the ability to apply a skill accurately and efficiently. We can think of this process as *a sequence of thinking that focuses on utilizing beneficial skills* (**FIGURE 2.4**).

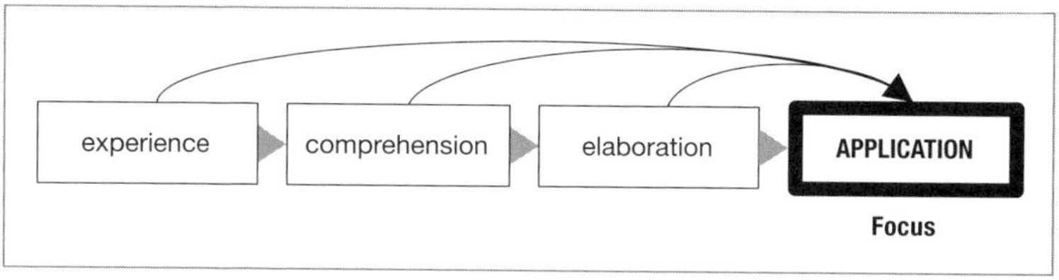

FIGURE 2.4 Core Processes Transforming Knowledge to Utilization

For example, if I understand the relationships of the components in an algebraic equation, I can find a solution for *x*. But I need data to start with. My teacher presents me with the equation 4x + 3 = 23 (experience) and asks me to find the value of *x*. I begin labeling and sorting the components (comprehension). I know that 23 represents the "answer" to the problem. I know that the problem contains a variable, for which I am trying to identify a value. I also recognize the mathematical processes within the problem: multiplication (4 times *x*) and addition (plus 3).

Now I explore relationships between those elements and compare them with reference points pulled from my long-term memory (elaboration). I remember in an equation, the "sides" are balanced; both have equal values. So, if remove the + 3 element on the left side, I must subtract an equal value from the equation's right side (23 - 3 = 20). I also know that multiplication's "opposite" operation is division. So, to find the value of *x*, I could divide the "answer" minus 3 by 4 [(23-3)/4]. My understanding of the relationships between the elements and my recall of relevant processes equips me to take action (application). I solve the problem: 20/4=5; *x*=5.

My thinking, focused on application, moves through the core processes to generate action. As I practice similar problems, my comprehension and elaboration processes shorten in duration to a point where I can act efficiently. Once I see the problem, I immediately know how to find the value for the variable. My understanding becomes utility.

Emotion: The Propeller That Drives Learning

Many educators hold extreme perspectives of emotion's relationship to learning. Some see no room for feeling in teaching while others value sentiment over scholarship. We fight a covert war pitting facts versus feelings, not realizing that neither extreme aids learning. "When we educators fail to appreciate the importance of students' emotions, we fail to appreciate a critical force in students' learning. One could argue, in fact, that we fail to appreciate the very reason that students learn at all."[3]

Facts and feelings dance inextricably through our neurological landscape. "There is a place…where explicit memories of emotional experiences and implicit memories meet," notes Joseph LeDoux, "—in working memory and its creation of immediate conscious experience."[4] Two neighbors in the brain, the amygdala and the hippocampus, contribute different inputs to two different memory systems. Sensory data channeled through the hippocampus is processed as factual, declarative data. New data channeled through the amygdala is processed as emotional data. Our working memory blends both the declarative and emotional data, providing us with a unified experience. Once the experience is over, the emotional data often morphs into declarative memory.

For example, a fourth-grade student may remember the excitement of her first day of kindergarten. She may recall the newness of the experience, seeing her teacher for the first time, and the layout of the classroom. Even though she recalls the excitement of the experience, she does not respond as if she is again entering kindergarten. She is not excited by the memory.

Sometimes a memory's emotional tag is dropped altogether. Can you remember anything emotional about learning that Earth is the third planet from the sun? For example, a child might be disappointed that it isn't closest to the sun, but you probably had a minimal emotional response to the fact. Yet repetition of the information enabled your brain to retain the fact but lose any associated emotional tags.[5]

However, the loss of memory can tip in the opposite direction. Emotional arousal tends to focus "attention on the 'gist' of an experience at the expense of peripheral details."[6] This process tends to be more common than memory of specifics. As a result, "our heads tend to be filled with generalized pictures of concepts or events, not with slowly fading minutiae."[7] And over time, the "gist" can devolve until only the amygdala's contribution, the emotion, remains.

In my early elementary years, I suffered convulsions any time my fever reached a certain level. This caused my parents and my pediatrician great concern, so I was hospitalized for a series of tests. One of them still makes me react: the spinal tap. Even while I write this, I'm feeling hot and tingly and my breathing is shallow, as if I'm anticipating something terrible is going to happen. I cannot recall the details—Who was in the room? What time of day was it? Did it actually hurt? What did the results show? I do not know any of these facts, but I vividly recall the blazing fear. If anyone even mentions this medical procedure, my mind and body respond.

What does this mean for teaching and learning? Memory construction—and therefore learning—includes emotional data. In fact, *emotion drives and enables learning*. It focuses a student's attention, allows her to find meaning, and feeds motivation.

Emotion and Attention

Emotion focuses attention for good or bad, as those of us who taught in the days following September 11, 2001, saw firsthand. Stress inhibits the additional processing necessary for learning. At the same time, an emotionally flat classroom also inhibits learning. Apathy is learning's nemesis, and a teacher who ignores the power of emotion creates an atmosphere of inattentiveness.

The key lies in the Goldilocks principle: to foster learning, teachers must generate emotion that's not too hot, not too cold, but just right. Too much emotion prevents new data from reaching the brain's processing centers. Too little emotion ensures that students will remain in a general, unfocused state of attention. A lack of focused attention prevents data from reaching the brain's processing centers.[8]

Emotion contributes more to learning than just attention. It enables students to construct meaning and understanding. In determining how much energy to devote to new data, the brain asks, "Have I seen it before?"[9] As the brain perceives that new data is connected to something it has previously experienced, it directs attention and energy toward constructing understanding of the new data. "Memory is enhanced by creating associations between concepts," and those associations construct meaning. When it comes to learning, the brain's motto is "Meaning before details."[10]

We need to engage students' emotions to gain their attention and promote processing of new data. But what emotions should we emphasize? Do we want students on the verge of tears prior to introducing fractions? (Not advisable.) Do we need to generate pep rally–level excitement prior to engaging students in reading *Hamlet*? (Also not advisable.) What emotions enhance learning without overwhelming the brain's ability to process new information?

Sustained Attention

The buttons were scattered on his desk, as one of my pupils bounced excitedly from foot to foot. "Look, Mr. W.!" he insisted. "See how these wires all lead into this thing here? That's where the numbers must get added and stuff!" I had no idea whether or not he was right, but I recognized the thrill of discovery in his voice. Carson had carefully—as carefully as ten-year-old hands allow—torn his calculator apart. Every machine or machine-like object sparked his curiosity. "What makes it do that?" he'd often ask. I learned to say, "I don't know, but I bet you can find out." One day he came into my classroom with the dismantled handset from an old telephone in hand. "Check this out, Mr. W." I'm not sure how much of the school curriculum Carson mastered that year, but I know how much he gained from his machine autopsies.

"Curiosity," claims creativity expert and filmmaker Erwin McManus, "is essential for life. Curiosity is essential for learning."[11] Curiosity taps into the desire to know. It is what drives us to find answers, explore new things, and resolve contradictions. In short, curiosity focuses and sustains attention. What Carson personified in the extreme can, even in lesser doses, foster learning. How, then, can we spark student curiosity?

One way is to create a sense of mystery, keeping an unknown factor active in our students' thinking while providing what is needed for them to make the "discovery." This method works with everyone. For example, I recently led an in-service program for teachers. Writing instruction was our focus, and on the third day of the program we examined how to coach developing writers. The teachers came from a wide range of levels, from kindergarten to college. To begin the morning, I gave each participant a wooden nut and bolt. I asked the teachers to hold the bolt by its head and position the nut at the bottom end. Then we turned the nut one full cycle, moving it slightly up the bolt. We did this a few times before I asked the teachers to place the bolt on the table. I explained that we'd examine coaching as it related to writing instruction, and that I wanted them to think about what the nut and bolt might have to do with it. I began presenting the key concepts of coaching, pausing occasionally to allow the teachers to think about the nut and bolt. (Are you wondering what associations they made? If so, it generates curiosity even secondhand!) They entered into the discussion of coaching wanting to solve the "mystery": What does this nut and bolt have to do with coaching? That sense of not knowing—of wanting to discover what someone had challenged them to find—focused and sustained their attention. When the group recognized that the bolt represented expectations and the nut represented coaching, they solved the mystery: cycles of coaching around consistent expectations generate upward movement or increased achievement.

Curiosity carries learning forward. Neurologist and teacher Judy Willis explains that such approaches provide just the right amount of challenge (not too hot, not too cold) to engage the amygdala at levels that "enhance the speed and efficiency of information flowing through into the memory storage areas of the brain."[12] Such "just right" stimulation, combining students' curiosity with new instructional material, engages their emotions and sustains their attention.

Judy Willis also shares an excellent example of mystery-sparked curiosity that even had her wondering about associations. Hoping for ways to energize the next day's math lesson for her middle school students, Dr. Willis visited a supermarket, seeking an inexpensive item she could display on the students' desks as they entered the classroom. She settled on a small vegetable, not knowing exactly how she would use it. The next morning, Dr. Willis started teaching the lesson without explaining the radishes the students discovered on their desks. At the lesson's conclusion, the students asked about the radishes. Still uncertain of the answers, Dr. Willis replied, "Why do you think I put a radish on your desk for today's lesson?" The students offered several explanations. They connected mathematical concepts with their sensory experience of the radish, making associations that seemed sensible to them. Though Dr. Willis could have "come up with something" to share as an explanation, the students' thinking generated more connections, and their discovery of these connections fostered deeper understanding and better memory formation. In short, the students were engaged in significant elaboration of the day's mathematical content prompted by its curiosity-generating pairing with a common vegetable.[13]

Motivation

As Dr. Willis's experience demonstrates, motivation drives the best learning. Yes, you can learn the multiplication tables under the threat of punishment or to "earn" that blue ring. But both the stick and carrot produce learning that tends to stop once the threat is avoided or the prize is obtained. Authentic learning requires a motivated learner.

"Motivation is the director of emotions." explains John Ratey.

"It determines how much energy and attention the brain and the body assign to a given stimulus."[14] While generally not considered an emotion, motivation "ties emotion to action." Our emotional response to a given stimulus generates the actions of our mind and/or body. For example, I'm a music lover. My mp3 player features performances from a wide variety of musical genres. My Internet Web browsers hold several bookmarks for sites that tell me when new recordings are coming out. I enjoy music even more when I know something about the artist, so I read anything I can find about my favorites. I am emotionally connected to music. My positive emotional response motivates me to take action—to read about music and musicians, to find new recordings (and sometimes vintage ones), to seek new artists whom I might enjoy. I do these things because my emotions propel me to act.

However, motivation generates more than activity. I also think deeply about music. I take pride in recognizing such details as a time signature change right when the lyrics take a new turn. Motivation generates the close listening, even though this process is more cognitive than concrete.

How can we motivate learners? If we use emotion to gain and direct their attention, how can we keep them advancing through the process of learning?

Here's one helpful principle: meaning is motivational. Because the brain constantly strives to make sense of the sensory data our experiences provide, finding meaning triggers the brain's reward system and increases the likelihood of our retaining the information. "The brain's determination of what is meaningful and what is not is reflected not only in the initial perceptual processes but also in the conscious processing of information," claims Patricia Wolfe. "Information that fits into or adds to an existing network has a much better chance of storage than information that doesn't."[15]

The brain is admirably designed to integrate new data with previous experiences. Association cortices, specialized regions spread throughout the brain, provide the bottom-up and top-down processing that empower perception. The bottom-up processing involves perceiving the data and "reporting" findings. For example, the crossing of two short lines is "reported" as the letter *x*. Once recognized, the new data gets top-down processing: the brain constructs associations between the new data and relevant previous experience.[16]

Comprehension mirrors the brain's bottom-up processing, and elaboration represents its top-down processing. Instruction that capitalizes on this natural neural functioning motivates learning.

Transfer

Emotion's influence does not stop with the initial stages of learning. Research findings suggest that "emotional processes are required for the skills and knowledge acquired in school to transfer to novel situations and to real life," claim Mary Helen Immordino-Yang and Antonio Damasio. "That is, emotion may play a vital role in helping children decide when and how to apply what they have learned in school to the rest of their lives." Emotion acts as a "rudder" in decision-making and reasoning. It enables the learner to use known content and skills in addressing the real world. Emotions act "like shelves," providing "...a repertoire of know-how and actions that allows people to respond appropriately in different situations," note Immordino-Yang and Damasio.[17]

Emotion influences every phase of learning, from raw

experience through application and intention. Overlaying emotion's contributions and learning's core processes reveals complementary interactions (**FIGURE 2.5**). Through experience, emotionally interesting data engages our senses; it *gains attention*. That attention *gains focus* as we comprehend—label and sort—the defining attributes of the new data. As we engage in elaboration, we construct understanding and *discover meaning* of the labeled and sorted data. Finally, as we use our understanding, we *respond to circumstances with know-how*. And, if truly engaged in learning, *curiosity drives us forward through the core processes*. Learning and emotion are complementary processes.

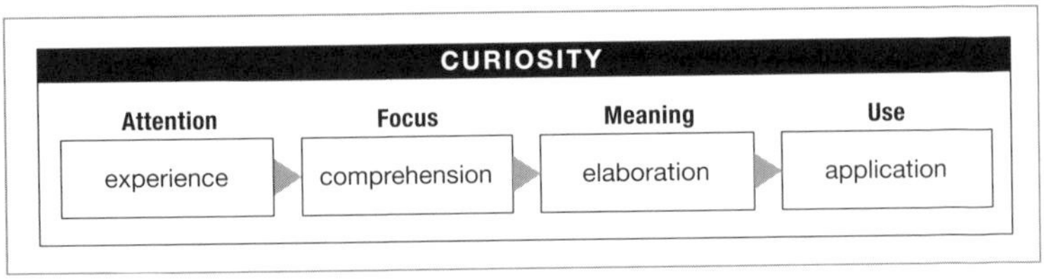

FIGURE 2.5 Core Processes and Emotion

Questions

1. Explain how the artists introduced in the chapter's opening produced their best artworks.

2. List the core processes. Why are application and intention combined in the core processes?

3. Relate the artist allies to learning's core processes. How do the artists' interactions illustrate those of the core processes?

4. What does a focus on each of the following core processes produce? What role does each product play in learning?
    - **experience**
    - **comprehension**
    - **elaboration**
    - **application**

5. Reexamine **FIGURE 2.5** and explain the relationship of emotion to learning's core processes.

Chapter 3

SUBJECT MATTER TYPES

Designing SKILL Instruction

A few years ago, my wife and I pursued the dream of building our own home. Julia ventured into a subdivision one day and called me via cell phone. "I'm not sure I know how to get home," she laughed, "but I've found where we want to build a house!" She had driven into a wooded subdivision set atop a large hill, and once I saw the site, I agreed with her. Our building adventure began as we purchased the lot, started reading about home design, and collected photos that fit our vision.

Having a blueprint developed proved critical in the construction process. While we could communicate directly with our builder regarding stylistic elements such as paint color, we needed the house to be framed soundly and function properly. The blueprint provided the needed direction.

Before we could give the architect the information needed to design the blueprint we had to answer some questions:

1. How do you want to live in the home? What functions will each room have?
2. What underlying feel do you want the home to have? What ideas/sensations/experiences do you want?
3. How do you want the rooms to connect? How do you hope to move within the space?

The answers to these questions would influence the content and cohesiveness of our home's design.

Designing instruction requires answers to similar questions:

1. What will your students be learning? What will they do with their learning?
2. What pattern(s) support(s) the instructional material? How will that/those pattern(s) connect to your students' prior experience?
3. How will you focus your students' attention and engage the mental processing needed to construct the learning? How will the flow of instruction mirror the brain's means of learning?

The cognitive steps—experience, comprehension, elaboration, application, and intention—interact to construct the timbers of learning. An effective teacher engages these processes, *but not in equal measure*. The subject matter being taught influences which phases are emphasized. Just as a construction blueprint guides home building to a predetermined outcome, an Architecture of Learning Blueprint guides teaching that produces true learning. By using the Blueprint as a template, the teacher can align subject matter types with their required cognitive processes.

A teacher begins designing effective instruction by first examining the subject matter and answering the related questions: What will your students be learning? and What will they do with their learning?

Discerning the Difference: Skills

"I don't get it! I can't identify them." Jaime's frustration began during the practice exercises and peaked as the class ended.

"If this is what's on the state test I might as well quit right now. I'll never pass it!"

I met Jaime while teaching remedial reading at a community college. Most of my students, like Jaime, had graduated from high school even though they possessed only middle-school reading abilities. Their eventual acceptance into college-level classes depended on their passing three levels of remedial reading. I taught the lowest level. To complicate matters, what they achieved in my class didn't influence their grades. Passing or failing depended entirely on a standardized state test they took. Several of the test's questions required the student to identify the main idea of a text passage, the very skill Jaime found so difficult.

"Okay, Jaime," I began, "let's go over it one more time—"

"That won't help," Jaime interrupted. "I can repeat your explanation word for word, but I still can't find the main idea!"

I suggested we try working through a short paragraph together. After Jaime read it, he could tell me the paragraph's topic, yet asking for more information triggered the comment: "I don't know *how* to find anything more than that." This revealed the real problem: I had taught what the required textbook suggested—the definition of *main idea*—but I had not given my students a strategy for identifying main ideas. Without a step-by-step process, Jaime lacked the knowledge needed to pick them out.

I began with what Jaime could do. "Okay, you can tell me the topic—who or what the paragraph is about. You've got one piece of the puzzle," I explained. "Identifying the main idea requires two more pieces. What facet of the topic does the paragraph discuss? And what does the writer want you, as the reader, to know about that facet? Let's try this. You said the paragraph is about Mark

Twain." Jaime nodded in agreement. "What part of Mark Twain's life is this paragraph about?"

Jaime scanned the paragraph again and said, "It's about his writing."

I smiled encouragingly. Two of the three pieces were in place. "Now, what does the writer want us to know about Mark Twain's writing?"

"Well," Jaime replied, "it talks about some of the stories he wrote, but that doesn't seem like what she wants us to know. I think she wants us to know that Mark Twain was funny."

"Great, Jaime!" I felt like we were on the brink of a breakthrough. "Now, take the three pieces—Mark Twain, his writing, and being funny—and put them into a statement."

Jaime hesitated, thinking. "Mark Twain's writing was funny?" It wasn't quite "Humor characterized Mark Twain's writing," but it was progress. I asked Jaime to restate the three "pieces" we had used (who or what, what facet, and what about it we should know). I wrote these in Jaime's notebook, and we worked through a few more examples. Jaime left equipped with a strategy for identifying main ideas. Even better, in the next class session, Jaime presented the strategy to the entire class. Immediately, students who had been struggling began identifying main ideas with increasing success. Jaime would go on to master the skill and pass the required standardized test. He just needed the right steps.

Students learn a *skill* when they *master a series of steps to efficiently accomplish a goal.* That can be skipping, forming the letter *a*, or identifying main ideas. The student reproduces a specific sequence of steps, develops proficiency through practice, and applies the skill as needed in real-world interactions.

Accuracy and efficiency characterize skill proficiency. For

example, elementary physical education instructors often teach students overhand throwing. The skill includes the following steps:

1. Stand with your side to the target.
2. Place the ball in your back hand.
3. Hold out your arms, forming a *T* while lifting your opposite foot.
4. Step with your opposite foot while bringing the ball over your head.
5. Release the ball and follow through by "scratching" your opposite knee.

Skills do not have to be physical. Reading comprehension, for example, requires several *cognitive* skills. A cognitive skill comprises a series of *thinking* steps that accomplish a goal. For example, when teaching students how to recognize cause and effect within a text, a teacher may outline a series of thinking steps, such as:

1. Identify what happened.
2. Consider what made (i.e., caused) that to happen.
3. State the relationship.

The teacher may then read aloud a story featuring cause-and-effect relationships and demonstrate the skill's steps. Eventually, during practice, students reproduce the thinking steps demonstrated by the teacher. Although the product—better understanding of a text—is achieved through cognitive rather than physical activity, the series of steps that accomplishes the task makes recognizing cause and effect a cognitive *skill*. Proficiency in applying this skill improves reading comprehension.

Making a skill second nature can be critical. Imagine a child playing an outfield position in a softball game when an opposing team member hits a ball past the infield. If she pauses, thinking, "To throw, I must stand with my side to the target and the ball in my back hand, bring my throwing hand up and back, forming a *T*. Now I must step with my opposite foot...," the batter may take an extra base, and the coach may be shocked speechless. Instead, the outfielder needs to return the ball to the infield immediately; she needs to apply the skill of overhand throwing automatically.

While overhand throwing requires enough proficiency to be done "without thinking," application of some skills actually engages refined methods of thinking. Throughout the semester, my community college students worked on several reading comprehension skills, such as the one Jaime mastered: identifying a text passage's main idea. Ideally, I wanted the students to recognize main ideas without deliberately proceeding through the steps. Stopping after every paragraph to ask the questions, identify the answers, and assemble a statement negatively influences reading rate. During *initial* practice, the students benefitted from systematically working through the steps. As they gained proficiency they also became more efficient, relying less on the deliberate three-step process. However, they could still use the strategy when a passage proved to be difficult.

Revising one's writing also uses skills that are open-ended. For example, revising modifiers requires that a student immediately know *what* to do, but *not* necessarily how to do it. Recognizing a modifier can be done quickly, but making a choice to keep or eliminate the modifier is not done "without thinking." That's not to mention the third option: changing the modifier to one that describes the noun better.

Regardless of differing forms, skills always feature a series of steps that produces a desired result—the ball gets thrown, the main idea gets identified, the sentence gets revised. Once a possible skill is identified, a teacher has to design the instructions on how to use it. He considers questions regarding the skill's pattern(s):

1. What pattern(s) support(s) the instructional material?
2. How will that/those pattern(s) connect to your students' prior experience?

By identifying a skill's pattern, the teacher can establish a reference point that fosters understanding in his students and helps them use the new skill.

Skill Patterns

The brain seeks patterns so it can recall relevant prior experiences to construct understanding. Prior memories help students think about how to address new circumstances. During instruction, students connect new skills and previous experiences that feature similar steps, similar concepts, or both. Skills often illustrate patterns in their series of steps.

For example, teachers in most disciplines want students to master the skill of citing and listing references. Structure and thoroughness characterize a well-referenced report or paper. The teacher plans to teach how to form in-text citations and end-of-text reference lists. Depending on the selected style (e.g., MLA vs. APA), the teacher presents the order, capitalization, and punctuation involved. This provides the students with a series of steps. For example, in developing the reference list, some of the steps involve finding a book's author's last name, first initial(s), the year the book was published, and the complete title. When generalized *conceptually*, this skill illustrates the relationship of completeness and credibility. For example, students may see this relationship represented by comparisons of completion and quitting. The teacher may ask if they've ever seen an athlete quit or give up before a competition was over. From the examples the students identify, the labeling and sorting of the characteristics of quitting too soon vs. completing the competition, and the discussion of how reliable or credible an athlete who gives up is (or is not), a pattern begins to emerge: completeness adds credibility.

Sometimes a more *literal* generalization works better. For example, science teachers want students to learn how to draw conclusions based on the results of an experiment. The steps for such a skill may include:

1. Conduct the experiment as directed.
2. Review in detail what happened during the experiment.
3. Review the results.
4. Ask, "How might the elements of the experience and the result relate?"
5. State your best, most supportable answer.

When generalized, these steps illustrate a simple pattern: observe, review, and conclude. Many experiences, such as viewing a series of photographs taken moments apart, engage students in illustrating the pattern. They review the events each photo shows, and conclude what happened to produce the results shown in the final photo. Such an experience provides reference points for understanding how to draw conclusions from experiments.

The brain can identify more connections to a pattern that is both common and succinct. The more connections the brain makes between the new material and prior experiences, the deeper the understanding it can construct of the new material. By recognizing a skill's underlying pattern, stating it succinctly, and providing a common experience that illustrates that pattern, the teacher activates a student's relevant prior knowledge to aid new learning.

Identifying Patterns:

SKILLS

1. Identify the skill's individual steps
2. Generalize the steps by removing context-specific terms
3. Rephrase the resulting sequence into a pattern statement

FIGURE 3.1 Steps for Creating Skill Pattern Statements

Blueprint Structure

Strands

Once the subject matter is recognized as a skill and its pattern is identified, a third set of questions guides the teacher in designing how to present it to the class:

1. How will you focus your students' attention and engage the mental processing needed to construct learning?
2. How will the flow of instruction mirror the brain's means of learning?

To teach a student a new skill, a teacher needs to focus on four processes:

SKILL LEARNING =

EXperience + **CO**mprehension + **AP**plication + **IN**tention.

The initial EXperience should contain a pattern-based reference point for understanding a skill's steps (e.g., finding a paragraph's main idea *is somewhat like* putting together a three-piece puzzle). COmprehension provides the required knowledge and the steps required to learn the skill (e.g., first, determine who or what the paragraph is about…). Because skills must be mastered, students consume significant instructional time developing accuracy and efficiency through practice. APplication uses the new skill over and over. INtention provides widened contexts for students to apply the skill. Because the focus of these four processes is to build students' skills, they form the rows, or "strands," of the Architecture of Learning Skill Blueprint (**FIGURE 3.2**).

EXperience	contains a pattern-based reference point for understanding a skill's steps
COmprehension	provides the required knowledge and the steps required to learn the skill
APplication	engages students in practicing new skills to develop accuracy and efficiency
INtention	provides widened contexts for students to apply the skill

FIGURE 3.2 Architecture of Learning Skill Focus Processes

Cells

The Skill Blueprint's strands in turn intersect with learning's four core processes—experience, comprehension, elaboration, and application—which form the Blueprint's columns. These intersections form *cells*. Each cell identifies the appropriate *core process* for that step of the strand. For example, the first strand, EXperience, and the first core process, experience, intersect to create the Blueprint's first cell, referred to as **EX-ex**. Moving sequentially, the EXperience strand intersects with the remaining core processes: comprehension (forming the **EX-co** cell), **el**aboration (forming the **EX-el** cell), and application (forming the **EX-ap** cell). Once instruction flows through the EXperience strand, it then moves into the COmprehension strand, the APplication strand, and the INtention strand (**FIGURE 3.3**). Like the EXperience strand, these intersect with the core processes to form cells. Each strand, therefore, comprises four cells. Let's see how this framework guides the design and delivery or instruction.

Architecture of Learning: SKILL BLUEPRINT					
		CORE PROCESSES			
		experience	comprehension	elaboration	application
FOCUS	EX	EX-ex	EX-co	EX-el	EX-ap
	CO	CO-ex	CO-co	CO-el	CO-ap
	AP	AP-ex	AP-co	AP-el	AP-ap
	IN	IN-ex	IN-co	IN-el	IN-ap

FIGURE 3.3 General Blueprint Structure

Designing Skill Instruction: An Example

The Skill Blueprint's influence on designing instruction can be seen from the very beginning of the process.

What will your students be learning? What will they do with their learning?

After considering how to teach students to revise writing by eliminating nonessential modifiers, Marcus, a middle school teacher, first recognizes the subject matter as a skill. It consists of a *series of steps*—a process—students will use to improve the quality of their writing.

Learning the new skill can be broken into four steps:

1. Identify the modifiers within a sentence.
2. Consider the word(s) each modifier describes.
3. Consider whether the modifier repeats the meaning of the targeted word or adds significant meaning to it.
4. If it repeats the meaning, eliminate it. Or, on the flip side, change the targeted word so the modifier can be eliminated. If the modifier in fact clarifies the intended meaning, keep it.

What pattern(s) support(s) the instructional material? How will that/those pattern(s) connect to your students' prior experience?

Generalized, these steps might be:

1. Identify the item to consider.
2. Examine its relationship to its target.
3. Keep what is needed but eliminate the rest.

The pattern begins to emerge when Marcus phrases these steps more efficiently:

Find it. Consider its relationships. Choose an effective action. By thinking about the steps in broader terms, Marcus identifies the skill's underlying pattern. He reduces the pattern to its imperatives: *Find, consider, and choose.*

Once the pattern has been stated, Marcus begins designing instruction based on the Skill Blueprint.

EXperience Strand

How will you focus your students' attention and engage the mental processing needed to construct the learning? How will the flow of instruction mirror the brain's means of learning?

Each cell within the EXperience strand (**FIGURE 3.4**) advances the students toward establishing a reference point for learning the new skill. The **EX-ex** activity illustrates the pattern previously identified by the teacher.

Architecture of Learning: SKILL BLUEPRINT

FOCUS	CORE PROCESSES: experience	comprehension	elaboration	application
EX	**EX-ex** Provide an experience that illustrates a pattern ◆ ◆ ◆ *This establishes a **reference point** for constructing understanding*	**EX-co** Engage students in identifying and sorting the experience's defining attributes ◆ ◆ ◆ *This establishes the critical components of the emerging pattern*	**EX-el** Guide pattern recognition and statement development ◆ ◆ ◆ *This enables a connection between the referential experience and forthcoming learning*	**EX-ap** Enable pattern identification within personal experiences ◆ ◆ ◆ *This establishes personal connections to the pattern and forthcoming learning*

FIGURE 3.4 EXperience Strand General Descriptors

To teach students how to revise writing by eliminating modifiers, Marcus begins with an activity that illustrates: *Find, consider, and choose*. What if, he thinks, I gave students a box of items and told them to use the items to construct an airplane that could fly across the room? Students would *find* items and *consider* each one in relation to the goal and to the other available items. They would then *choose* to use some items and eliminate others. This illustrates the pattern, he decides, so he makes it the **EX-ex** activity.

Before his students recognize the pattern, they must comprehend the experience. Instruction moves into the **EX-co** cell, where the teacher guides student review and sorting of the experience. While student activity may be effective here, teacher-directed questioning and discussion often produce optimal results.

After his students have constructed the planes, Marcus asks them, "What just happened? What were the steps you took?" As Marcus guides the discussion, students articulate the experience in sequence:

1. We received a box of items.
2. We used some of the items to complete a task.
3. We had some items left over.

Marcus continues engaging student thinking with additional questions: "How did you decide which items to use? Did any groups use items that other groups left out of the finished product? Were any items chosen at first but then refused? Why weren't they used?" This questioning prompts the *students* to mentally organize the experience rather than Marcus reviewing and organizing it for the students.

Like **EX-co**, the next cell, **EX-el,** directs the students' attention back to the illustrative experience (**EX-ex**). A combination of questioning, contemplating, and conversation often helps them to elaborate.

Marcus asks, "Can you see any patterns emerging from building the airplanes?" With continued questioning and guidance, Marcus leads students to "discover" the pattern. (Occasionally, the teacher needs to explicitly state the pattern.) Students then discuss and explain *how* the experience *illustrates* the pattern: Find, consider, choose.

Students expand and use their understanding in the EXperience strand's final cell, **EX-ap**. To enable students to recognize personal illustrations of the pattern, Marcus restates the pattern in a flowchart (see **FIGURE 3.5**). Students then use their understanding of the pattern to identify illustrations from their own backgrounds. They can then organize these personal experiences into flowcharts, replacing the pattern's steps with personal examples of something found, something considered, and something decided or chosen. These personal reference points provide several potential connections for students to construct an understanding of how to revise writing by eliminating modifiers.

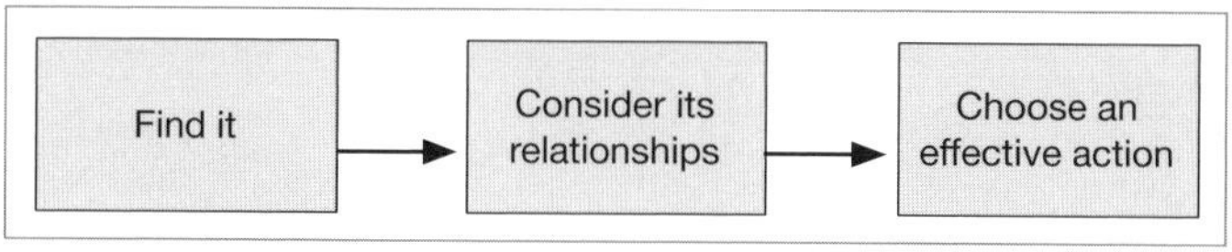

FIGURE 3.5 Pattern Presented in Flowchart (**EX-ap**)

For example, the students may relate the pattern to packing for a vacation. If the plan is to spend time at the beach, heavy sweaters and winter coats do not need to be packed even though they are normally found in the student's closet. Considering the relationship of the destination to the article of clothing reveals what is and is not needed.

As you move through the four core processes, the EXperience strand flows like a single activity (**FIGURE 3.6**). Comprehension, elaboration, and application direct the students' attention to a personal experience that illustrates the pattern and establishes it as a reference point. Instruction then moves into the COmprehension strand.

Architecture of Learning: SKILL BLUEPRINT Skill: Revising Modifiers					
		CORE PROCESSES			
		experience	comprehension	elaboration	application
FOCUS	EX	Plane Construction	Guided Review	The Plane Pattern	Pattern Examples from Experience

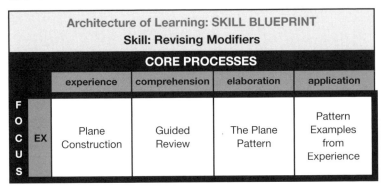

FIGURE 3.6 Unit EXperience Strand

COmprehension Strand

The COmprehension strand covers the skill's "how to" information. The teacher presents and models the skill's steps (**CO-ex**), helps students state and reorganize them (**CO-co**), guides students to recognize connections between the new skill and the previously established reference point(s) (**CO-el**), and engages students in initial, guided practice of the new skill (**CO-ap**) (**FIGURE 3.7**).

Architecture of Learning: SKILL BLUEPRINT

		CORE PROCESSES			
		experience	**comprehension**	**elaboration**	**application**
FOCUS	EX	EX-ex	EX-co	EX-el	EX-ap
	CO	**CO-ex** Present new content and/or skill processes to be mastered ◆ ◆ ◆ *This provides the new material to be learned*	**CO-co** Engage students in identifying and organizing the critical components of the new material ◆ ◆ ◆ *This establishes the new* ***knowledge*** *students must acquire*	**CO-el** Direct students to overlay new material, reference point (EX-ex), and/or personal reference points (EX-ap) ◆ ◆ ◆ *This initiates merging of the new and known to construct understanding*	**CO-ap** Facilitate guided and supported practice or summarization of the new material ◆ ◆ ◆ *This reveals and helps establish student knowledge of the new material*

FIGURE 3.7 COmprehension Strand General Descriptors

In **CO-ex**, the teacher presents the new skill, listing its individual steps and demonstrating how one follows the other. *Simply telling students the steps is insufficient for mastering a skill.* The skill's steps *must be modeled by a teacher*, both in isolation and as a complete process, so students can accurately replicate them. Students need to "do" the skill. Demonstrating *how-to* fosters learning *to do.*

This may be because demonstration actually encourages the brain to engage. Specialized neurons known as *mirror neurons* make practicing "in the head" possible. Neurologist Richard Restak details an example that explains how mirror neurons function:

> [A] perception-action matching system exists in the human brain. Imagine yourself watching me reach out and grasp the cup of tea that now sits on the small table next to my word processor. As you observe my hand reaching for the cup, the motor cortex in your brain will also become highly active in the same areas you would use if you reached out to pick up that teacup...No, that doesn't mean you can taste my tea. But it does mean that I'm directly affecting your brain as you watch me go through the motions of drinking my tea...Think for a moment of the implications of this. You can activate my brain if you can attract my attention enough to get me to watch what you're doing...[1]

When a teacher repeatedly performs a sequence of steps, her students' mirror neurons may enable their own preliminary practice of the same steps. In other words, as a teacher demonstrates a skill, students mentally rehearse it.

For example, Marcus introduces the steps for eliminating modifiers, explaining and demonstrating each step thoroughly. He then thinks aloud as the skill's steps are used to improve several examples. He does not call on students for their input yet. Instead, he explains and performs the process to all of his students:

> I have a paragraph here on the board. I'm going to revise it by working through it sentence by sentence, checking my modifiers and making improvements wherever I can. The first sentence reads, "Ellis Island, the first entry point for many traveling immigrants, lay within sight of New York City." The first step I want to take is identify the modifiers. I'm going to underline them as I find them. I see *first*, *entry*, *many*, and *traveling*. Now,

> for step two, I need to consider the words in the sentence that these modifiers modify. The modifier *first* modifies *point*. The *first point* for immigrants. That doesn't really make sense. The first point of what? Oh wait, my next modifier is *entry*, and it also modifies *point*. The *entry point* for immigrants. If it is the entry point, it has to be the first part of the United States that the immigrants encounter, right? So, it seems like *first* repeats the meaning of *entry*, and *entry* seems like a clearer modifier for *point*. So, I'm going to eliminate *first* but keep *entry*. Now my next modifier is *many*...

Demonstrating the skill, as Marcus does through thinking aloud, moves instruction naturally toward application. Before practicing the skill though, students need to review and sort its steps as the teacher demonstrated.

In the **CO-co** activity, referring students to the flowchart they created in the EXperience strand (**EX-ap**), Marcus has students create a similar flowchart, first detailing and then illustrating the skill's steps (**FIGURE 3.8**). This engages students in visualizing and organizing the skill, and it provides an opportunity for a teacher to assess each student's knowledge. Who identifies the steps and orders them correctly? Who needs additional instruction, demonstration, or guidance? Who seems confused by one or more of the steps? Marcus keeps these questions in mind as he moves around the classroom and observes the students' work.

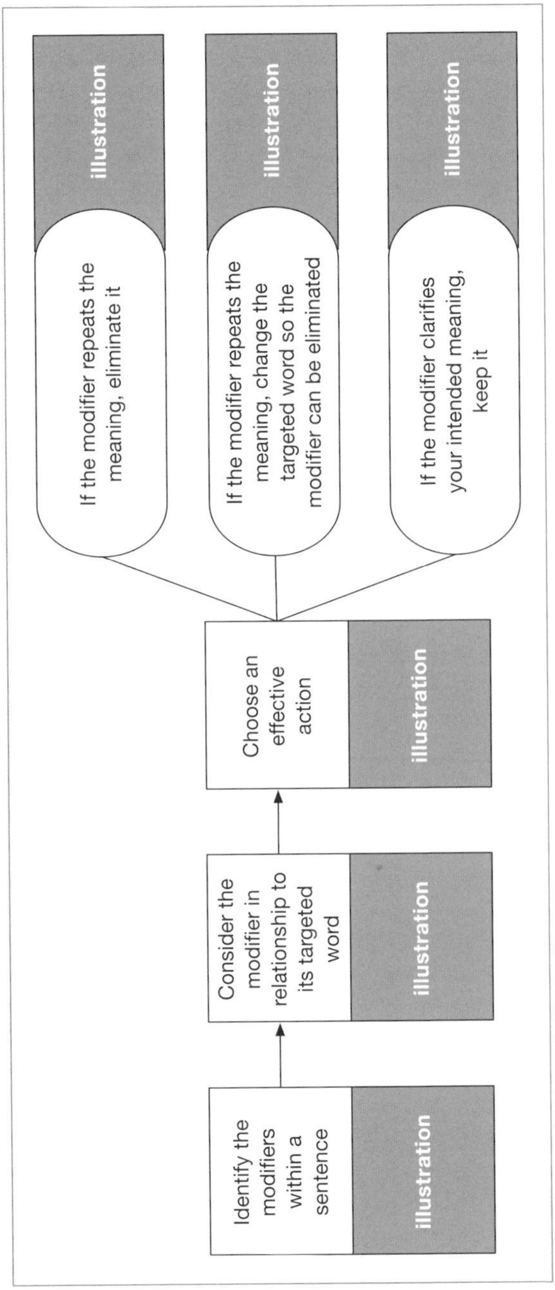
Identify the modifiers within a sentence
illustration
Consider the modifier in relationship to its targeted word
illustration
Choose an effective action
illustration
If the modifier repeats the meaning, eliminate it
illustration
If the modifier repeats the meaning, change the targeted word so the modifier can be eliminated
illustration
If the modifier clarifies your intended meaning, keep it
illustration

FIGURE 3.8 Detailed Flowchart of Skill's Steps (**CO-co**)

Marcus engages his students in comparing the flowcharts developed during the EXperience and COmprehension strands by completing an open-ended sentence: "Revising writing by eliminating nonessential modifiers is like the airplane assembly experience because...." Marcus has the students write down their initial responses first before sharing and discussing them. To strengthen connections between the new material and meaningful reference points, Marcus directs the students to examine their personal examples developed during the EXperience strand (**EX-ap**), identify one or two that relate to the skill, and explain their connections: "My experience of_____ is like revising writing by eliminating nonessential modifiers because..."

In the strand's final cell, **CO-ap**, students initially practice the skill with their teacher providing guidance and immediate feedback to ensure accuracy. This is *not* an assignment students should complete for homework and turn in for later feedback. Instead it should be conducted in the classroom with immediate instructive feedback.

For example, Marcus writes, "The man slowly plodded down the alley" on the board and has the students copy the sentence. He then directs them to use the skill's steps to evaluate the sentence's modifiers. Marcus then asks a student to demonstrate the skill by "thinking aloud," speaking throughout the process, "I see the word *slowly* in the sentence. It modifies the word *plodded*. *Plodded* means to walk slowly. Since *slowly* repeats the meaning, I will eliminate it." The teacher repeats this activity with additional sentences to help students develop their capability. Each time they proceed step-by-step through the skill's steps.

Skills in other disciplines have similar COmprehension strands. For example, a math teacher teaching students to plot ordered pairs on a graph would explain and demonstrate the skill's steps:

1. Identify the *x*-coordinate, the first number in the ordered pair, and find that position on the *x*-axis.
2. Identify the *y*-coordinate, the second number in the ordered pair, and find that position on the *y*-axis.
3. Find the spot where the *x*-axis and *y*-axis positions intersect.
4. Mark that point.

The students would then restate and sequence the steps, possibly by creating a flowchart. The teacher then guides the students in making connections between the skill's steps and examples of the pattern, possibly relating it to identifying street intersections on a map, which would have been explored in the EXperience strand. Students would then practice plotting points as the teacher stays nearby to offer direction as needed.

The COmprehension strand equips students with the knowledge of how to use the skill (**FIGURE 3.9**). Learning proceeds from the teacher's explanations and demonstrations to the students' initial attempts at evaluating modifiers. This equips students to employ their newfound knowledge during the APplication Strand.

Architecture of Learning: SKILL BLUEPRINT Skill: Revising Modifiers					
		CORE PROCESSES			
		experience	comprehension	elaboration	application
FOCUS	EX	Plane Construction	Guided Review	The Plane Pattern	Pattern Examples from Experience
	CO	Revising Writing: Modifiers	Sequencing the Steps	Modifier Revisions and Experience	Initial Practice, Instructive Feedback

FIGURE 3.9 Unit COmprehension Strand

APplication Strand

The APplication strand repeats several times to provide the practice that develops skill proficiency. The strand's cell sequence prompts deliberate thinking prior to applying the skill. As the practice continues, the center cells (**AP-co** and **AP-el**) merge and shorten, indicating increased efficiency with the skill (**FIGURE 3.10**).

Architecture of Learning: SKILL BLUEPRINT

CORE PROCESSES

FOCUS	experience	comprehension	elaboration	application
EX	EX-ex	EX-co	EX-el	EX-ap
CO	CO-ex	CO-co	CO-el	CO-ap
AP	**AP-ex** Present a scenario or problem ◆ ◆ ◆ *This initiates practice*	**AP-co** Engage students in identifying the relevant contextual components (e.g., pattern illustrated by the scenario) and/or skill-related components (e.g., steps of the skill process) ◆ ◆ ◆ *This initiates pre-application thinking*	**AP-el** Provide opportunity to compare anticipated steps with the pattern ◆ ◆ ◆ *This confirms or redirects the student's intended use of the skill*	**AP-ap** Provide opportunity to use the skill to address the scenario ◆ ◆ ◆ *This initiates skill* ***utilization*** *to produce a result or solution*

FIGURE 3.10 APplication Strand General Descriptors

In **AP-ex**, a teacher presents his students with resources and reasons to practice the skill. For example, Marcus gives the students copies of an essay featuring several modifiers. Reading the essay initiates the strand's remaining activities.

Progressing to **AP-co**, students review the skill's steps and begin *thinking through* how to apply the skill. For example, students reread the distributed essay sentence by sentence. With each sentence, they *find* any modifiers, identify and *consider* each modifier's target and the modifier's role in relation to it, and *choose* to keep or eliminate the modifier. Stopping to think about each decision enables higher-quality responses. *The student does* *not actually make the revision to the essay yet*, but thinks through what changes may be beneficial. Marcus may initially guide the students through this thinking, but such direction lessens as students continue to practice.

The **AP-el** activity provides an evaluative pause between deliberately thinking through the skill and actually using it. For example, Marcus directs the students to ask themselves, "Does the way I am considering this modifier illustrate the pattern: *Find, consider, and choose*?" If not (e.g., the student may have identified a modifier and changed it without identifying its targeted word or considering its relationship to the targeted word), the student rethinks the decision by applying the skill's three steps (**AP-co**). If he correctly used the skill—i.e., if the thinking mirrors the pattern of find, consider, and choose—he is ready to take action.

In the APplication strand's final cell, **AP-ap**, students act upon their decisions. In this example, Marcus's pupils actually revise a sentence's modifiers or leave the text as it is.

Similarly, with the math unit, students would practice plotting ordered pairs on a graph. The teacher supplies the pairs to be plotted, the students work through the steps of the skill, compare their thinking with the pattern (perhaps "Interesting points form where things intersect." Does my potential point show things intersecting?), and then plot the ordered pair. The teacher would still be available to offer help, but the students would work with increasing independence and efficiency.

The APplication strand flows as a series of related activities (**FIGURE 3.11**). Unlike the EXperience and COmprehension strands, the APplication strand repeats multiple times. Repeating the strand provides the practice necessary to transform knowledge to utility.

Architecture of Learning: SKILL BLUEPRINT Skill: Revising Modifiers					
		CORE PROCESSES			
		experience	comprehension	elaboration	application
F	EX	Plane Construction	Guided Review	The Plane Pattern	Pattern Examples from Experience
O C U	CO	Revising Writing: Modifiers	Sequencing the Steps	Modifier Revisions and Experience	Initial Practice, Instructive Feedback
S	AP	An Essay to Revise	Working the Skill	Pattern Pause	Revising

FIGURE 3.11 APplication Strand for for Revising Modifiers

INtention Strand

The INtention strand promotes transfer of a learned skill by widening the contexts in which students experience the skill's application (**FIGURE 3.12**).

Architecture of Learning: SKILL BLUEPRINT				
	CORE PROCESSES			
FOCUS	experience	comprehension	elaboration	application
EX	EX-ex	EX-co	EX-el	EX-ap
CO	CO-ex	CO-co	CO-el	CO-ap
AP	AP-ex	AP-co	AP-el	AP-ap
IN	**IN-ex** Present a scenario or problem from a wider context ◆ ◆ ◆ *This initiates recall and transfer of mastered material*	**IN-co** Provide a way to identify and organize the IN-ex scenario ◆ ◆ ◆ *This exposes the relevant scenario components and its emerging pattern(s)*	**IN-el** Provide opportunity to identify commonalities of new scenario and content or skill ◆ ◆ ◆ *This promotes the use of learned concepts and skills in addressing the scenario*	**IN-ap** Provide opportunity to make a prediction/use the skill to address scenario ◆ ◆ ◆ *This represents transfer, true **integration** of the new learning*

FIGURE 3.12 INtention Strand General Descriptors

To begin the INtention strand (**IN-ex**), Marcus has the students generate a short story or a written report. Students then identify modifiers within the written text and deliberate over whether or not to make a change (**IN-co**), compare their thinking with the established pattern to be sure they're applying the skill correctly (**IN-el**), and take appropriate action, revising the text or leaving it as is (**IN-ap**). Repeating these steps for each modifier produces completed revisions, enabling students to develop final drafts of their writing. The INtention strand mirrors the APplication strand, but it widens the context for using the skill. This process, creating an original work and revising it, simulates the "real world" practice of writers. It encourages students to begin integrating the skill into their interactions with real-world scenarios.

In the unit on plotting points on a graph, the teacher engages students in thinking similar to the APplication strand, but with actual data. For example, the teacher may have the students plot their scores on video games (played at home) over several days, or the class may plot the number of books they read each week, or plot scores on various challenges, such as word puzzles, logic puzzles, and number puzzles. In addition to actually plotting data they generate, the students see how plotted data provides opportunities for interesting comparisons. Did my video game performance improve over time? Did I score better on word puzzles, logic puzzles, or number puzzles? The INtention strand's emphasis on using the skill in different contexts deepens and extends learning as students discover new uses for the skill and the results from applying it.

Applying a skill in isolation (as in the APplication strand) differs from applying a skill within a context (as in the INtention strand). Applying the skill in a new context typically requires more thinking than using it during classroom practice. An analogy can be drawn to aspiring drivers. They usually earn a learner's permit before being allowed behind the wheel of a car, and initial driving in a confined context (e.g., an empty parking lot) often follows. To earn the learner's permit, the wannabe driver must possess knowledge of driving and the laws that govern it. Driving in a confined context prompts practice of that knowledge and develops driving skills. However, as anyone who has learned to drive has experienced, the *knowledge* required to earn the driver's permit and the initial use of driving skills in an empty parking lot (practice in isolation) differs significantly from safely driving a car in varying traffic and road conditions (application in a widened context). Continued coaching from an experienced driver increases achievement and accelerates learning as the fledgling driver moves from the parking lot to the interstate. This difference—practicing a skill in a confined context vs. applying it in widened contexts—distinguishes the APplication and INtention strands, and learning continues to deepen as teachers provide instructive feedback throughout both strands.

The INtention strand also deepens learning by engaging students in recall of previous learning. Researchers Karpicke and Roediger claim that additional studying once material is learned produces no effect on the recall required for transfer, but *repeatedly recalling the material increases the likelihood of the later recall that enables transfer.* "If a person wants to remember an event or some information over the long term," suggests Roediger, "it must be actively engaged, and retrieving information from memory serves that purpose well…Repeated retrieval over time is critical to effective, long-term retention."[2] By presenting scenarios that require using previously learned skills throughout the school year, teachers engage students in "repeated retrieval." This increases the likelihood of their long-term retention, which is critical to the transfer of learning from the classroom to the world at large.

For example, Marcus could plan to repeat the INtention strand for every writing assignment throughout the rest of the school year. Students would engage in revising writing by eliminating nonessential modifiers multiple times, and each recall of the skill would promote future recall and increase the likelihood of future use.

Teaching, like Marcus's, which carries students from referential experience to integrated learning, requires intentionally designed instruction. The completed Architecture of Learning Skill Blueprint for revising modifiers illustrates such instruction (**FIGURE 3.13**). It recognizes what students will do with their learning (use the skill to improve writing quality), connects new material to prior experiences via pattern-based (find, consider, choose) reference points, and mirrors the brain's means of learning through the focus strands and their interactions with the core processes (**FIGURE 3.14**).

Architecture of Learning: SKILL BLUEPRINT Skill: Revising Modifiers				
	CORE PROCESSES			
FOCUS	experience	comprehension	elaboration	application
EX	Plane Construction	Guided Review	The Plane Pattern	Pattern Examples from Experience
CO	Revising Writing: Modifiers	Sequencing the Steps	Modifier Revisions and Experience	Initial Practice, Instructive Feedback
AP	An Essay to Revise	Working the Skill	Pattern Pause	Revising
IN	Student-Generated New Material	Working the Skill	Pattern Pause	Revising & Final Drafts

FIGURE 3.13 Unit INtention Strand

FIGURE 3.14A on following pages

Architecture of Learning:

FOCUS	CORE: experience	CORE: comprehension
EX	**EX-ex** Provide an experience that illustrates a pattern ◆ ◆ ◆ *This establishes a* ***reference point*** *for constructing understanding*	**EX-co** Engage students in identifying and sorting the experience's defining attributes ◆ ◆ ◆ *This establishes the critical components of the emerging pattern*
CO	**CO-ex** Present new content and/or skill processes to be mastered ◆ ◆ ◆ *This provides the new material to be learned*	**CO-co** Engage students in identifying and organizing the critical components of the new material ◆ ◆ ◆ *This establishes the new* ***knowledge*** *students must acquire*
AP	**AP-ex** Present a scenario or problem ◆ ◆ ◆ *This initiates practice*	**AP-co** Engage students in identifying the relevant contextual components (e.g., pattern illustrated by the scenario) and/or skill-related components (e.g., steps of the skill process) ◆ ◆ ◆ *This initiates pre-application thinking*
IN	**IN-ex** Present a scenario or problem from a wider context ◆ ◆ ◆ *This initiates recall and transfer of mastered material*	**IN-co** Provide a way to identify and organize the IN-ex scenario ◆ ◆ ◆ *This exposes the relevant scenario components and its emerging pattern(s)*

FIGURE 3.14A Skill Blueprint Before

SKILL BLUEPRINT	
P R O C E S S E S	
elaboration	application
EX-el Guide pattern recognition and statement development ◆ ◆ ◆ *This enables a connection between the referential experience and forthcoming learning*	**EX-ap** Enable pattern identification within personal experiences ◆ ◆ ◆ *This establishes personal connections to the pattern and forthcoming learning*
CO-el Direct students to overlay new material, reference point (EX-ex), and/or personal reference points (EX-ap) ◆ ◆ ◆ *This initiates merging of the new and known to construct understanding*	**CO-ap** Facilitate guided and supported practice or summarization of the new material ◆ ◆ ◆ *This reveals and helps establish student knowledge of the new material*
AP-el Provide opportunity to compare anticipated steps with the pattern ◆ ◆ ◆ *This confirms or redirects the student's intended use of the skill*	**AP-ap** Provide opportunity to use the skill to address the scenario ◆ ◆ ◆ *This initiates skill utilization to produce a result or solution*
IN-el Provide opportunity to identify commonalities of new scenario and content or skill ◆ ◆ ◆ *This promotes the use of learned concepts and skills in addressing the scenario*	**IN-ap** Provide opportunity to make a prediction/use the skill to address scenario ◆ ◆ ◆ *This represents transfer, true* ***integration*** *of the new learning*

Architecture of Learning: SKILL BLUEPRINT Skill: Revising Modifiers				
	CORE PROCESSES			
FOCUS	experience	comprehension	elaboration	application
EX	Plane Construction	Guided Review	The Plane Pattern	Pattern Examples from Experience
CO	Revising Writing: Modifiers	Sequencing the Steps	Modifier Revisions and Experience	Initial Practice, Instructive Feedback
AP	An Essay to Revise	Working the Skill	Pattern Pause	Revising
IN	Student-Generated New Material	Working the Skill	Pattern Pause	Revising & Final Drafts

FIGURE 3.14B Skill Blueprint After

Blueprint "Rhythm" and Flow

The Blueprint strands reveal a simple consistency (**FIGURE 3.15**). Within every strand, core cognitive processes direct how the instruction will progress, establishing a natural rhythm: data is introduced (ex), identified and reorganized (co), so emerging patterns can be recognized and compared with previous experience (el), resulting in new understanding used to demonstrate a level of mastery (ap). The underlying instructional rhythm, input→processing→output, directs the flow of every strand.

CORE PROCESSES			
experience	comprehension	elaboration	application
Sensory data is introduced...	*identified and reorganized...*	*so emerging patterns can be recognized, resulting in new understanding...*	*used to demonstrate a level of mastery*
Input →	*Processing*	→	*Output*

FIGURE 3.15 The Blueprint Strand "Rhythm"

As the rhythm repeats through the strands, teachers and students flow seamlessly from new exposure to the transfer of new learning within expanding contexts (**FIGURE 3.16**).

FOCUS		
	EX	Students construct airplanes. Teacher guides review and sorting of the experience's details and the identifying of the pattern: find, consider, choose. The students identify personal examples that illustrate the pattern.
	CO	Teacher presents and demonstrates the action sequence for revising modifiers. Students review and sort the action sequence steps. Teacher guides student thinking about the new skill and its connection to the pattern and its referential illustrations. Teacher guides initial practice of the new skill.
	AP	Students read text provided for skill practice. Students use the skill to consider modifier revisions, check consistency of their skill use and its underlying pattern, then make the desired revision. Students repeat this process until all practice is completed.
	IN	Students generate text passages, such as a report or short story. Students use the skill to consider modifier revisions, check consistency of their skill use and its underlying pattern, then make the desired revision. Students repeat this process until all revisions are completed. Teacher repeats the strand multiple times throughout the school year.

FIGURE 3.16 The Skill Blueprint Strand "Rhythm" for Example Unit

Questions

1. What is a skill? List three examples from your experience as a teacher or student.

2. What role do patterns play in skill learning? What is the source for identifying skill patterns?

3. What are the strands of the Architecture of Learning Skill Blueprint? Why are these the strands?

4. How are cells formed on the Blueprints?

5. Review **FIGURE 3.15** and explain the basic consistency found in each strand.

6. Review Marcus's unit. What would you expect students to master as a result of his instruction?

Chapter 4

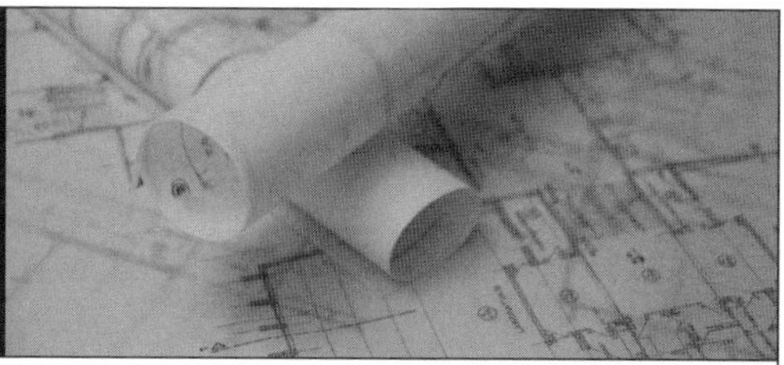

SUBJECT MATTER TYPES

Designing CONTENT Instruction

Surprises happen, especially during large projects like building a house. One day Julia and I visited our home's construction site to find a wall we didn't know would exist. Actually, it's more of a wide post than a wall, but since we weren't expecting it, it looked like a wall. A conversation with our builder revealed that the "wall" had been included in the blueprint and was needed because it provided support at a critical point. Without it the structural integrity of the house would be compromised. What we hadn't noticed was needed, the architect and builder had wisely included. A well-designed blueprint can help ensure a sound outcome.

The same is true of the Architecture of Learning Content Blueprint. It prevents teachers from overlooking a process that supports students as they strive to understand new content. It helps teachers focus on the right learning processes at the right time.

A teacher begins developing the Content Blueprint by examining the subject matter and answering the related questions: What will your students be learning? and What will they do with their learning?

Discerning the Difference: Content

The fourth-graders carefully carried their projects into the classroom, impatient to share them. New Jersey, their home state, played a dramatic role in the American Revolution on several occasions. Washington crossed the Delaware River to fight the Hessians in the Battle of Trenton; Mary Ludwig Hays became the folklore heroine “Molly Pitcher” at the Battle of Monmouth. Plus, Washington’s troops suffered a harsh winter at a Morristown encampment. The state’s history captivated me in my first year of teaching, and I hoped my passion would rub off on my nine- and ten-year-old students. Thinking a project would generate enthusiasm, I assigned one with rather vague directions. “Be creative,” I told my class. “Surprise me!”

I spent much of the the morning warning students not to reveal the projects until the afternoon social studies period. When lunch and recess ended, the unveiling began. I’d like to say that the results astonished and impressed me. They did, but for all the wrong reasons. In one display, a muscled, modern-day action figure stood in the bow of a plastic block boat to show Washington crossing the Delaware. Round-bottomed, wobbly “colonists” fought reptilian ninja “Hessians” at the Battle of Trenton, which apparently occurred atop a massive sheet cake. A late-eighties boy band, cut out of a magazine and mounted on index cards, called to a teenage pop diva for water at Monmouth. Scattered among the confusion were a few stand-out projects—the Battle of Trenton retold as a comic strip with close-to-accurate drawings, a map of Washington’s movements that showed how the state became the “crossroads of the Revolution”—but they were rare. Most projects were comical but not credible, failing to convey accurate information or engage the students in deepened thinking about New Jersey’s Revolutionary role. I had directed my students toward hands-on doing that failed to spark the minds-on thinking needed to construct a true understanding of New Jersey's role.

Students learn *content* when they *build an understanding of new information*. Students gain insights (Aha!) by recognizing patterns that emerge from the content's defining details and relating them to previous experiences or known concepts. For example, a student may relate the human musculoskeletal system to a construction crane. The student overlays the new (musculoskeletal system) with the previously experienced (construction crane) to construct understanding. (The musculoskeletal system supports the body and enables its movement.) As students identify additional connections between the new and known, the emerging understanding lays the groundwork for future thinking—for analyzing current conditions, guiding evaluative thinking, and making decisions.

In contrast to the step-by-step *action* that reveals skill mastery, understanding *ideas* and their *relationships* indicates mastery of content. As students think about new content, they form mental images and forge associations between the new content and other ideas and experiences. These associations are often expressed through statements of comparison (e.g., This is like that in such-and-such a way, but different in such-and-such a way) or statements featuring figurative language (e.g., warm water is a hurricane's gasoline).

Deeper understanding increases the likelihood of recall, which increases content's value for future thinking. When the brain perceives patterns in a context, it triggers retrieval of related content. The brain can then use the retrieved content as a reference for analysis, critical thinking, and problem-solving.

Consider a social studies unit on ancient Greece. Its facts

and cultural comparisons can contribute to a student's depth of understanding about a wide array of subjects. For example, a teacher may want her students to understand ancient Greece's political and cultural contributions. By recognizing the contributions ancient cultures have made to contemporary society, students develop respect for the past and deepen their understanding of the present. Additionally, by examining how ancient Greece solved its problems, students can gain direction for responding to today's challenges.

Before designing the unit's instruction, the teacher needs to consider questions regarding the content's pattern: *What pattern(s) support(s) the instructional material? How will that/those pattern(s) connect to your students' prior experience?* By identifying content patterns, the teacher can establish a reference point that deepens the student's understanding of the new content.

Content Patterns

To recognize emerging patterns, a teacher explores the material's specifics and identifies connections between them (which are often causal in nature). *The relationships reveal the pattern.* A science unit on the earth's structure illustrates this. The subject matter emphasizes understanding how the earth is composed, including the following ideas:

1. Scientists believe the earth's structure includes three layers: the core, the mantle, and the crust.
2. According to plate tectonic theory, solid plates that "float" on the semi-solid mantle make up the earth's crust.
3. The core and mantle contain magma, a molten rock.
4. Magma can reach the earth's surface, becoming lava, through openings in the mantle and cracks in the earth's crust.

5. Earthquakes occur when the plates of the earth's crust move, spreading apart, pushing together, or sliding by one another.
6. Earthquakes can cause openings in the earth's crust through which volcanoes may form.
7. Because of its composition, the "Ring of Fire" in the Pacific experiences frequent earthquakes and volcanic eruptions.

The unit includes information on the earth's surface and on the earth's internal structure. These two dimensions, the outside and inside, interact. The relationship between earth's surface integrity and rising magma illustrates the reciprocal relationship: magma rises and reaches the surface through cracks in the earth's surface, where it can harden and form new land masses and mountains. Such interaction illustrates a pattern: "The internal can affect the external; the external can affect the internal."

By identifying such patterns, a teacher helps students recognize meaning within the subject matter. As stimuli enter the brain, neural networks search for patterns. When patterns are recognized, the brain recalls relevant prior experiences and merges new stimuli with known concepts to construct meaning and understanding. If no patterns emerge, the brain may find the stimuli interesting for its novelty, but this attention will quickly wane. As learning expert Pat Wolfe explains, "Sustained attention [to] something that you can't figure out or that makes no sense is not only boring, it's almost impossible."[1]

Identifying Patterns:
CONTENT

1. Review the material and list or map its significant concepts.
2. Select the two most significant concepts.
3. Identify the relationship between the two major concepts (e.g., cause and effect).
4. State the relationship in a way that it relates to the material and is general enough to allow for experiential illustrations.

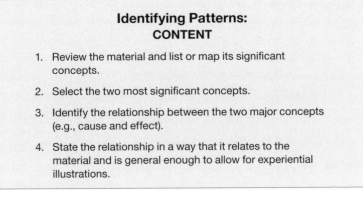

FIGURE 4.1 Steps for Creating Content Pattern Statements

Meaningful content in one subject area often connects to meaningful content in others. For example, since the earth's structure illustrates the dual influence of internal and external elements, a study of character in literature can supply an interesting reference point. A character's "internal" beliefs and values influence her "external" behavior; a character's "external" experiences and interactions influence her "internal" beliefs and values. You could also overlay the disciplines in reverse. The pattern illustrated by earth's structure may provide a reference point for understanding a fictional character.

Consider a high school teacher or college professor preparing a unit on Romanticism's influence on literature. In examining Romanticism's origins, the teacher notes its relationship to the Enlightenment. Romanticism's emphasis on intuition, sensory experience, and imagination was a reaction to the previous period's emphasis on reason, science, and rationality. Romanticism emphasized values that the Enlightenment largely rejected.

The ideas of *reaction* and *opposite* seem important. Consulting a dictionary—which is often helpful in identifying content-based patterns—the teacher finds that *react* is defined as "to respond, especially with opposition, to something." In many ways, Romanticism defined itself as anti-Enlightenment to the point where some described it as a movement from the rational to the irrational. The two eras are *opposites*. With two major ideas, *reaction* and *opposite*, identified, the relationship between them reveals an emerging pattern. Romanticism pushed away from Enlightenment's pull. The Enlightenment stressed certain values, often to the "-nth" degree, and the unfulfilling overreliance on those values provoked discontentment. This prompted a reaction, or push, in the opposite direction. Stating this relationship as a pattern, the teacher thinks, "A pull in one direction can cause a push (i.e., a reaction) in the opposite direction." That pattern captures the essence of Romanticism, and connects widely with human experience, making it valuable as an organizing structure for the new content.

As with the science unit example, this pattern crosses disciplinary boundaries. For example, the American Civil War may be viewed as several "pushes" against "pulls." Abolitionists pushed away from slavery's pull. States' rights advocates pushed away from Federalism's pull. Even with a shared belief in abolition, the pull of Quaker pacifism contrasts with the push of John Brown's actions. Lincoln's push away from bitterness, as implied in the Second Inaugural Address, contrasts with the pull of bitterness—conflict's inevitable result, as illustrated in John Wilkes Booth's assassination of Lincoln. Current events frequently illustrate this same pattern. Elections may reveal a country's pushing away from the pull of its current political direction. Pending legislation may reveal organized groups pushing against the pull of existing laws they feel impact their rights. Individuals may push away from the pull of expected conformity.

Patterns have the power to extend well beyond the curriculum's stated aim. Patterns "allow one to cross disciplinary boundaries and transfer simple ideas in one realm of human experience to another realm."[2] The more patterns we use to process our experiences, the richer we are in understanding.

What are the uses of patterns? They:

1. Create a connection to students' experiences
2. Establish a reference point for processing new content
3. Enable elaboration by relating the new and the known
4. Embed a cross-discipline benefit in the curriculum
5. Deepen understanding

The pattern, "A pull in one direction can cause a push in the opposite direction," embodies all these benefits. It also raises questions that the topic's content will answer, such as: What pull? What was the original direction and its opposite? What were the forces behind both the pull and the push? How was the push in the opposite direction communicated?

Content and Learning Processes

Once the subject matter is recognized as content and its pattern is identified, the third set of questions guides the teacher in designing the unit's instruction: *How will you focus your students' attention and engage the mental processing needed to construct the learning? How will the flow of instruction mirror the brain's means of learning?*

To transform an uninformed learner into someone with the depth of understanding that can empower effective thinking, the teacher focuses on four processes:

CONTENT LEARNING =

EXperience + **CO**mprehension + **EL**aboration + **IN**tention

Because these processes represent the focus of the teacher's content instruction, they establish the strands of the Architecture of Learning Content Blueprint (**FIGURE 4.2**). **EX**perience provides a pattern-based reference point for constructing an understanding of new content specifics. **CO**mprehension provides the new content's defining details. **EL**aboration engages the thinking needed to identify associations between the pattern-based reference point and the new content. (Because content comprises concepts to be understood, elaboration plays a prominent role in content learning.) **IN**tention provides widened or new contexts for using content understanding in logical analysis, problem-solving, and decision-making.

FOCUS	**EXperience**	establishes a pattern-based reference point for new learning; contributes a reference point for new learning
	COmprehension	presents students with new material to sort and pattern; contributes new learning's knowledge component
	ELaboration	engages students in merging new material with known reference points; contributes deepening understanding of concepts
	INtention	widens the contexts in which new learning possesses value and establishes a foundation for developing wisdom by engaging students in context analysis, evaluative thinking, decision-making, and skill application; contributes integration as students use new learning in widened contexts

FIGURE 4.2 Focus Processes of the Content Blueprint

The Content Blueprint

As they do in the Skill Blueprint, learning's core processes form the columns of the Content Blueprint, which intersect with the strands to create cells (**FIGURE 4.3**). Instruction flows through the strands, as it does in the Skill Blueprint, and moves from EXperience to INtention.

Architecture of Learning: CONTENT BLUEPRINT					
		CORE PROCESSES			
		experience	comprehension	elaboration	application
FOCUS	EX	EX-ex	EX-co	EX-el	EX-ap
	CO	CO-ex	CO-co	CO-el	CO-ap
	EL	EL-ex	EL-co	EL-el	EL-ap
	IN	IN-ex	IN-co	IN-el	IN-ap

FIGURE 4.3 Content Blueprint General Structure

The Content Blueprint's influence on teaching can be seen by following a teacher through the design and delivery of instruction.

What will your students learn? What will they do with their learning?

Helen, a high school history teacher, faces the challenge of making Byzantine history interesting for her students. She knows the material possesses value beyond her end-of-unit test. The people, patterns, and principles of the era could inform her students' thinking about contemporary situations and even aid their problem-solving and decision-making. Her curriculum guide includes the following objectives for the unit:

1. Identify the major people groups and their contributions to Byzantine culture and history.

2. Examine the influence of significant rulers such as Justinian the Great.
3. Identify significant individuals of the period and their cultural contributions.

The subject matter, Helen notes, emphasizes that students need to understand concepts; it represents content.

What pattern(s) support(s) the instructional material? How will that/those pattern(s) connect to your students' prior experience?

Helen directs her energy toward identifying an underlying pattern. She quickly notices the three objectives' frequent emphasis on the ideas of *contributions* and *influence*. These ideas connect the unit's specifics, such as the historical individuals. Consulting a dictionary, Helen notes the following definitions:

> ***contribution***: the part played by a person or thing in bringing about a result or helping something to advance
>
> ***influence***: the capacity to have an effect on the character, development, or behavior of someone or something, or the effect itself.

Both terms specify causes ("part played by a person or thing," "capacity to have an effect") and effects ("a result," "an impact"). However, cause and effect, while being an important concept, is too broad to be a pattern statement. Additional ideas need to be considered. Examining the objectives again, Helen notes that people are the identified causes ("people groups," "significant rulers," "Justinian the Great," "significant individuals"), and that the effects spread across significant spheres ("culture and history," "cultural contributions"). These ideas (people, cause and effect, wide influence) reveal a common thread, and Helen's resulting pattern statement expresses the relationship: *Individuals and groups can influence other individuals, groups, and culture.*

At first the statement seems too obvious, too simple. However, as Helen considers it more deeply, several thought-provoking questions arise. Who is influencing? Who or what is influenced? Are the influences positive? negative? neutral? Do the influences last? The unit's important concepts and their interrelationships address the questions raised by the pattern statement. The pattern provides a framework for organizing the content and connecting it to the students' experience.

EXperience Strand

How will you focus your students' attention and engage the mental processing needed to construct the learning? How will the flow of instruction mirror the brain's means of learning?

The EXperience strand establishes a reference point that illustrates the pattern. Each cell within the strand moves students toward recognizing and understanding the pattern's presence in their own experiences.

Helen begins by considering how to illustrate the pattern: "Individuals and groups can influence other individuals, groups, and culture." For the **EX-ex** activity, she decides to engage the students in a somewhat familiar scenario. First she asks a few students to step briefly outside the classroom. Once they are out in the hallway, she distributes two different items—red-striped mint candies and green-striped candies—to the remaining students and instructs them on what to do next. When one student reenters the room, students holding the red-striped mint candy (the majority) wave their candies. Helen tells the entering student to choose either the red- or green-striped candy. When the second student reenters, a good friend clearly reveals the candy he received as Helen instructs the entering student to choose a candy. The scenario repeats with other attempts at influencing each entering student's choice.

All of this fun is providing the data for the **EX-co** activity. As in the Skill Blueprint, the **EX-co** activity has students review and order the experience.

Helen uses thought-prompting questions to engage students in identifying and sorting the data: What happened as each student entered? What factors were considered when choosing the mint? Were the entering students influenced by any factors? What did the class or individual students do to influence the decisions? How many students were affected by this? (Most likely all of the entering students would have been influenced in some way. Even those who chose the opposite of the intended influence likely did so to avoid conforming. This intentional response represents an influenced choice as well.) As students discuss the questions in small groups or as a whole class, Helen helps them recognize significant ideas and how they connect.

The **EX-el** activity guides students to recognize the pattern. In this case, Helen decides to use questioning to move students closer to the pattern. "Based on the relationships between the prominent ideas our experience illustrates, what statement could we make?" Helen continues questioning students in order to help them verbalize the pattern: *Individuals and groups can influence other individuals, groups, and culture.* If necessary, Helen states the pattern and guides students to recognize how it's illustrated by the experience.

Moving to the **EX-ap** activity, the discussion switches to examples beyond the classroom. Where else, in your experience, have you seen this pattern illustrated?

For example, after showing them a definition of *influence,*

Helen asks the students to identify five contemporary, well-known individuals or groups that have influence. Following a discussion of possible examples, Helen directs the students to create a list of individuals or groups they personally have been influenced by and individuals, groups, or areas (i.e., aspects of culture) they personally have influenced. Both lists—contemporary and personal examples—provide powerful reference points for the unit's content. To help students visualize these reference points, Helen displays a flowchart (**FIGURE 4.4**) showing how influence works and asks students to follow its structure to illustrate their own examples. These flowcharts are kept for later reference.

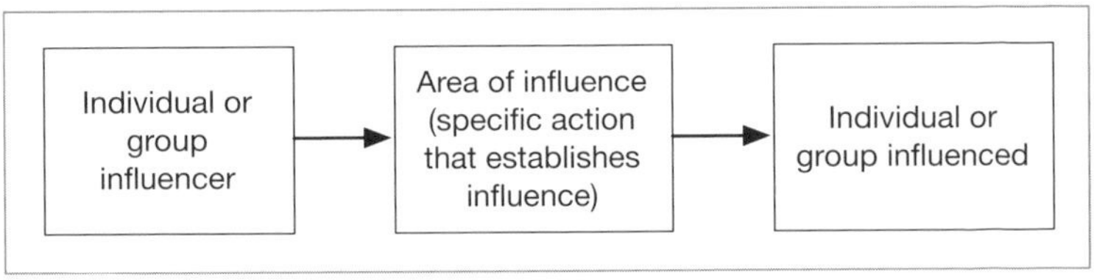

FIGURE 4.4 Influence Flowchart

The Content Blueprint's EXperience strand comprises related activities that form a sequence (**FIGURE 4.5**), and though the pattern source differs, the EXperience strands of the Skill and Content Blueprints share the same purpose: to provide a basis for thought, illustrating a pattern and establishing a reference point related to the forthcoming material.

Architecture of Learning: CONTENT BLUEPRINT Content: Byzantine History					
		CORE PROCESSES			
		experience	comprehension	elaboration	application
FOCUS	EX	Candy and Influence	Influence Analysis	Pattern of Influence	Our Examples of Influence

FIGURE 4.5 Unit EXperience Strand

COmprehension Strand

The COmprehension strand introduces the unit's new content. It can be presented by a number of effective methods, but capturing and sustaining the students' attention is critical. For homework, they may receive a textbook reading assignment with instructions to identify and reorganize key concepts using a graphic organizer. A lecture or informative video presentation the next day may be a helpful follow-up activity, during which highlighted elements from carefully selected overviews can help focus the students' attention. If they do not actively attend to the critical details, the students' ability to process the content will be limited and inhibit learning.

In presenting new content, teachers must keep in mind the brain's need for small doses of information. Often called "downtime," the brain needs to process new content in manageable chunks.[3] A teacher who lectures for forty-five minutes straight promotes less learning than a teacher who lectures for ten minutes, engages students in processing new material, and then resumes the lecture for another brief period. If the new content requires extended presentation time, frequent downtime activities that foster comprehension and elaboration should be planned.

Accordingly, Helen plans a variety of presentations for **CO-ex**. The students read textbook sections devoted to the Byzantine Empire. Helen follows up the textbook reading with lectures that present additional material and help connect the various details. Helen also shows a brief documentary video on Justinian the Great. Mindful of the students' need to process the material in limited chunks, Helen plans multiple "processing pauses" that feature activities emphasizing comprehension and elaboration.

From each information source, Helen directs her students to identify Byzantine influencers, the influential actions, and the resulting effect or contribution. She then has the students organize their findings into three-box flowcharts similar to the general sample created during **EX-ap** (**FIGURE 4.4**). The results provide a basis for formative assessment of how well students identify the key concepts and recognize ways they relate. Formative assessment and instructive feedback at this point lets both Helen and her students know that the critical knowledge components have been correctly identified and organized.

After each comprehension activity, Helen directs the students to compare the Byzantine influencers on their flowchart with the contemporary and personal examples identified during the **EX-ap** activity. This **CO-el** activity encourages students to explore connections between the new content and meaningful reference points. The connections may be anything justifiable, including areas of influence (e.g., law, the arts), roles (e.g., leaders, artists, thinkers), or contributions (e.g., codes, paintings, ideas). For example, a student may identify a connection between Byzantine ruler Justinian and a legislator who proposed changes to a law, explaining that both influenced (or sought to influence) legal elements. Such connections may be relatively simplistic, as deeper processing will occur in the ELaboration Strand.

The final activity of the COmprehension strand, **CO-ap**, engages students in processing the new content through producing something; students develop *evidence* of their content knowledge. Any activity requiring use of the new content's critical elements is appropriate.

Helen directs her students to their three-box flowcharts (**CO-co**) and has them either write a summary of the Byzantine era's influences or develop a series of sketches that illustrate a Byzantine influencer and the resulting influence. The results provide another opportunity for her assessment and instructive feedback.

The COmprehension strand equips students with knowledge of the content's important details. Learning proceeds from the teacher presenting source material to the students producing evidence that they know and can organize the content. Like the EXperience strand, it flows as a single activity: presentation, recognition and organization of key ideas, connection to known reference points, and evidence of new knowledge (**FIGURE 4.6**). This equips students to transform the new knowledge into understanding during the ELaboration strand.

Architecture of Learning: CONTENT BLUEPRINT Content: Byzantine History					
		CORE PROCESSES			
FOCUS		experience	comprehension	elaboration	application
	EX	Candy and Influence	Influence Analysis	Pattern of Influence	Our Examples of Influence
	CO	Byzantine Influencers	Organizing Byzantine Influences	Influence Connections	Summarizing Byzantine Influence

FIGURE 4.6 Unit COmprehension Strand

ELaboration Strand

Understanding, "a realization that the learner experiences about the power of an idea,"[4] distinguishes learning that lasts a lifetime from knowledge recalled just long enough to take a test. "As he organizes things in new arrangements and attaches them to the networks that represent his prior knowledge," explains James E. Zull, "each learner creates his own understandings."[5] The EXperience and COmprehension strands provide a reference point and new content. The ELaboration strand merges the two to deepen understanding (**FIGURE 4.7**).

Architecture of Learning: CONTENT BLUEPRINT					
		CORE PROCESSES			
		experience	comprehension	elaboration	application
FOCUS	EX	EX-ex	EX-co	EX-el	EX-ap
	CO	CO-ex	CO-co	CO-el	CO-ap
	EL	**EL-ex** Reconnect to the established reference point OR present a supplementary reference point ◆ ◆ ◆ *This initiates deeper conceptual blending to foster deeper understanding*	**EL-co** Guide student labeling and reorganizing of both the reference point (EL-ex) and the new knowledge components (CO-ex) ◆ ◆ ◆ *This enables the pattern(s) of the new material to emerge and initiates deeper blending of the new and known*	**EL-el** Create opportunity to blend data (all ex cells) ◆ ◆ ◆ *This deepens understanding of new material as it associates with and differentiates from known experience*	**EL-ap** Facilitate a means of communicating or portraying deepened understanding ◆ ◆ ◆ *This reveals and increases student understanding*

FIGURE 4.7 ELaboration Strand General Descriptors

The **EL-ex** activity simply establishes the two elements students will "overlay"—like encyclopedia acetate pages—and blend to deepen understanding of the new content.

Helen directs the students to record several Byzantine influencers (previously listed on their flowchart during **CO-co**) and contemporary or personal examples of influence (developed during the **EX-ap** activity) on individual index cards. This establishes the two elements students will be blending.

The next activity, **EL-co**, engages students in an in-depth analysis and organization of the two elements. Students focus on each individual item and identify its important details. They do this for both the new content and the known concepts. The deeper the analysis, the richer the coming elaboration can be.

Helen directs her students to record significant characteristics, both Byzantine and contemporary, on the back of each corresponding index card. The students record as many details that explain the individual, his or her influential actions, and the resulting influence (**FIGURE 4.8**).

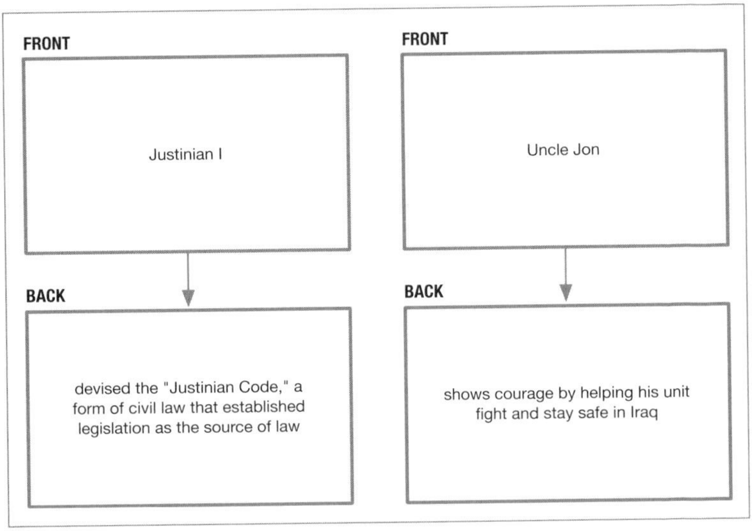

FIGURE 4.8 Example of Student Index Cards

Blending new content with known experience to produce meaningful connections provides the **EL-el** focus. The teacher may use questioning to prompt deeper thinking and increased understanding.

Helen directs the students to arrange and survey the index cards, thinking about the influences they represent. Helen then directs the students to identify associations between the Byzantine influence and the contemporary influence. When they identify a significant connection, the students place the index cards side by side and write brief notes to explain how the subjects connect. This continues, possibly as homework, until each new content element (Byzantine influences) pairs with at least one pattern-illustrative (contemporary) element (**FIGURE 4.9**).

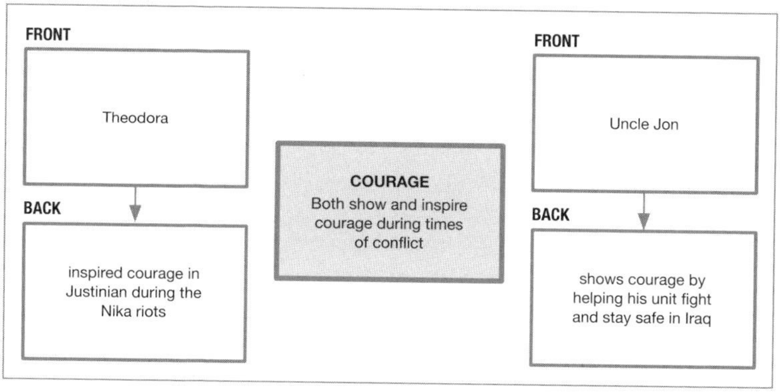

FIGURE 4.9 Example of Student Index Card Pairings and Explanation

As an effective alternative, Helen could have the students arrange all the index cards on a large sheet of paper and draw connecting lines between them to create a concept map. On each line, students would record the ideas that connect one subject to the other. The resulting web encourages multiple connections between elements and produces new insights that deepen understanding (**FIGURE 4.10**). Similar activity could also be completed using computer- or Internet-based graphic organizers.

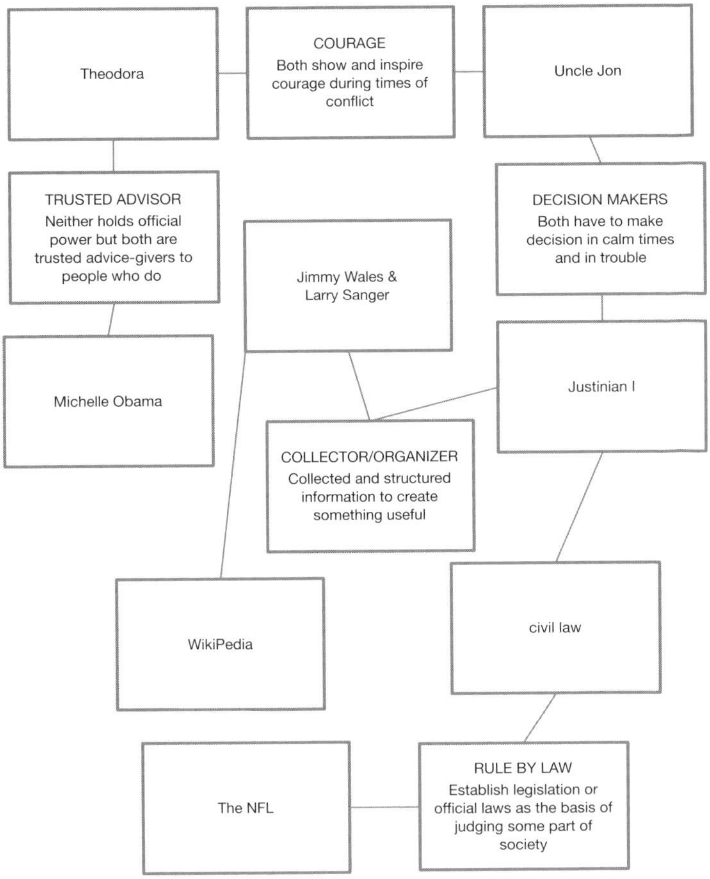

FIGURE 4.10 Partial Example of Student Index Card Web

In many ways, the cognitive activity of the **EL-el** cell represents the culmination of the unit's objectives. New content relates to an understood reference point, constructing insights that may be used to analyze current conditions (i.e., the "real world") and guide critical thinking and decision-making.

New insights gained via the blending of the new and known need to be expressed. The **EL-ap** activity engages students in communicating their understanding of the new content.

Helen directs the students to select one or two of their connected index card sets—perhaps those they think represent the most significant connections. The students then write an explanation of the connections between the two influencers and how each illustrates the pattern: *Individuals and groups can influence other individuals, groups, and culture.* For example, a student may write:

> Theodora and Michelle Obama seem to have much in common. Both married men who became leaders. Theodora's husband, Justinian I, ruled over the Byzantine Empire. Michelle Obama's husband was elected President of the United States. As a result, both women possess influence even though they were/are not in official positions of leadership. Both women also demonstrate confidence. When Michelle Obama spoke during the campaign to elect her husband she always seemed self-assured enough to ignore those who criticized her. Theodora showed amazing confidence during the Nika riots. When her husband and his empire were in danger, she spoke confidently and convinced Justinian to stay and fight rather than run and hide. Though they are separated by thousands of years of history, both women influenced their worlds.

Like the preceding strand, the ELaboration strand flows as a series of related activities (**FIGURE 4.11**). Two inputs—new and known data—are identified, each critical element is analyzed and sorted, the two inputs are "overlaid" to promote blending and understanding, and new understandings are communicated. This equips the students to transform their deepened understanding into integrated concepts for thinking. The Blueprint's final strand, INtention, helps initiate this transformation.

Architecture of Learning: CONTENT BLUEPRINT Content: Byzantine History					
CORE PROCESSES					
		experience	comprehension	elaboration	application
FOCUS	EX	Candy and Influence	Influence Analysis	Pattern of Influence	Our Examples of Influence
	CO	Byzantine Influencers	Organizing Byzantine Influences	Influence Connections	Summarizing Byzantine Influence
	EL	Index Cards of Influence	Detailing the Cards	More Influence Connections	Connection Explanations

FIGURE 4.11 Unit ELaboration Strand

INtention Strand

The INtention strand engages students in using their new content understandings in critical thinking, problem solving, contextual analysis, and decision-making. It directs attention to circumstances that relate to the new content and promotes thinking about how new content understanding can be used as a basis for conclusions.

For example, to begin the strand (**IN-ex**), Helen distributes a news article detailing a current Supreme Court case and asks students to read it (**FIGURE 4.12**). The article provides the data to be discussed throughout the strand.

In the **IN-co** phase, students identify and sort out the critical details of the case. The students establish knowledge of the widened context. Helen directs her students to identify the key ideas (e.g., individuals, issues, events) presented in the news article. She uses questioning to help guide her students' thinking when necessary, and helps them identify the article's critical details.

The **IN-el** step reintroduces the recently learned content by connecting it with a real-world example. Pattern recognition sparks the connection and subsequent thinking.

Once students have identified the news article's critical details, Helen asks them if they see any patterns emerging. If necessary, she reminds them of the pattern: *Individuals and groups can influence other individuals, groups, and culture*. Helen then directs them to explore connections between the case and Byzantine-era influences. Helen uses questions as needed to guide this elaborative thinking: "Can you identify areas (specific governance procedures, rights of a group, etc.) that were influenced by the Byzantine era and could potentially be influenced by the ruling in this case?" "In light of what we know about Byzantine-era influence, how might the ruling in this case influence subsequent cases, generations, or societies?" "How would a decision in this case relate to the concept of civil law?"

The **IN-ap** activity brings this deepened thinking to a point of making independent decisions. Students draw conclusions, make predictions, offer advice, or propose solutions. To support these, the students refer back to their new content understanding.

For example, Helen asks her students to make predictions about the current case, using Byzantine-era examples as justification. These may be informally written (i.e., each student drafts ideas) and then discussed in small groups or as a whole class. Throughout the discussion, Helen reminds students to show how understanding Byzantine influences informs their conclusions about the contemporary court case. (Look how relevant Byzantine history suddenly becomes!) Note that students are *not* asked to provide an opinion on the case. The purpose of the INtention strand is to *use understanding of the unit's content* (the Byzantine era) *to comprehend and evaluate contemporary conditions*. Having students share their personal, often uninformed and unjustified opinions about the case does not address the **IN-ap** objective, which is to make the unit's content a basis for examining current events.

Architecture of Learning: CONTENT BLUEPRINT Content: Byzantine History				
FOCUS	CORE PROCESSES			
	experience	comprehension	elaboration	application
EX	Candy and Influence	Influence Analysis	Pattern of Influence	Our Examples of Influence
CO	Byzantine Influencers	Organizing Byzantine Influences	Influence Connections	Summarizing Byzantine Influence
EL	Index Cards of Influence	Detailing the Cards	More Influence Connections	Connection Explanations
IN	Influence in the News	News Analysis	History and the News	Looking Ahead

FIGURE 4.12 Unit INtention Strand

To optimize the value of content understanding, students benefit from repeated INtention strands with different scenarios and connections to different units of study throughout the year.

Students could be directed to the real-world scenario (**IN-ex**), asked to identify and label another element that exhibits similarities with a previous unit of study (**IN-co**), to find connections (**IN-el**), and predict or advise (**IN-ap**). The value of accumulated knowledge increases each time students use it to appraise present circumstances. Recalling content comes more easily as students rehearse the new material in light of previous units, and understanding continues to deepen as students merge contemporary elements with ideas from prior learning.

For example, Helen may direct students back to the article (**IN-ex**), ask them to list the people involved in the court case (**IN-co**), and then direct students to compare these people with individuals studied during an Ancient Egypt unit that emphasized the relationship between personalities and actions (**IN-el**). Students explore connections between Ancient Egyptian personalities and individuals involved in the contemporary court case. These connections inform their predictions about attitudes or actions individuals may take during the case (**IN-ap**).

Teaching like Helen's that elevates students from first exposure to integrated thinking requires intentionally designed instruction. The completed Architecture of Learning Content Blueprint for teaching the Byzantine Empire illustrates how such instruction works (**FIGURE 4.13**). It recognizes what students will do with their learning (construct an understanding of new information and use that understanding in thinking). It identifies an underlying pattern that connects new content with known concepts (individuals and groups can influence other individuals, groups, and culture). It mirrors the brain's means of content learning through the focus strands and their interactions with the core processes. A teacher *can* be certain content instruction will match content learning by using the Content Blueprint as a guide to design sound instruction of a unit.

This flow of instruction can also be seen in other subject areas, such as an elementary math unit. Knowing what a percentage represents and its relationship to fractions and decimals are important concepts for higher math but difficult ideas for young students. While most math units include related skills, such as adding decimals, the concepts and connections between percentages, decimals, and fractions are so critical that instruction that focuses on helping students just understand these ideas makes sense. When understanding is the target, the Content Blueprint guides teaching.

In the EXperience strand of such a unit, Matt, the teacher, shows examples of the same item represented in multiple forms. For example, paintings and photographs of the same landmark (e.g., the Brooklyn Bridge). Matt follows this by showing his students multiple representations of the same monetary amount (e.g., a $1.00 bill, 4 quarters, ten dimes, and 100 pennies). He focuses the students' discussion on how the same thing can be represented in different ways, leading to the students recognizing the pattern: The same idea can be shown in different formats. Matt then has the students identify additional examples of the pattern from their own experiences.

In the COmprehension strand, Matt reviews any formats previously taught, introduces new formats, and helps students recognize the relationships between them. Following explanations of each format, he works through several examples, thinking aloud so students become familiar with how to process the related formats. For example:

> I see in a newspaper article that nine out of ten people prefer the candy CrunchyTarts to the candy SofteeSweets. Hmm, nine out of ten. That's a pretty big difference. If I express that as a fraction, I put the size of the whole group, *10*, as the denominator because ten represents the whole. The part of the group that prefers CrunchyTarts is nine, so I put *9* in the numerator. Now I can see nine out of ten represented as a fraction. Hmm, when I say the fraction out loud, nine-tenths, it makes me think of another way to represent the same amount. The first place to the right of the decimal is the tenth's place. It's like the denominator in my fraction. So, if nine-tenths is the amount I want to show in a decimal, I can write "0.9," which represents "nine-tenths." So

> far, I've got nine out of ten, $\frac{9}{10}$, and 0.9. I can still show this quantity in one more format. Let's see, percentages are always based on 100 representing the whole group. If I want to show the quantity as a percentage, it will be a certain number out of 100%. If my fraction is $\frac{9}{10}$, I can multiply the bottom by 10 to get a denominator of 100, and if I multiply the denominator, I need to multiply the numerator by the same number to keep the fractions equal. That gives me $\frac{90}{100}$, which we often present as 90%. So, nine out of ten, $\frac{9}{10}$, and 0.9 are also equal to 90%; they all show the same quantity. I can write 9 out of 10, $\frac{9}{10}$, 0.9, or 90% of people prefer CrunchyTarts to SofteeSweets.

Such demonstration and thinking aloud would need to be repeated multiple times with the emphasis placed on both the unique features of each form and the relationships between them. Matt then has the students write definitions for percentage, fraction, and decimal expressed in their own words. Next, Matt asks the students to explain how their definitions and the examples presented in the think-aloud demonstrations relate to the pattern: The same idea can be shown in different formats. Discussion focuses on how each distinct format represents an equal quantity and how each representation shows that quantity. For example, students connect the denominator of $\frac{9}{10}$ with the first place to the right of a decimal point and connect the percentage with the fraction $\frac{90}{100}$. Matt takes every opportunity to connect the idea of a whole being shown by the denominator of a fraction so students recognize that a whole can be represented by 1.0, 10, and 100 even though the number of individual items making up the whole can vary. The COmprehension strand ends with the students developing their own think-aloud demonstrations with a different quantity as Matt assesses and provides instructive feedback.

The ELaboration strand for this unit engages students in deeper thinking about the various formats and, especially, the mathematical connections between them. Matt begins the strand by having students review the definitions they wrote for each format (**EL-ex**) and identify the defining characteristics of each. For example, a fraction has a numerator that shows the number of items in relation to the number of items in the whole, which is represented by the denominator (**EL-co**). He then reminds students of the pattern, *The same idea can be shown in different formats*, and asks them how the various formats with their distinct characteristics also illustrate the pattern. After some discussion, Matt asks the students to convey, in a nonverbal form, the characteristics of each format and how all the formats can represent the same quantities (**EL-el**). The results may be as concrete or abstract as the students wish. Then, as if they were preparing an explanation to be posted with their graphic, the students write a brief statement that describes the relationship of the graphic to the pattern (**EL-ap**).

For the INtention strand, Matt collects news reports that feature a quantity expressed in a fraction, percentage, as a decimal, or in phrasing (e.g., 7 out of 10). The students review each article (**IN-ex**), identify the quantity and in which form it is stated (**IN-co**), explain why it could also be expressed in the other formats—how it can illustrate the unit's pattern (**IN-el**), and convert the quantity into each of the other forms and explain why the varied forms still represent the same quantity (**IN-ap**).

By designing his instruction this way, Matt emphasizes the thought processes that will help his students build an understanding of the relationship between fractions, decimals, and percentages. *This understanding prepares them for instruction in calculating each form and solving problems that present quantities in mixed forms.*

Architecture of Learning:

FOCUS \ CORE	experience	comprehension
EX	**EX-ex** Provide an experience that illustrates a pattern ◆ ◆ ◆ *This establishes a **reference point** for constructing understanding*	**EX-co** Engage students in identifying and sorting the experience's defining attributes ◆ ◆ ◆ *This establishes the critical components of the emerging pattern*
CO	**CO-ex** Present new content and/or skill processes to be mastered ◆ ◆ ◆ *This provides the new material to be learned*	**CO-co** Engage students in identifying and organizing the critical components of the new material ◆ ◆ ◆ *This establishes the new **knowledge** students must acquire*
EL	**EL-ex** Reconnect to the established reference point OR present a supplementary reference point ◆ ◆ ◆ *This initiates deeper conceptual blending to foster deeper understanding*	**EL-co** Guide student labeling and reorganizing of both the reference point (EL-ex) and the new knowledge components (CO-ex) ◆ ◆ ◆ *This enables the pattern(s) of the new material to emerge and initiates deeper blending of the new and known*
IN	**IN-ex** Present a scenario or problem from a wider context ◆ ◆ ◆ *This initiates recall and transfer of mastered material*	**IN-co** Provide a way to identify and organize the IN-ex scenario ◆ ◆ ◆ *This exposes the relevant scenario components and its emerging pattern(s)*

FIGURE 4.13A Content Blueprint Before

CONTENT BLUEPRINT

P R O C E S S E S	
elaboration	**application**
EX-el Guide pattern recognition and statement development ◆ ◆ ◆ *This enables a connection between the referential experience and forthcoming learning*	**EX-ap** Enable pattern identification within personal experiences ◆ ◆ ◆ *This establishes personal connections to the pattern and forthcoming learning*
CO-el Direct students to overlay new material, reference point (EX-ex), and/or personal reference points (EX-ap) ◆ ◆ ◆ *This initiates merging of the new and known to construct understanding*	**CO-ap** Facilitate guided and supported practice or summarization of the new material ◆ ◆ ◆ *This reveals and helps establish student knowledge of the new material*
EL-el Create opportunity to blend data (all *ex* cells) ◆ ◆ ◆ *This deepens* ***understanding*** *of new material as it associates with and differentiates from known experience*	**EL-ap** Facilitate a means of communicating or portraying deepened understanding ◆ ◆ ◆ *This reveals and increases student understanding*
IN-el Provide opportunity to identify commonalities of new scenario and content or skill ◆ ◆ ◆ *This promotes the use of learned concepts and skills in addressing the scenario*	**IN-ap** Provide opportunity to make a prediction/use the skill to address scenario ◆ ◆ ◆ *This represents transfer, true* ***integration*** *of the new learning*

Architecture of Learning: CONTENT BLUEPRINT Content: Byzantine History					
		CORE PROCESSES			
		experience	**comprehension**	**elaboration**	**application**
FOCUS	EX	Candy and Influence	Influence Analysis	Pattern of Influence	Our Examples of Influence
	CO	Byzantine Influencers	Organizing Byzantine Influences	Influence Connections	Summarizing Byzantine Influence
	EL	Index Cards of Influence	Detailing the Cards	More Influence Connections	Connection Explanations
	IN	Influence in the News	News Analysis	History and the News	Looking Ahead

FIGURE 4.13B Content Blueprint After

Blueprint "Rhythm" and Flow

Like those of the Skill Blueprint, the Content Blueprint strands reveal a simple consistency (**FIGURE 4.14**). Within every strand, core cognitive processes direct how the instruction progresses, establishing a natural rhythm: data is introduced (ex), identified and reorganized (co), so emerging patterns can be recognized and compared with previous experience (el), resulting in new understanding used to demonstrate a level of mastery (ap). The underlying instructional rhythm, input→processing→output, directs the flow of every strand.

CORE PROCESSES			
experience	**comprehension**	**elaboration**	**application**
Sensory data is introduced...	*identified and reorganized...*	*so emerging patterns can be recognized, resulting in new understanding...*	*used to demonstrate a level of mastery*
Input ⟶		*Processing* ⟶	*Output*

FIGURE 4.14 The Blueprint Strand "Rhythm"

As the rhythm repeats through the strands, teachers and students flow seamlessly from experiential background to the transfer of new leaning within expanding contexts (**FIGURE 4.15**).

FOCUS	EX	Students experience choices made with attempted influence. The experience is reviewed and sorted to recognize the pattern: Individuals and groups can influence other individuals, groups, and culture. Students identify personal examples of influences and their experiences as influencers.
	CO	Teacher presents content on the Byzantine Empire. Students identify and sort Byzantine Influencers by creating flowcharts and make quick comparisons with the referential experience (EX-ex) and personal examples (EX-ap). Students write a summary of the influence evident in the Byzantine Empire.
	EL	Students list Byzantine and personal influences on index cards and identify key characteristics of each. Students then pair the Byzantine influences with a personal influence and explain how one relates to the other.
	IN	Students read about a contemporary court case and identify and sort its critical details. The teacher guides students to recognize the pattern of influence evident in the court case and engages students in thinking about it by referencing the Byzantine Empire. Students draw conclusions that they support with evidence from their understandings of the Byzantine Empire.

FIGURE 4.15 The Content Blueprint Strand "Rhythm" for Byzantine Empire Unit

Questions

1. What characterizes content? List three examples from your experience as a teacher or student.

2. What role do patterns play in content learning? What is the source for identifying content patterns?

3. What are the strands of the Architecture of Learning Content Blueprint? Why are these the strands?

4. Explain the basic consistency found in each strand.

5. Review Helen's unit. What would you expect students to master as a result of her instruction? Do the same for Matt's unit.

Chapter 5

SUBJECT MATTER TYPES

Designing COMBINATION Instruction

It's our moving day, but a problem comes up. The small patch of front lawn lacks sod, and an inspector who must sign the occupancy permit refuses to do so. The house is incomplete, according to the inspector, because the lawn lacks grass. What he saw that Friday afternoon implied that what he could not see would remain incomplete. As a result, we could stay in the house, but until the permit was signed, we could not turn on the heat or hot water. We had already vacated our temporary apartment, so we spent a few chilly early spring days unpacking boxes and talking about how good the heat and a hot shower would eventually feel.

The following Monday, our builder, drawings in hand, met with the inspector. The drawings revealed what the inspector could not see on the surface. Utility connections had been made according to code, and with the exception of sod, which would be laid that week, all digging and pipe laying was complete. Satisfied that the home passed inspection, the inspector signed the permit. Heat and hot water never felt so good!

Because the inspector could not see beyond the surface, he could not sign off on the permit. Additional information drawn from the context would have altered his initial decision. Once the *underlying patterns were shown* to him, he permitted occupancy.

Partial learning can produce similar results. Students who master certain skills but lack the conceptual understanding necessary to recognize where those skills are valuable lose opportunities to apply them in life. It's as if they have money in their wallets that they can never spend.

Discerning the Difference: Combination

"Now?" he asked.

"Tell me what you see in the scenario," I requested.

Ryley knew his math. Given a sheet of practice exercises, he could supply answers with remarkable speed. But word problems stumped him. His parents grew concerned when Ryley's standardized test performance did not reflect the skills of the young mathematician they saw doing daily homework.

As Ryley entered middle school, the annual standardized test required responses to an increasing number of word problems. This contrasted with his early math instruction at another school, which emphasized rote memorization of facts and skill sequences. Ryley could rattle off an acrostic or other mnemonic for nearly every multistep mathematical process. "Dogs Must Seek Biscuits," he explained, "really means divide, multiply, subtract, and bring down."

"When you had to answer word problems in math class, how did you know which operation to use?" I asked.

"That was easy," Ryley explained. "Whatever we were practicing was what we were studying. When we practiced adding, I just needed to add to answer all the word problems."

Aha! The problem with standardized test performance became clear. The word problems he faced now were not clustered by type. To solve the word problems—and to use math in real life—

Ryley needed to understand the patterns associated with each mathematical operation and be able to recognize those patterns within scenarios, both real and portrayed in word problems.

"Ryley, what does addition look like?" I asked.

"You know, it has numbers with a plus sign between them," he responded.

"Show me what addition looks like," I challenged, "without using any numbers."

Ryley gave me a blank stare and then responded, "You can't do that. You have to have numbers to add."

He had great skills, but he did not know when to use them. His know-how lacked the conceptual understanding needed to use the right skills at the right time.

Students learn combination subject matter when they recognize a context-based pattern and use the appropriate skill for problem-solving. Two steps characterize combination subject matter: the student recognizes what defines the problem's context, and applies a skill to address it. In other words, the student accurately "reads" a scenario, identifying an underlying pattern that triggers recall and use of a relevant skill.

Consider long division. To apply the correct skill, a learner must identify the need for division by recognizing that a group of things must be separated into smaller, equally sized groups. Recognizing this pattern triggers her recall of the steps she must take to calculate a quotient.

Imagine Ryley working through a mathematics section of a standardized test featuring several word problems. For example:

> Mrs. Jones owns a candy store. A new shipment of Big Bubble Gumballs just arrived. There are 144 gumballs in the shipment.

> Mrs. Jones tells Jerry to put an even number of gumballs in each of the twelve display jars. How many gumballs should Jerry put in each jar?

To solve this problem, Ryley must recognize that a large number of items (144 gumballs) needs to be separated into twelve equally sized groups (the display jars). Recognition of the context-based pattern precedes the decision to use division.

Now extend the context. Fifteen years after the standardized test question with Jerry and Mrs. Jones, Ryley leads a summer camp program. During an activity session, 45 children need to be separated into 11 teams of equal (or close to equal) size. Ryley must again recognize that a quantity of something (45 children) needs to be separated into 11 equally sized groups (teams). "Ah!" figuratively shouts his brain, "Division!" At this point Ryley applies the correct math skill to determine team sizes and group the children accordingly. Ryley divides the children into 10 teams of 4 and one team of 5.

Accurate analysis and application characterize mastery of combination subject matter. The student can "read" a situation, determining the patterns that define it. Her ability to respond with an appropriate skill also increases. Applying the skill follows discerning the context. As the student develops ability *in both elements*, combination learning deepens.

Before designing the instruction of combination material, a teacher must consider questions regarding the combination's pattern: *What pattern(s) support(s) the instructional material? How will that/those pattern(s) connect to your students' prior experience?* By identifying combination patterns, the teacher can establish a useful reference point.

Combination Patterns

To recognize the pattern(s) within combination subject matter, a teacher needs to explore the patterns of scenarios in which the skill proves valuable. Though combination subject matter ultimately requires applying the right skill, it first requires reading the context. Because the one comes before the other, the contextual pattern provides the pattern for instruction.

For example, a language-arts unit on adjectives may require both content and skill components:

1. Content—understanding an adjective's critical attributes.
2. Skill—revising to improve adjective use.

Notice the interdependent relationship of the two. While many teachers merely teach students the defining attributes of adjectives, this knowledge is of little value without being able to use the associated skill. Conversely, teaching students to revise writing by improving adjective use requires knowing how to identify adjectives. The need to learn both makes this subject matter a combination.

Recognizing this, the teacher should explore the relationship between adjectives and other sentence elements to identify a pattern. An adjective, he thinks, names an attribute of a noun; it describes a noun. Adjectives are defined by their relationship to a noun. This relationship matters because some words can play several roles. For example, *red* can be a noun (the color red…), an adjective (the red car), or even a proper noun ("Hey, Red!"). As you can see, merely memorizing a list of adjectives will not work. Students must understand the defining attributes of adjectives.

The idea also relates to the skill element. In determining if an adjective is necessary, students need to consider its relationship to the noun it modifies. This relationship influences whether the adjective is eliminated, changed, or kept as is. The relationship prompts thinking about both the conceptual understanding (What makes an adjective an adjective?) and the associated skill (How are adjectives used effectively?). In analyzing sentences, students may identify the nouns, then identify any terms describing or stating attributes of the nouns. In usage, students may examine their nouns, evaluate each noun's meaning, and either use a more descriptive noun (*mansion* instead of *house*) or add a clarifying adjective (an *opulent* house). Understanding the relationship of adjectives to nouns enables students to successfully complete both tasks.

Convinced this is a useful pattern, the teacher states it succinctly: "Relationship reveals identity." Wow, he thinks, that is potentially a powerful pattern because it can be transferred to many areas of study and illustrated in many life experiences. If students understand this pattern and can plug in the related grammatical aspects (adjectives and nouns), they can achieve both the identification and usage goals of the unit.

Identifying Patterns:
COMBINATION

1. Focus on the material's contextual element.
2. Review the material and identify the defining attributes of the context that will require the associated skill. What pattern, recognized within the context, will trigger recall of the associated skill?
3. State the pattern using general terms.

FIGURE 5.1 Steps for Creating Combination Pattern Statements

Writer Mark Tredinnick explains that from patterns "meaning arises." He continues:

> How does that happen? It happens because a writer or speaker puts words into an order in which we have learned to recognize a pattern of relationships and so can derive the meaning that particular pattern makes. It happens because of the innate human avidness for story, for relationship and causality. It happens because of the human gift for seeing and attributing meaning to patterns—and for storing and repeating them in mind and body and speech. We humans make sense of our life and the world we live in by learning how things interact, what causes what....[1]

Patterns are meaningful. They are what the brain seeks, and they are the trigger for appropriate action. They enable students to read contexts and apply appropriate skills. Patterns promote learning, recall, and transfer. They are a critical component of combination instruction.

Combinations and Learning Processes

Once the subject matter is recognized as a combination and its pattern is identified, the third set of questions guides the teacher in designing instruction: *How will you focus your students' attention and engage the mental processing needed to construct the learning? How will the flow of instruction mirror the brain's means of learning?*

To transform an unresponsive student into one who can analyze a scenario and choose the right skill, the teacher focuses on all five learning processes.

COMBINATION LEARNING =

EXperience + **CO**mprehension + **EL**aboration + **AP**plication + **IN**tention

Because these processes represent the teacher's focus, they establish the strands of the Architecture of Learning Combination Blueprint (**FIGURE 5.2**). EXperience provides a reference point for the subject matter's pattern. COmprehension presents the defining details of the pattern and how to employ the associated skill step-by-step. ELaboration engages students in understanding the contextual pattern. This understanding triggers recall of associated skills. Students gain proficiency in using the skill through APplication. INtention widens the contexts in which students analyze contexts and apply the appropriate skill.

FOCUS	EXperience	establishes a pattern-based reference point for new learning
	COmprehension	presents students with new material to sort and pattern
	ELaboration	engages students in merging new material with known reference points to deepen understanding
	APplication	engages students in practicing new skills to develop accuracy and efficiency
	INtention	widens the contexts in which new learning possesses value and establishes a foundation for developing wisdom by engaging students in context analysis, evaluative thinking, decision-making, and skill application

FIGURE 5.2 Focus Processes of the Combination Blueprint

Learning's core processes form the columns of the Combination Blueprint and intersect with the strands to create cells (**FIGURE 5.3**). Instruction flows through the strands, from establishing a reference point to engaging students in choosing the right skill and applying it.

Architecture of Learning: COMBINATION BLUEPRINT					
		CORE PROCESSES			
		experience	comprehension	elaboration	application
FOCUS	EX	EX-ex	EX-co	EX-el	EX-ap
	CO	CO-ex	CO-co	CO-el	CO-ap
	EL	EL-ex	EL-co	EL-el	EL-ap
	AP	AP-ex	AP-co	AP-el	AP-ap
	IN	IN-ex	IN-co	IN-el	IN-ap

FIGURE 5.3 The Combination Blueprint

The Combination Blueprint's influence on designing instruction can be seen by following a teacher through the design and teaching process. As always, it starts with two questions:

What will your students be learning? What will they do with their learning?

Elisa, an early elementary teacher, finds the following objective in her first grade curriculum guide: "solve simple story problems by adding together numbers between 1 and 20." Two steps will be required to accomplish the objective:

1. The children need to recognize two groups must merge into one large group—the pattern of addition.
2. They must actually "do the math" (the skill of adding) to find the sum.

The material *combines* both a conceptual recognition element (the pattern) and a skill element (the adding). It is combination subject matter.

What pattern(s) support(s) the instructional material? How will that/those pattern(s) connect to your students' prior experience?

Elisa begins thinking about an underlying pattern. By this point in the year, her students have learned foundational addition and understand commutative properties (a+b=b+a), but their recognizing the need to add based on *contextual* elements will be new. Elisa thinks deeply about this problem. *When two groups merge to form one group, I will need to add to know how many individual items compose the larger, combined group. When I recognize a context or a story problem illustrating this pattern, I add to find a sum.* She puts these thoughts into a succinct statement using terms familiar to first-graders: *When two groups are put together to make one group, the new group has a larger number of items.* With the pattern statement identified, Elisa begins designing the unit.

EXperience Strand

How will you focus your students' attention and engage the mental processing needed to construct the learning? How will the flow of instruction mirror the brain's means of learning?

As in the other Blueprints, the EXperience strand first establishes a reference point that illustrates the pattern. Each cell within the strand moves students toward recognizing and understanding the pattern (**FIGURE 5.4**).

To illustrate the pattern for students, Elisa develops an activity for **EX-ex** that she thinks will work well. She gives her students a variety of small items—two students each receive a few pink erasers, two students each receive a few paper clips, and other pairs receive other items. After counting their items individually, Elisa tells her students to find the classmate that has the same kind of item. Each one should count the classmate's items. Then they should merge both sets of items into one group and count the combined items. This illustrates that a larger group forms when two smaller groups merge. It provides the point of reference for understanding the pattern of addition.

This simple but effective experience provides the data for the **EX-co** phase. This activity engages students in reviewing and ordering the experience.

Using questions, Elisa guides students to recognize that the combined groups are larger than the original groups. "How many items did you have to start?" she asks the first-graders. "How many did your partner have? What happened when you put your items together—how many did you have then? When were there more items—when you each had a group, or when you put the two groups together?" Elisa continues these questions throughout the **EX-co** activity to help her students label and sort the data provided by the experience.

Knowing the importance of the pattern, Elisa decides to include another example—a second **EX-ex** activity. It will provide another reference point for the pattern. Elisa places the students into groups of two to four each and asks the students to count the people in their group. She then instructs them to link arms to form a short chain (not a circle), and then to find another group and stand facing them. Elisa asks the students to count the students in each other's chains, and then tells the first student in each chain to link arms to create one longer chain (not a circle) of students. The students proceed to count the people in the combined group. Elisa repeats the process until the whole class links into one line. Each time a count is taken, Elisa directs the students to notice how the combined groups are larger than either of the two original groups. She then uses similar questions based upon this second experience to help students identify and organize the new data.

This naturally generates an emerging pattern. The **EX-el** activity guides students to recognize the pattern.

Again asking her first-graders questions, Elisa leads them to recognize that when two groups are put together into one group, the new group contains a larger number of items. Elisa displays the pattern statement with an illustration of two smaller groups (e.g., a group of red dots and a group of blue dots) combining to form a larger group. The visual will provide a reminder for students who may not be able to read the statement by themselves.

Advancing to the **EX-ap** activity, the discussion switches to examples beyond the classroom experience. It engages students in recognizing the pattern from their own experiences.

Elisa refers to the red and blue dots. She asks the students to explain to her what the display is showing, and then encourages the students to illustrate similar examples. Elisa also uses the manipulatives in her classroom. Students illustrate the pattern by creating and combining groups with the manipulatives.

The Combination Blueprint's EXperience strand moves from one related activity to another (**FIGURE 5.4**), and provides a basis for thought, illustrating a pattern and establishing reference points related to the forthcoming content. It emphasizes the pattern students will see in a scenario where the associated skill proves valuable.

Architecture of Learning: COMBINATION BLUEPRINT Combination: Story Problems Requiring Addition					
		CORE PROCESSES			
		experience	comprehension	elaboration	application
FOCUS	EX	Merging Groups	Seeing the Groups Merge	Seeing the Pattern	Examples of the Pattern

FIGURE 5.4 Unit EXperience Strand

COmprehension Strand

The COmprehension strand introduces the unit's new content and skill to students. For combination units, this includes both reinforcing the pattern and providing the steps needed to learn the skill.

In **CO-ex**, Elisa emphasizes the skill's sequence of steps:

1. Read the story problem.
2. Find the story's numbers.
3. Think about the question. What does it ask you to show in an equation?
4. Write the equation.
5. Solve the equation and label the result.

Interestingly, these steps actually mirror the core learning processes: experience (reading the word problem), comprehension (noting the details of the story problem), elaboration (recognizing the pattern as being that of addition), and application (forming the equation and solving the problem).

Elisa models the steps for her children, knowing that they need to recognize the concept and apply the skill. *It is critical that she model both elements.* Elisa accomplishes this by thinking aloud:

> John has seven balloons. Susan also has seven balloons. Together, how many balloons do John and Susan have? Hmm. There are two groups of balloons. John has one group of balloons, and Susan has another group of balloons. The question being asked is: how many balloons do John and Susan have when their groups are put together? So there are two smaller groups, John's balloons and Susan's balloons. They are put together to make one larger group. That's what addition is! So, to answer

> the question, I want to add the number of balloons John has to the number of balloons Susan has. Let's see, John has seven balloons, so I will write a 7. Susan also has seven, so I will write another 7. And I know that I want to add, so I will write a plus sign between the two numbers. I end up with 7+7=. Let me think a moment. Oh, yes! I know that 7+7=14. So, together, John and Susan have 14 balloons. I'm going to write 14 at the end of my equation and add the label *balloons* so I can tell someone else what there are 14 of.

Elisa shares similar thinking-aloud monologues with several different story problems.

After students have listened to the teacher's thinking aloud and realize the importance of both recognizing the concept and applying the skill, they are prepared to sort this new knowledge. For the **CO-co** activity, Elisa asks her students to illustrate the five steps on index cards and then place the cards in order. She then listens as students refer to the illustrations while explaining the five steps to a partner. Elisa closely monitors each student's explanations and provides feedback as needed.

In the **CO-el** step, Elisa again asks questions to help students merge the reference point (**EX-ex**) with the newly introduced material. She asks:

1. What did you notice when you put groups of items together?
2. How do your illustrations show the pattern?
3. What do the story problems we're studying have in common with those examples?

Elisa then reads several story problems aloud. As a story problem is read aloud (with frequent pauses), Elisa directs the students to close their eyes to better "see" the story's details (like a movie) in their mind. For example, Elisa reads, "Joe has three toy trucks," and then instructs the students to imagine a boy playing with three toy trucks. Once Elisa reads the entire story problem, she asks the students to describe how the story illustrates the pattern. Elisa uses questioning and verbal support to help the first-graders form an explanation.

The final cell of the COmprehension strand (**CO-ap**) engages students in guided practice. Because this is a combination unit, the conceptual element (i.e., the pattern of addition) receives further attention.

Elisa reads several more story problems aloud and guides students through the thinking needed to recognize the pattern of addition in each one. After a few guided examples, Elisa reads another story problem and asks students if it represents the pattern of addition, and if so, how. As she senses the students gaining confidence, Elisa introduces story problems that do *not* illustrate the pattern. She discusses with the students what is different about those examples, reemphasizing the characteristics that indicate addition as the associated skill. After this pattern recognition practice, the class works together to solve a story problem. Elisa directs their attention to the pattern illustrated by the story problem and supports their use of the five-step process to find the answer.

Architecture of Learning: COMBINATION BLUEPRINT Combination: Story Problems Requiring Addition					
		CORE PROCESSES			
		experience	comprehension	elaboration	application
FOCUS	EX	Merging Groups	Seeing the Groups Merge	Seeing the Pattern	Examples of the Pattern
	CO	Addition: The Pattern and the Skill	Reorganizing Addition	Addition Connections	Seeing and Adding

FIGURE 5.5 Unit COmprehension Strand

While different in level, this same flow of instruction can be seen in a high school unit on the literary device of allusion. Geoff, a high school English teacher, concludes that students need to understand the concept of allusion and be able to apply thinking skills to interpret allusions. He chooses a pattern that emphasizes the understanding component: *Things borrowed remind us of their owners.* In the EXperience strand, Geoff presents students with an object and explains the circumstances surrounding his borrowing it from its owner. He emphasizes that because the item belongs to its owner, he thinks of the owner each time he sees it (**EX-ex**). He then has the students discuss the following questions:

1. Have you ever borrowed something that you had in your possession for an extended period?
2. What did you think when you saw the borrowed object?
3. What does it mean to borrow something?
4. What is the relationship between the thing that is borrowed and its owner? between the thing borrowed and the borrower?
5. What could someone borrow from you that would reveal something about you? What would it say about you?

6. Can you tell something about a borrower from the thing(s) he borrows? Explain.

Geoff has the students discuss these questions in small groups and then leads a whole class discussion of the ideas (**EX-co**). He then guides them to recognize the pattern: *Things borrowed remind us of their owners* (**EX-el**). Since students have already shared some of their own examples, he asks the class for a few of the best examples that illustrate the pattern (**EX-ap**).

In the COmprehension strand, Geoff explains the concept of allusion and shares several examples with the class. He also details a sequence of questions that can guide thinking about allusions:

1. To what does the allusion refer? Where or from whom did the writer borrow the allusion?
2. What do you know about the original source of the allusion?
3. How does what you know about the original source relate to the current text?
4. What does that relationship reveal about the current text? What does the author intend to communicate by the allusion?

Geoff then demonstrates this associated skill sequence by reading allusions and thinking aloud through the questions. He addresses both what an allusion is and how to interpret one (**CO-ex**). Geoff asks the students to develop a definition of *allusion* in their own words and to convert his list of questions into a flowchart to show their sequence (**CO-co**). He then reminds the students of the pattern, *Things borrowed remind us of their owners,* and asks the students to explain how allusions are another example of it (**CO-el**). He ends the COmprehension strand by reading a few allusions to the students and guiding their initial use of the skill sequence to interpret them (**CO-ap**).

The COmprehension strand introduces new material, emphasizing the pattern recognition that triggers the associated skill (**FIGURE 5.5**). Without pattern recognition, students will possess a skill they cannot use because they cannot recognize contexts where it can be used. This conceptual prerequisite to application is the reason combination units comprise all five learning processes as strands, including elaboration.

ELaboration Strand

In this phase, students continue to process the relationship between the pattern and its associated skill. The ELaboration strand helps students connect the two so that they can read a scenario and respond with appropriate action.

To initiate the ELaboration strand, Elisa displays another visual representation of the pattern (**FIGURE 5.6**). She asks the students to examine the visual and explain what they see to a partner. The visual provides the data for the strand's remaining activities.

Elisa guides the students in labeling and sorting the data by asking questions, such as: What do you notice in this upper section of the picture? What happens in this lower section?

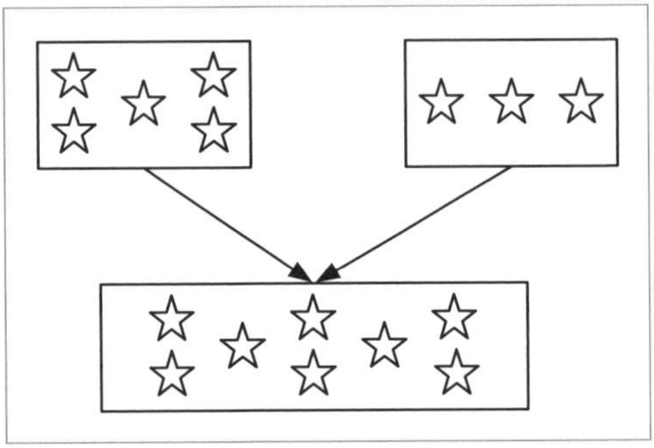

FIGURE 5.6 Visual Representation of Addition Pattern

Once the students recognize two separate groups coming together to form one larger group in the picture, they are ready to deepen their understanding of the pattern and the associated skill. For example, students need to understand that two merging groups form one larger group (conceptual knowledge), which is an addition process, expressed mathematically using "+" and "=" (skill knowledge).

For **EL-el**, Elisa has the students develop their own illustrations of addition, and write the mathematical equation it represents. For example, a student may draw a picture of a birthday party with six children at a table and two more coming through the door, mathematically represented as 6+2=. By creating illustrations and adding the associated equation, students combine understandings of the pattern and the mathematical equation. Elisa simplifies the activity (illustrations without a context, like **FIGURE 5.6**) for some students and supports them as necessary.

The deepened understanding of the pattern and associated skill increases student interest in using the skill to address a scenario. Elisa displays one of the student-created illustrations with its associate equation concealed. With her guidance and support, the first-graders discuss how the illustration shows the pattern of addition, express its pattern as a mathematical equation, and then solve the equation.

		Architecture of Learning: COMBINATION BLUEPRINT Combination: Story Problems Requiring Addition			
		CORE PROCESSES			
		experience	comprehension	elaboration	application
F	EX	Merging Groups	Seeing the Groups Merge	Seeing the Pattern	Examples of the Pattern
O C	CO	Addition: The Pattern and the Skill	Reorganizing Addition	Addition Connections	Seeing and Adding
U S	EL	Pattern Illustrations	Illustrations Analysis	New Illustrations	Adding Our Illustrations

FIGURE 5.7 Unit ELaboration Strand

Notice how the ELaboration strand (**FIGURE 5.7**) instills confidence in the students. Students are not only equipped for the APplication strand, but eager for it! This process can be seen in the high school literature unit, too. With knowledge of allusions and a skill sequence they can use to interpret allusions, students are ready for deeper thinking about the concept. Geoff begins the ELaboration strand by explaining to the students that they are going to borrow something from a well-known work to convey a quality about themselves. For example, they may want to borrow a character trait from the main character of a movie they recently saw. Geoff gives the students time to think about this (**EL-ex**). He then asks the students to write down what they are going to borrow and then to list ways it could be shown visually. For example, a student has great respect for the loyalty a character showed and may recall that the character's loyalty was mirrored in his pet dog. The student may list the dog as a way the borrowed idea, or allusion, could be shown visually (**EL-co**). Geoff then has the students sketch themselves and include the allusion in their drawing. For example, the student focused on loyalty may draw the movie character's dog standing by his side. Geoff asks the students to consider how their resulting sketches illustrate the pattern (**EL-el**). How does the drawing reveal something borrowed and what does it make the viewer think? Geoff ends the ELaboration strand by having the students write brief explanations of their self sketches, explaining the allusion and what it reveals (**EL-ap**).

APplication Strand

This strand (**FIGURE 5.8**) resembles the Skill Blueprint's APplication strand. The teacher provides scenarios that prompt a mental review of the pattern and skill, suggests a pause to check thinking against the pattern, and encourages use of the skill to address the scenario.

With Elisa's guidance and support, the students listen to a short story problem (**AP-ex**), identify the important details (i.e., numbers) within the story problem (**AP-co**), consider the pattern the short story illustrates (e.g., are two groups coming together to form one larger group?) (**AP-el**), and then solve the problem and label the result (**AP-ap**). This series of steps repeats for several short story problems, allowing the students enough practice so that they can recognize a story problem that requires addition by themselves and then do the addition to find the sum. Elisa lessens her guidance and support as students gain accuracy and confidence, but she continues to assess them formatively and supply feedback as needed. Such practice prepares students for the INtention Strand.

Architecture of Learning: COMBINATION BLUEPRINT Combination: Story Problems Requiring Addition					
		CORE PROCESSES			
		experience	comprehension	elaboration	application
F	EX	Merging Groups	Seeing the Groups Merge	Seeing the Pattern	Examples of the Pattern
O C	CO	Addition: The Pattern and the Skill	Reorganizing Addition	Addition Connections	Seeing and Adding
U	EL	Pattern Illustrations	Illustrations Analysis	New Illustrations	Adding Our Illustrations
S	AP	Story Problem	Story Problem Analysis	Checking the Pattern	Solving the Story

FIGURE 5.8 Unit APplication Strand

Again, the high school literature unit reveals a similar flow of instruction. Geoff presents students with works of literature that feature allusions (**AP-ex**). Students read the literature and work through the skill steps when they encounter an allusion (**AP-co**). Geoff reminds them to relate their findings to the pattern statement, especially as they consider what the author intends to communicate through the allusion (**AP-el**). Geoff asks the students to write their own brief interpretations of the allusion and then engages them in a full class discussion (**AP-ap**). Ultimately, the students use their understanding of allusions to discover examples and use the associated skill to interpret them.

INtention Strand

The INtention strand promotes using skills to respond to real-life scenarios. Students read such examples to identify patterns that trigger recall of associated skills. The skills can then be applied to reach solutions. The INtention strand can immediately follow the APplication strand or be designed for later. Each time students experience INtention strand activities, they recognize widening contexts in which the pattern and the associated skill are beneficial.

Elisa's INtention strand (**FIGURE 5.9**) mirrors her APplication strand with one important exception: the data (**IN-ex**) comes from a real-world scenario that illustrates the pattern of addition and requires using it. While she arranges for such scenarios to "occur," Elisa stays alert for "teachable moments" that spring up spontaneously. For example, on the way inside from recess, one loving student brings her three yellow dandelions. Another student carries in five more. A teachable moment! She points out the pattern—two groups, one of three and one of five, become one larger group when she places them together in a styrofoam cup "vase" on the teacher's desk That triggers the associated skill (3+5=?), and the students experience a "real world" context in which to apply addition.

Architecture of Learning: COMBINATION BLUEPRINT
Combination: Story Problems Requiring Addition

FOCUS	CORE PROCESSES: experience	comprehension	elaboration	application
EX	Merging Groups	Seeing the Groups Merge	Seeing the Pattern	Examples of the Pattern
CO	Addition: The Pattern and the Skill	Reorganizing Addition	Addition Connections	Seeing and Adding
EL	Pattern Illustrations	Illustrations Analysis	New Illustrations	Adding Our Illustrations
AP	Story Problem	Story Problem Analysis	Checking the Pattern	Solving the Story
IN	Addition in the World	Scenario Analysis	Checking the Pattern	Solving the Scenario

FIGURE 5.9 Unit INtention Strand

The high school literature unit follows a similar approach. Geoff provides a variety of materials throughout the school year, such as political speeches, editorials, and other works of literature (**IN-ex**). He challenges students to identify allusions with the materials and use the associated skill to interpret them (**IN-co**). He reminds students of the pattern and asks how the examples illustrate it (**IN-el**). Finally, he engages the students in discussing the meaning of the allusion and possibly in evaluating whether or not the allusion works within its context (**IN-ap**). Does it remind us of something that truly adds to the meaning, or does it lack significance or even create confusion?

Widening the contexts in which the students can use their learning promotes transfer. The INtention strand increases the likelihood that material learned in school will influence a student's interactions with the world.

FIGURE 5.10A on following pages

Architecture of Learning:

	CORE: experience	CORE: comprehension
FOCUS: **EX**	**EX-ex** Provide an experience that illustrates a pattern ◆ ◆ ◆ *This establishes a **reference point** for constructing understanding*	**EX-co** Engage students in identifying and sorting the experience's defining attributes ◆ ◆ ◆ *This establishes the critical components of the emerging pattern*
CO	**CO-ex** Present new content and/or skill processes to be mastered ◆ ◆ ◆ *This provides the new material to be learned*	**CO-co** Engage students in identifying and organizing the critical components of the new material ◆ ◆ ◆ *This establishes the new **knowledge** students must acquire*
EL	**EL-ex** Reconnect to the established reference point OR present a supplementary reference point ◆ ◆ ◆ *This initiates deeper conceptual blending to foster deeper understanding*	**EL-co** Guide student labeling and reorganizing of both the reference point (EL-ex) and the new knowledge components (CO-ex) ◆ ◆ ◆ *This enables the pattern(s) of the new material to emerge and initiates deeper blending of the new and known*
AP	**AP-ex** Present a scenario or problem ◆ ◆ ◆ *This initiates practice*	**AP-co** Engage students in identifying the relevant contextual components (e.g., pattern illustrated by the scenario) and/or skill-related components (e.g., steps of the skill process) ◆ ◆ ◆ *This initiates pre-application thinking*
IN	**IN-ex** Present a scenario or problem from a wider context ◆ ◆ ◆ *This initiates recall and transfer of mastered material*	**IN-co** Provide a way to identify and organize the IN-ex scenario ◆ ◆ ◆ *This exposes the relevant scenario components and its emerging pattern(s)*

FIGURE 5.10A Combination Blueprint Before

COMBINATION BLUEPRINT

PROCESSES	
elaboration	**application**
EX-el Guide pattern recognition and statement development ◆ ◆ ◆ *This enables a connection between the referential experience and forthcoming learning*	**EX-ap** Enable pattern identification within personal experiences ◆ ◆ ◆ *This establishes personal connections to the pattern and forthcoming learning*
CO-el Direct students to overlay new material, reference point (EX-ex), and/or personal reference points (EX-ap) ◆ ◆ ◆ *This initiates merging of the new and known to construct understanding*	**CO-ap** Facilitate guided and supported practice or summarization of the new material ◆ ◆ ◆ *This reveals and helps establish student knowledge of the new material*
EL-el Create opportunity to blend data (all *ex* cells) ◆ ◆ ◆ *This deepens **understanding** of new material as it associates with and differentiates from known experience*	**EL-ap** Facilitate a means of communicating or portraying deepened understanding ◆ ◆ ◆ *This reveals and increases student understanding*
AP-el Provide opportunity to compare anticipated steps with the pattern ◆ ◆ ◆ *This confirms or redirects the student's intended use of the skill*	**AP-ap** Provide opportunity to use the skill to address the scenario ◆ ◆ ◆ *This initiates skill **utilization** to produce a result or solution*
IN-el Provide opportunity to identify commonalities of new scenario and content or skill ◆ ◆ ◆ *This promotes the use of learned concepts and skills in addressing the scenario*	**IN-ap** Provide opportunity to make a prediction/use the skill to address scenario ◆ ◆ ◆ *This represents transfer, true **integration** of the new learning*

Architecture of Learning: COMBINATION BLUEPRINT Combination: Story Problems Requiring Addition				
	CORE PROCESSES			
FOCUS	experience	comprehension	elaboration	application
EX	Merging Groups	Seeing the Groups Merge	Seeing the Pattern	Examples of the Pattern
CO	Addition: The Pattern and the Skill	Reorganizing Addition	Addition Connections	Seeing and Adding
EL	Pattern Illustrations	Illustrations Analysis	New Illustrations	Adding Our Illustrations
AP	Story Problem	Story Problem Analysis	Checking the Pattern	Solving the Story
IN	Addition in the World	Scenario Analysis	Checking the Pattern	Solving the Scenario

FIGURE 5.10B Combination Blueprint After

Blueprint "Rhythm" and Flow

Like the Skill and Content Blueprints, the Combination Blueprint strands reveal a simple consistency (**FIGURE 5.11**). Within every strand, core cognitive processes direct how the instruction progresses, establishing a natural rhythm: new data (e.g., a new topic) is introduced (ex), identified and reorganized (co), so emerging patterns can be recognized and compared with previous experience (el), resulting in new understanding used to demonstrate a level of mastery (ap). The underlying instructional rhythm—input→processing→output—directs the flow of every strand.

CORE PROCESSES			
experience	comprehension	elaboration	application
Sensory data is introduced...	*identified and reorganized...*	*so emerging patterns can be recognized, resulting in new understanding...*	*used to demonstrate a level of mastery*
Input →		*Processing* →	*Output*

FIGURE 5.11 The Blueprint Strand "Rhythm"

As the rhythm repeats through the strands, teachers and students flow seamlessly from experiential background to the contextual analysis and appropriate skill application. This can be seen in Elisa's early elementary mathematics unit (**FIGURE 5.12**) and the general flow of the Blueprint (**FIGURE 5.13**).

FOCUS	EX	Students experience one larger group being formed from two smaller groups. With teacher questioning and guidance, the experience is reviewed and sorted to recognize the pattern: When two groups get put together to make one group, the new group has a larger number of items. Students Develop personal illustrations of the pattern.
	CO	The teacher presents characteristics of the pattern and models the action sequence for solving addition-oriented word problems. Students review the material by creating and sequencing each step. The teacher guides students to recognize the pattern within the word problems and engage in initial, guided practice with word problems.
	EL	Teacher displays an illustration of the pattern. The students analyze the illustration and then create their own illustrations, adding the mathematical equation that fits the illustration. The illustrations are displayed individually with equations hidden for students to "read" the scenario and state the correct equation.
	AP	Word problems are presented. Students identify the critical information within the problem, consider whether or not the problem illustrates the pattern, and then solve the problem.
	IN	Teacher creates scenarios that illustrate the pattern, engages students in identifying the critical information within the scenario, considering whether or not the problem illustrates the pattern, and solving the problem.

FIGURE 5.12 The Combination Blueprint Strand "Rhythm" for Elementary Math Unit

F O C U S		C O R E: experience	C O R E: comprehension
	Rhythm of the strand	*Sensory data is introduced…*	*identified and reorganized…*
	EX	**EX-ex** Provide an experience that illustrates a pattern ◆ ◆ ◆ *This establishes a **reference point** for constructing understanding*	**EX-co** Engage students in identifying and sorting the experience's defining attributes ◆ ◆ ◆ *This establishes the critical components of the emerging pattern*
	CO	**CO-ex** Present new content and/or skill processes to be mastered ◆ ◆ ◆ *This provides the new material to be learned*	**CO-co** Engage students in identifying and organizing the critical components of the new material ◆ ◆ ◆ *This establishes the new **knowledge** students must acquire*
	EL	**EL-ex** Reconnect to the established reference point OR present a supplementary reference point ◆ ◆ ◆ ***This initiates deeper cognitive blending to foster deeper understanding***	**EL-co** Guide student labeling and reorganizing of both the reference point (EL-ex) and the new knowledge components (CO-ex) ◆ ◆ ◆ ***This enables the pattern(s) of the new material to emerge and initiates deeper blending of the new and known***
	AP	**AP-ex** Present a scenario or problem ◆ ◆ ◆ *This initiates practice*	**AP-co** Engage students in identifying the relevant contextual components (e.g., pattern illustrated by the scenario) and/or skill-related components (e.g., steps of the skill process) ◆ ◆ ◆ *This initiates pre-application thinking*
	IN	**IN-ex** Present a scenario or problem from a wider context ◆ ◆ ◆ *This initiates recall and transfer of mastered material*	**IN-co** Provide a way to identify and organize the IN-ex scenario ◆ ◆ ◆ *This exposes the relevant scenario components and its emerging pattern(s)*
		Input →	***Processing***

FIGURE 5.13 The Blueprint "Rhythm" and Flow

PROCESSES	
elaboration	**application**
so emerging patterns can be recognized, resulting in new understanding…	*used to demonstrate a level of mastery*
EX-el Guide pattern recognition and statement development ◆ ◆ ◆ *This enables a connection between the referential experience and forthcoming learning*	**EX-ap** Enable pattern identification within personal experiences ◆ ◆ ◆ *This establishes personal connections to the pattern and forthcoming learning*
CO-el Direct students to overlay new material, reference point (EX-ex), and/or personal reference points (EX-ap) ◆ ◆ ◆ *This initiates merging of the new and known to construct understanding*	**CO-ap** Facilitate guided and supported practice or summarization of the new material ◆ ◆ ◆ *This reveals and helps establish student knowledge of the new material*
EL-el Create opportunity to blend data (all *ex* cells) ◆ ◆ ◆ *This deepens **understanding** of new material as it associates with and differentiates from known experience*	**EL-ap** Facilitate a means of communicating or portraying deepened understanding ◆ ◆ ◆ *This reveals and increases student understanding*
AP-el Provide opportunity to compare anticipated steps with the pattern ◆ ◆ ◆ *This confirms or redirects the student's intended use of the skill*	**AP-ap** Provide opportunity to use the skill to address the scenario ◆ ◆ ◆ *This initiates skill **utilization** to produce a result or solution*
IN-el Provide opportunity to identify commonalities of new scenario and content or skill ◆ ◆ ◆ *This promotes the use of learned concepts and skills in addressing the scenario*	**IN-ap** Provide opportunity to make a prediction/ use the skill to address scenario ◆ ◆ ◆ *This represents transfer, true **integration** of the new learning*
Processing →	***Output***

Blueprints and Curriculum

Now that we have reviewed the Architecture of Learning Blueprints, I should point out that they should not be used for every topic in a teacher's curriculum. Not everything a teacher teaches during the course of a year requires a Blueprint. Some topics are introductory, exposing students to subject matter that will be major units only in future grades. Some topics are review, reminding students of learning covered in major units in previous years. These topics do not need the step-by-step procedures provided by Architecture of Learning.

Major instructional units, those that define the grade level, do deserve the attention and instruction Architecture of Learning provides. For example, when I taught fourth grade, long division was a major topic. Students had been introduced to it in previous years, and it was treated as a review unit in future grades. Following this principle, it was appropriate to develop the unit using an Architecture of Learning Blueprint. In contrast, double- and triple-digit addition were review topics. It was not necessary to use a Blueprint for these topics.

A recent anecdote further illustrates this principle. A first-grade teacher decided to design a mathematics unit on an Architecture of Learning Blueprint. In past years, only a fifth of her students mastered the subject matter, even though it was a major topic in first grade. When she taught her unit designed on a Blueprint, 89 percent of the students mastered the subject matter—nearly a 70 percent increase in student success. Imagine if students came to your class having had instruction developed on Architecture of Learning Blueprints for all their major units in previous grades. They would likely be far more prepared for the subject matter studied in your grade level.

Questions

1. What characterizes combination subject matter? List three examples from your experience as a teacher or student.

2. What role do patterns play in combination learning? What is the source for identifying combination patterns? Why?

3. What results from instruction that emphasizes the skill component of combination subject matter but neglects the pattern component?

4. What are the strands of the Architecture of Learning Combination Blueprint? Why are these the strands?

5. Explain the role of the ELaboration strand in the Combination Blueprint. Why is it included—why not just move from COmprehension to APplication?

6. Review Elisa's unit. What would you expect students to master as result of her instruction? Do the same with Geoff's unit.

Chapter 6

CREATING COHERENCE

Aligning Learning, Teaching, and Assessment

Imagine yourself as a student of abstract art history. Your teacher walks into class with three tubes of paint. She holds each tube up, one at a time, for the class to see. "This particular shade of yellow is the yellow Jackson Pollock used in his painting *Yellow, Gray, and Black*," she explains. She then holds up the gray and explains it is the gray used in the same painting, as is the tube of black paint. She discusses the critical attributes of each shade—"The yellow is really more of a mustard with strong hints of orange." You find this detailed information fascinating, even though you've never seen the painting using these colors. The teacher then announces, "To be sure you've learned today's lesson well enough to think critically, we are going to have a test. You will each receive a blank canvas and a palette with large dollops of this yellow, gray, and black paint. After receiving your materials, re-create Jackson Pollock's painting as closely as possible." Hands, including yours, immediately go up around the room. The teacher replies, "I know that I have not shown you this painting. Remember, I am testing to see how well you *can think* about the material."

Seem unfair? The teacher explained the isolated facts thoroughly. Why do you feel cheated? If you just "put on your thinking cap," could you be successful? Would your results be an accurate and fair representation of your abilities and understanding?

Haphazard assessment can give a flawed impression of a student's true achievement. Educator and parent Ken O'Connor relates an experience that illustrates this method and the justification often used to support it:

> Throughout his high school career, my son had great difficulty completing tests within the set time limit, often leaving unfinished work that lowered his grade. I will never forget one year when his English teacher came up to me in the local supermarket and said, "You know your son's grades don't accurately reflect what he knows and understands in English." My response was that if she was confident in this judgment, she should make the appropriate changes in his grade to reflect her belief. She replied, however, that she could not do this because all his scores had to be averaged to determine the report card grade. To me, this teacher had a misconception of what a grade represented.[1]

The teacher recognized the difference between the student's abilities and his grade but chose to record the misrepresentative grade anyway. Such misalignment diminishes the integrity of both the teacher and the school. So we have to ask ourselves: What causes this disparity? Let's observe three teachers as they complete an end-of-marking-period ritual.

While preparing report cards, Miss Snyder, Mr. Stilman, and Mrs. Sheffield discover a disturbing trend. Miss Snyder notices that Jimmy, who reads well below grade level, earned enough points from assignments and assessments to have a *C* in reading—a passing grade that inaccurately represents his progress. Mr. Stilman notices the same problem. Through points given for completed homework and corrected work, Joanie earned a passing grade in math. Mr. Stilman knows she will experience frustration and likely failure next year because she hasn't mastered basic concepts, despite what her grade appears to indicate. Mrs. Sheffield sees a different problem with Justin's language grade. The *D* that indicates he is failing results from his poor sentence-diagramming skills. However, Justin's writing capacities indicate a deep understanding of grammar and a level of communication that exceeds grade-level expectations. Oh well, each teacher concludes, how can you give a grade other than what the point values indicate? The three teachers knowingly communicate grades that are false representations of each student's true achievement. They create a disparity between a student's abilities and what they communicate about those abilities.

In Architecture of Learning, the learning process guides the teaching process, which leads to the assessment process. Such coherence between teaching, learning, and assessment is essential for producing learning that is "integrative so that it lasts."[2] Assessing a subject in ways that differ from how we taught it places our integrity as professionals in question.

Assessment *for* Learning: Instructive Feedback

The test given at the end of a unit should represent a miniscule percentage of actual classroom assessment. Most assessment should be *formative* as opposed to *summative*. Formative assessment *forms* the student as the teacher monitors progress and provides feedback. A teacher's assessment activities *while a student is learning* can significantly influence her achievement.

Researchers Paul Black and Dylan Wiliam describe formative assessment as any activity that provides information about student learning and enables teachers to adapt teaching to meet student needs.[3] Such activity resonates with the original meaning of *assessment*. The word *assess* has its origins in the Latin term *assidere*, meaning "sit by." Formative assessment is a vital teacher-student dialogue, a "sitting by" that improves teaching and increases learning. Educators and authors Grant Wiggins and Jay McTighe remind us that such feedback is essential: "Learning requires regular, timely, and user-friendly feedback to understand goals, produce quality work, and meet high standards."[4] Assessment experts Leahy, Lyon, and Wiliam describe this as "assessment *for* learning rather than assessment *of* learning,"[5] and Grant Wiggins argues for more of it:

> Here's a radical idea: We need more assessment, not less.
>
> Seem crazy? Substitute *feedback* for *assessment*, and you'll better understand what I mean. The point of assessment in education is to advance learning, not to merely audit absorption of facts. That's true whether we're talking about that fourth-period pop quiz, the school play, or the state test. No one ever mastered a complicated idea or skill the first—or fifth—time. To reach any genuine standard, we need lots of trials, errors, and adjustments based on feedback.
>
> Think of assessment, then, as information for improving.[6]

Educators and authors Susan M. Butler and Nancy D. McMunn also describe assessment's role as a means of increasing learning:

> Classroom assessment is of vital importance to student learning. Research demonstrates that student achievement is increased

> (particularly for low student achievers) by the use of classroom assessment when such assessment features good feedback to students about their performance, sets clear standards for learning, is ongoing so it can be used to monitor student growth and progress, and is used to modify instruction to meet the needs of the student...Such classroom assessment promotes assessment *for* learning rather than assessment *of* learning.[7]

Teachers increase learning through instructive feedback, a major component of formative assessment. Instructive feedback is "teacher-student interaction in which the comparison of student work with defined levels of proficiency provides the student with direction for future work and increased proficiency."[8] According to researcher John Hattie, it is "the most powerful single modification that enhances achievement,"[9] and Paul Black and Dylan Wiliam call instructive feedback "the heart of effective teaching."[10]

Instructive feedback follows a four-step cycle. First, a student shows his level of understanding while practicing a skill or processing new content. For example, in learning to handwrite the letter *q*, students generally practice forming the letter. In a more advanced class, learning the cause-effect sequence of the water cycle, students may develop detailed diagrams. Both their practice of the skill and their grasp of the topic can produce a basis for instructive feedback.

Second, the teacher compares the student's work with defined standards. The teacher identifies:

1. Elements in the student's work that conform to the standards

2. The overall level of proficiency the student's work represents
3. Elements the student does and does not appear to understand
4. Ways the student can achieve greater proficiency

Though generally done quickly, the teacher's review yields details that shape the final steps of the cycle.

During the third step's pivotal dialogue, the teacher begins by identifying what the student has done well and appears to understand. The teacher then asks her to comment on the work completed thus far. This gives the student an opportunity to correct the teacher's perceptions, offer additional evidence of understanding, or ask important questions about the material. The teacher follows with questions of clarification, if necessary, and encourages the student to respond. This dialogue, a balance of encouragement and exhortation, creates an environment that enhances learning.

In the cycle's final step, the teacher and student develop an improvement plan. The teacher offers specific suggestions of what the student can do to achieve more. In forming the plan, the teacher refers to established standards (often detailed on a rubric) and suggests specific, concrete actions the student can take. As the student acts on the plan, new evidence of understanding is produced, returning the four-step process to its start.

My wife's interactions with piano students illustrate the instructive feedback cycle. A student plays a previously assigned and practiced piece (step 1). My wife then comments on the performance, saying things like, "You played the introduction well. The timing was correct and you played it expressively" (step 2). She then asks the student what he thought about the piece and listens carefully. In response, she interacts accordingly and then offers a suggestion: "Let's look at this middle section and tap the rhythm together" (step 3). Together, they discuss how to practice the piece, especially the sections that need more work (step 4). The next week, if the student has practiced as directed, the performance improves.

Professor of biology James E. Zull suggests that providing teacher feedback triggers the learner's sense of progress. This sensation ignites activity in the brain's basal structures, neural regions associated with pleasure and reward. Such "active learning," claims Zull, makes learning "pleasurable and effective for developing concepts and applications."[11]

Research confirms that increasing instructive feedback increases learning. Robert J. Marzano found that students who had teachers that consistently provided timely and specific feedback scored anywhere from 21 to 41 percentage points higher on standardized tests than students who had teachers that failed to provide such feedback.[12] Neurologist and classroom teacher Judy Willis offers one reason for this dramatic impact: "One of the most successful strategies for engaging students' brains in their lessons comes from personal connection and accountability."[13] Through frequent instructive feedback, teachers connect with individual students, hold them accountable, provide an opportunity for a student's questions, and optimize learning and achievement.

Based on Learning, Revealed by Teaching

Instructive feedback helps align learning, teaching, and assessment, but how do we fairly assess student achievement? What relationship should testing have to instruction? Architecture of Learning Blueprints aid teachers in activating learning processes, but tests frequently require more knowledge and skill than teachers have taught. A teacher, for example, may present isolated factual content during instruction and then ask a "critical thinking" test question that requires a synthesis and evaluation of the material. When asked about this inconsistency, teachers often respond that it is a way to tell who has "really learned" the material. But this practice and the justification offered for it reveal a lack of understanding about how learning develops. If an assessment requires learning that the teacher failed to foster, it asks students, in effect, to reproduce a painting after only seeing separate tubes of paint. We certainly want students to build their own understanding of instructional material, but our teaching, not our assessment, needs to enable this.

The Architecture of Learning Blueprints help teachers develop assessments based on learning and revealed through teaching. The Blueprints create "critical intersections" (**FIGURE 6.1**). These points, where a focus process (strand) meets itself in the core processes (column), can guide a teacher's choice of testing material and how the test asks a student for the material. By engaging in formative assessment and developing summative assessments based on a unit's critical intersections, a teacher imbues educational practice with integrity.

FOCUS	experience	comprehension	elaboration	application
EX	Critical Intersection: **Reference Point**	EX-co	EX-el	EX-ap
CO	CO-ex	Critical Intersection: **Knowledge**	CO-el	CO-ap
EL	EL-ex	EL-co	Critical Intersection: **Understanding**	EL-ap
AP	AP-ex	AP-co	AP-el	Critical Intersection: **Utilization**
IN	IN-ex	IN-co	IN-el	Critical Intersection: **Integration**

FIGURE 6.1 The Architecture of Learning Critical Intersections

Critical Intersection EX-ex: The Reference Point

A Blueprint's first cell forms its first critical intersection: **EX-ex.** While this cell does not produce material for assessment, it influences the other critical intersections. The **EX-ex** activity features an experience that illustrates a pattern. That experience becomes the "reference point" for the learning—the understood element to which the mind returns again and again as it constructs understanding of new material.

Critical Intersection CO-co: The Knowledge Component

The **CO-co** intersection represents the unit's *knowledge component.* It features the unit's factual material and answers the question, "Does the student know the essential details and how to effectively organize them?" In terms of learning a skill, the knowledge component includes the skill's individual steps and their correct sequence. For example, if a student is trying to identify the main idea of a text passage, the knowledge component includes knowing a definition of *main idea* and the three steps that guide main idea identification. It is *not* actually identifying a main idea from a passage. In units featuring content, the critical details of the material compose the knowledge component. Such components for a unit on Romanticism include the definition of *Romanticism* and a list of major Romantic authors. In combination units, the knowledge component includes knowing the pattern and the associated skill's sequence of steps. For example, the knowledge components of an early elementary unit on solving word problems requiring addition include stating or describing the pattern that suggests addition as a solution and stating the steps for finding a solution by using addition. In short, if it can be recited and/or organized, it is probably a knowledge component.

This suggests two important implications, one for designing instruction and one for developing assessments. First, the **CO-co** activity should clearly engage the students in restating and reorganizing the knowledge components. If the activity fails to emphasize an important element of the unit's essential knowledge, the activity needs to be redesigned or expanded. By reviewing the **CO-co** intersection this way, a teacher can self-coach and improve instructional design. (Think of this as self-provided instructive feedback!) When I review an Architecture of Learning Blueprint, the **CO-co** activity is the first element I examine. If the unit's foundational knowledge is not represented there, it is the first thing I work with a teacher to improve.

For example, recently while working with a mid-elementary teacher on a science unit, I noticed her test included a section for cloud types and associated weather conditions. As we reviewed her unit, I noted that the students never sorted these associations themselves. We examined her **CO-co** cell and found other details being addressed but nothing about cloud-weather connections. The teacher told students about the associations, *but the students never processed these details.* We revised her **CO-co** activity so that the students actually processed the knowledge required to successfully complete that section of the test.

Second, the **CO-co** critical intersection should inform assessment. What students are asked to recall on a test and the way they are asked to reorganize the data should clearly relate to the **CO-co** activity. For example, on a test for identifying main ideas, I may ask the students to write a definition of *main idea* and to write, in order, the steps used to identify main idea. The assessment's knowledge component should echo the content and form of the unit's **CO-co** critical intersection. This pulls together teaching and assessing of the learner's comprehension of the unit's content.

When instruction and testing do not align this way, students are placed at an unfair advantage. For example, a Spanish teacher may teach individual vocabulary terms, asking students to match Spanish terms with English definitions in the **CO-co** stage of the unit. However, on the test, the teacher may ask the students to translate sentences in which some words appear in a different form because they are used in context. Not only do students lack the experience of interpreting sentences, they may also lack basic knowledge of words forms and the influence of context. The teacher's testing has a tentative relationship to her teaching.

Critical Intersection EL-el: The Understanding Component

The **EL-el** intersection, which appears in the Content and Combination Blueprints, represents a unit's *understanding* *component.* It comprises the unit's interrelated ideas and their connections to students' prior experiences. It answers the question, "Does the student demonstrate understanding through connections of new and known concepts?" For example, within a unit on the Byzantine Empire, students may identify influencers and influences in the Byzantine era and from their personal experiences, relate the Byzantine influencers to personal influencers, and explain how the personal examples are illustrative of the Byzantine examples. A student may, for example, relate the Byzantine Church to a modern political party, explaining that both possessed significant influence over the thinking of leaders. A student's ability to identify and explain such connections reveals an understanding of the unit's content.

An assessment of student understanding should be a part of the assessment "package" for a unit. While it may be included in a test at the unit's conclusion, it may also be based on student work produced prior to the final test. For example, within the Byzantine Empire unit, the teacher could expand the **EL-ap** activity by asking students to identify corresponding contemporary illustrations for every influencer and influenced area, individual, or group detailed in the unit's new material and write a multi-paragraph essay explaining each illustration. Such an assignment could be completed partially in class, creating opportunities for instructive feedback, and partially for homework. The resulting evidence would reveal the student's understanding of the unit's critical ideas, the relationships between them, and the connections between these related ideas and experience. A rubric would then guide the teacher's evaluation of the completed essay.

Critical Intersections AP-ap and IN-ap: The Utilization and Integration Components

The **AP-ap** intersection, which appears in the Skill and Combination Blueprints, represents the unit's *utilization component.* It emphasizes the sequence of steps used to accomplish a goal—i.e., the actual doing of the skill—and answers the question, "Does the student know how to achieve the desired result by applying the skill?" For example, if the skill is overhand throwing, the student's ability to throw a ball overhand in isolation, *not* within a wider context such as a softball game, represents the utilization component. If the skill is multiplication of two-digit numbers by single-digit numbers, a student's ability to calculate correct products represents the utilization component.

One additional critical intersection exists in each Blueprint. The **IN-ap** cell represents the ability to use new knowledge within a new context, the unit's *integration component.* It answers one of three questions:

1. When placed in a relevant context, does the student apply the skill accurately and with adequate efficiency?
2. Does the student use conceptual understanding to analyze current conditions and make predictions or generate solutions?
3. Does the student use conceptual understanding to analyze current conditions and apply the associated skill for a satisfactory result?

For skills, the integration component refers to a student's ability to replicate the process within a context—to transfer the learning. For example, with identifying main idea, integration would be demonstrated by his ability to independently identify the main idea of a new nonfiction text passage.

With content, integration is illustrated by a student's ability to apply her understanding to new contexts. "The learner begins to integrate, to continually make connections and create new wholes out of multiple parts: his or her knowledge and ability, individual abilities needed in a given situation, and abilities and the situation or context."[14] By engaging in activities requiring integration, a learner "extends, deepens, and secures" understanding and capability.

For example, the unit on Romanticism required students to consider how a pull in one direction can cause a push (or reaction) in the opposite direction. A teacher may read a news article detailing a current movement in cultural values, such as increased movement to technology-based, less expensive customer service, and ask the students to discuss its content. The teacher may then ask the students to consider content understandings they have constructed, apply these to the scenario detailed in the article, and offer some insights, such as predictions, advice, or potential solutions to problems. (You should note that such thinking will need to be modeled and practiced with instructive feedback several times before you can expect students to extrapolate on their own.) Some insights may be discussed, and the teacher may then ask the students to compose a response to the article, such as a letter to the editor, using their insights on Romanticism to explore and explain reactions to the contemporary movement.

Such an activity would likely take place sometime after the unit has been completed, and a rubric would guide evaluation. However, since the INtention Strand is most effective when repeated multiple times throughout the year, such a formal approach is not always required or justified. In fact, most INtention Strands are best approached informally, allowing students to explore the relationship of their new understanding to contemporary circumstances. The teacher who frequently uses such an informal approach in short interactions (only occasionally requiring a more detailed, formal response for evaluation) uses the proper balance.

Within a Combination Blueprint, the **IN-ap** cell merges both the new concept and associated skill within a widened context. For example, within a math unit on division, a teacher may arrange a scenario in which students experience the need to separate items or people into equally sized groups. The students analyze the context to identify this pattern and apply the associated skill (division).

Being able to use new content and skills represents authentic learning. Educator and assessment expert Eeva Reeder claims, "The degree to which students grasp a concept can be *reliably* inferred only when they can somehow apply the concept in an authentic context. In other words, students cannot reasonably claim to understand what they cannot demonstrate."[15] Integration is the evidence of authentic learning.

Assessment *of* Learning: Summative Assessment

Thorough assessment reveals student knowledge (represented by the **CO-co** cell), understanding (represented by the **EL-el** cell), and/or utilization (represented by the **AP-ap** cell), and integration (represented by the **IN-ap** cell) of new material. A teacher can design connections between the content and method of assessment and the content and method of instruction by using the unit's critical intersections as a guide.

Knowledge components are clearly defined and can often be assessed via "traditional" methods (e.g., multiple choice, matching, fill in the blank). However, alignment between the **CO-co** cell and the testing methods should be obvious. For example, if in class students identify the major events of the antebellum period prior to the Civil War and arrange those events in sequential order, a multiple-choice test is unlikely to mirror the form even though it may cover the same details. A stronger alignment would be created if students were given a list of events and asked to sequence them in a timeline.

Assessing the understanding (**EL-el**), utilization (**AP-ap**), and integration (**IN-ap**) components requires additional thought and effort. While each of these elements possesses levels of proficiency, determining a student's achievement is nearly impossible with "traditional" test structures. Labeling a statement as true or false, selecting an option from a choice of four, or matching two corresponding ideas (e.g., term and definition) reveals little, if any, depth of understanding, ability in utilization, or transfer of learning (integration).

Rubrics enable assessment beyond the knowledge level by providing "an outline of the criteria" used to determine student achievement.[16] A descriptive rubric is one practical and helpful form. It details the evidence associated with various achievement levels. The specific labels assigned to these levels vary, but here are four terms that would work: *exemplary, proficient*, *adequate*, and *not yet*.

For instance, the teacher who required the students to pair influences from their own experiences with influences of the Byzantine era could assess the resulting connections in this fashion (see **FIGURE 6.2**).

	Exemplary	Proficient	Adequate	Not Yet
Connections & Explanations	Student work features connections (with explanations) between Byzantine and contemporary influences, revealing relationships between both broad and specific ideas (e.g., connecting Justinian with the authors of the Constitution, explaining that both created codes that influenced later systems of governance, and both created codes that designated legislation as the source of laws)	Student work features connections (with explanations) between Byzantine and contemporary influences, revealing recognition of links based on relationships, such as cause and effect or prototype and later forms (e.g., connecting Justinian with the Pilgrims, explaining that both created "codes" that became the basis for later documents establishing legal systems)	Student work features connections (with explanations) between Byzantine and contemporary influences, revealing recognition of links across broad areas (e.g., connecting Justinian's contribution of codifying law with a current judge because both influence issues of law)	Any responses not meeting the Adequate descriptors

FIGURE 6.2 Sample Rubric

Adequate work might be described as identifying connections between the ideas, revealing recognition of links across broad areas (e.g., a student connects Justinian's contribution of codifying law with a judge because both influence issues of law). In contrast, proficient work might be described as identifying connections between the ideas, recognizing links based on relationships, such as cause-effect or prototype-later forms (e.g., a student connects Justinian with the Pilgrims, explaining that both created "codes" that formed foundations for future legal systems). Exemplary work might be described as identifying multiple connections and explanations that reveal relationships between both broad and specific ideas (e.g., a student connects Justinian with the authors of the Constitution, explaining that both created codes that influenced later systems of governance, and both created codes that designated legislation as the source of laws). Adequate means the student can articulate connections that reveal a basic understanding. Proficient means the student can articulate more than one-to-one connections, explaining related ideas and their relationships. Exemplary describes the student that can articulate both broad connections and significant, detail-based connections.

The question naturally arises: Isn't this a subjective assessment? The answer is both yes and no. The teacher does make a judgment regarding the level of achievement, but she bases this judgment on *predetermined* standards. The standards reveal consistency between expectations (i.e., objectives) and achievement. Because rubrics set out predetermined descriptors of established standards, they can help ensure evaluative integrity. Assessing more than factual recall requires such an approach.

Assessment *for* and *of* Learning: Rubrics and Instructive Feedback

However, the most significant contribution rubrics make to learning is their role in instructive feedback. This cycle of feedback revolves around established achievement standards (see **FIGURE 6.3**). Prior to assigning a task that will produce evidence for review, the teacher must consider how various levels of achievement will be gauged. What are the defining characteristics of achievement that is adequate? proficient? exemplary? When students have this information before them (e.g., copies of the rubric distributed in the **CO-ex** cell), the rubric serves as a guide for the desired depth of learning, and it provides a tool for instructive feedback. The teacher can review student work and plan for improvement by referencing the rubric. For example, a teacher may note a student's connections made during the **EL-el** activity indicate one-to-one, surface-level connections that, though not incorrect, reveal only a beginning understanding. The teacher may commend the student for recognizing these connections and then suggest the student consider broader areas of connection. The rubric provides a "place to go" in giving feedback and establishing the "next step" in the student's efforts.

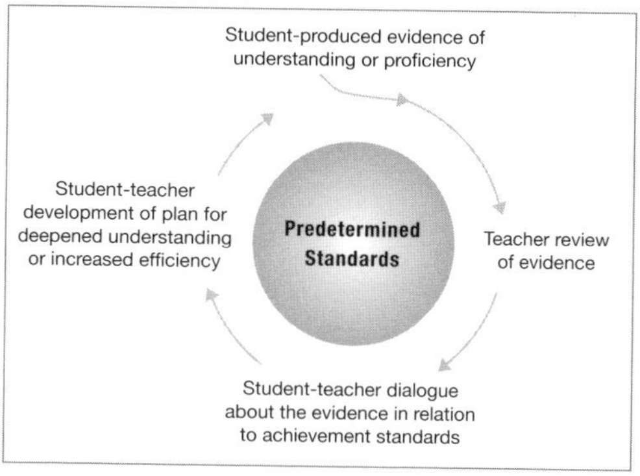

FIGURE 6.3 Instructive Feedback Cycle[17]

Tests, papers, and projects, for which grades are assigned, should be structured to assess student knowledge, understanding, and/or utilization, and possibly integration. Again, the critical intersections of the unit's Blueprint provide guidance for form and content. The knowledge component, as indicated previously, can be addressed via "traditional" testing methods. All the other levels may or may not require rubric-based assessment, depending on the new subject matter's structure.

For example, a unit on long division designed on a Combination Blueprint possesses all the critical intersections. The knowledge component may be addressed by asking the students to state or identify the pattern that indicates the need for division and to identify the steps used in calculating a quotient. The understanding component may ask the students to identify an illustration of a pattern and explain how it exemplifies separating a larger group into equally sized smaller groups. The utilization component may be assessed simply through a series of long-division equations for which students calculate quotients, and a series of word problems for which students identify those requiring long division and calculate their quotients. (In this case, a rubric would not be needed to assess utilization.) The integration component, if addressed during instruction, may ask the students to identify and explain a realistic situation, based on actual or imagined experience, to which division could be applied, state the equation representing the situation, and find its quotient (**FIGURE 6.4**).

Grade 4, Long Division Test

KNOWLEDGE

Examine the following word problem:

> Jack has a jar with 96 pieces of candy inside. He wants to share the candy with his basketball team. All together, there are 8 people on his team. How many pieces of candy should Jack give each person?

Using the space below, explain how you know to use division in answering the question. What pattern does the word problem present? (4 points)

Referring to the same word problem, write the correct order of operations for solving the problem (4 points).

UNDERSTANDING

In the space below, draw a picture that shows the pattern of division. If necessary, write an explanation of your picture. Use the rubric to guide your response. (This is the same rubric we used during the unit!)

	Exemplary 10 points	Proficient 7 points	Adequate 4 points	Not Yet
Division Illustration	• Student's illustration includes a realistic context in which the use of division is sensible	• All Adequate descriptors, plus... • Student correctly restates the illustration in a mathematical equation	• Student's illustration accurately depicts the pattern of division	• Any responses not meeting the Adequate descriptors

FIGURE 6.4 Sample Assessment with Knowledge, Understanding, Utilization, and Integration Components

Grade 4, Long Division Test

UTILIZATION
Solve the following division equations (1 point each; 10 points).

$32 \div 8 =$	$49 \div 7 =$	$83 \div 9 =$	$51 \div 6 =$	$13 \div 3 =$
$26 \div 2 =$	$79 \div 8 =$	$44 \div 4 =$	$38 \div 7 =$	$67 \div 5 =$

Solve the following story problems that require division. Do not solve any story problems that do not require division (1 point each; 5 points).

Sue has 14 balloons to give 7 children. How many balloons should Sue give each child?

Jack has $2.00. Fred has $1.50. How much money do Fred and Jack have all together?

Grant had 63 cookies that he gave 21 of his classmates. How many cookies did each classmate get?

Zane has 5 bags. There are 4 baseball cards in each bag. How many baseball cards does Zane have?

I want to put the same number of jelly beans in each bag. I have 48 jelly beans and 4 bags. How many jelly beans should I put into each bag?

INTEGRATION
Write about a real-life situation in which you could use division and write the equation that would provide the correct quotient. (You may write your situation into a word problem.) Then use division to find the quotient and explain how it solves or addresses the situation. Use the rubric to guide your response. (This is the same rubric we used during the unit!)

	Exemplary 7 points	Proficient 5 points	Adequate 3 points	Not Yet
Division Situation	• All Proficient descriptors, plus… • Student explains how using division successfully addresses the situation	• All Adequate descriptors, plus… • Student solves the associated equation and labels the quotient	• Student presents a situation in which division provides a solution and correctly writes the associated mathematical equation	• Any responses not meeting the Adequate descriptors

FIGURE 6.4 [continued] Sample Assessment with Knowledge, Understanding, Utilization, and Integration Components

Similarly, a summative assessment for a content unit can feature knowledge, understanding, and integration components (**FIGURE 6.5**). The knowledge component may, for example, ask students to recall the major characters and events of a Shakespearean play. The understanding component may require students to write an essay that explores the relationship of the unit's referential pattern, elements of the play, and connections to personal experiences. Finally, the integration components may engage students in analysis of a contemporary situation and require a response, such as a prediction or advice, which references play elements as support. However, the teacher must ensure such assessment prompts are consistent with the teaching activities of the represented critical intersections.

Ideally, these components correspond to grading intervals. For example, the knowledge component and utilization component (combined, since both the content and skill are essential) should possess enough points to place the student in the adequate or "*C*-range" of a school's grading system. The understanding component should possess enough weight (i.e., points) to move the student into the proficient or "*B*-range" of a school's grading system. The integration component should possess enough weight to move the student into the exemplary or "*A*-range" of a school's grading system. A student who answers all traditional questions correctly and has exemplary scores on all the rubric-based sections would earn a perfect score (e.g., 30 out of 30 possible points, or 100%).

High School English: Macbeth

KNOWLEDGE

Match the following characters and descriptions:

_____1. Weird Sisters	**A**. Thane of Glamis who becomes Thane of Cawdor and murderer of King Duncan
_____2. Banquo	**B**. Witness of the prophecy concerning Macbeth who is murdered for his suspicions
_____3. Macbeth	**C**. Ambitious woman who is eventually overcome by a guilty conscience
_____4. Malcom	**D**. Son of Banquo; escapes the murderers sent by Macbeth

[section continues]

Multiple Choice

_____ 11. Who was described as "lesser than Macbeth, and greater"? Why?

A. Fleance because he becomes king

B. Banquo because he becomes king

C. Banquo because he does right but is never king

D. Lady Macbeth because she can influence Macbeth

[section continues]

FIGURE 6.5 Sample Assessment with Knowledge, Understanding, and Integration Components

High School English: Macbeth

UNDERSTANDING

As we read *Macbeth*, we discussed and wrote about the influence one's view of one's self can have over one's actions. Summarize the elements of *Macbeth* that address this idea and include illustrations from your own experiences. Explain logical correlations between the play, the pattern, and your own experiences. (Note: the rubric used to evaluate your response is the same rubric we used for our in-class writing during the unit.)

	Exemplary 20 points	Proficient 16 points	Adequate 12 points	Not Yet
Understanding Essay	• All Proficient descriptors, plus... • Response integrates play elements and personal experiences in such a way that one mirrors the other—personal experiences are described/explained in relation to play elements, creating obvious correlations between the two	• All Adequate descriptors, plus... • Response includes examples from personal experience that illustrate the pattern	• Response summarizes elements of the play that illustrate the pattern: Individuals tend to act in alignment with how they view themselves	• Any responses not meeting the Adequate descriptors

[space for writing included]

INTEGRATION

Select one of the newspaper clippings from the table. Review the article carefully. Write a description of any similarities you see between the scenario explained in the clipping and the play *Macbeth*. Then, using your understanding of *Macbeth*, offer a prediction of what could occur in the scenario or offer advice to those involved in the scenario. Your response does not need to be lengthy! (Note: the rubric used to evaluate your response is the same rubric we used for our in-class writing during the unit.)

[space for writing included]

	Exemplary 10 points	Proficient 8 points	Adequate 6 points	Not Yet
Integration Response	• Response features significant correlations between the contemporary scenario and the play plus... • Response includes prediction(s) or advice that are well supported/defended/justified with clearly explained references from the play	• Response features significant correlations between the contemporary scenario and the play plus... • Response includes prediction(s) or advice that addresses the contemporary scenario and references the play	• Response describes minimal correlations between the contemporary scenario and the play	• Any responses not meeting the Adequate descriptors

FIGURE 6.5 [continued] Sample Assessment with Knowledge, Understanding, and Integration Components

Note that achieving the unit's objectives without any evidence of greater achievement earns the student a grade of adequate (i.e., a *C* in most grading systems). To earn higher grades, the student must produce evidence within the proficient and/or exemplary levels. This is an idea teachers often find difficult to grasp and apply. In the past, teachers may have considered achieving a unit's objectives to represent *A*-level work. With such an approach, a school actually has a covert pass-fail grading system. An *A* is a passing mark; the student has achieved the objectives. A *B* or lower is a failing mark; the student did not achieve the objectives. However, teachers and schools generally consider a *C* to represent passing. In such a system, a student who earns a *C* has not mastered the objectives for the grade level and will not be prepared to achieve those of the next grade level, creating a spiral of failure disguised as acceptable achievement.

The problems this situation creates became obvious to me a few years ago. I worked with a school that was dissatisfied with its students' reading achievement. As a result, it decided to add a class period for some students. The class featured a lengthened meeting time and included some reading instruction. In addition to data from standardized test results, we asked teachers of earlier grades to recommend students they believed would benefit from the appended English class. Three dozen students (about 25 percent of the class) were recommended by the teachers. They thought each of these students was below expected achievement in reading. However, when we reviewed the report card grades of these students, all but one of them had earned either an *A* or a *B* in reading in every marking period of the previous three years. The school was communicating proficiency had been achieved even though its teachers knew the students were not performing at grade level. (You can imagine the response of some parents when they were informed their child had been recommended for an added class featuring instruction for "struggling" readers.) These problems diminish a school's integrity and impair a student's academic development.

The outcome of such flawed grade reporting became clear in the community-college remedial reading classes I taught. When polled, very few students, about 15 percent, recalled ever receiving either additional help in reading or report card grades indicating they were not meeting the school's grade-level expectations. Yet they had reading achievement deficits of four to seven years. I find it difficult to believe that only 15 percent of their teachers recognized a problem. More likely, embedded grading systems generated "good" grades while students were actually failing. Students suffer the consequences of grade misrepresentation. Though they may feel good about their high marks while in school, their confidence suffers greatly when new circumstances prevent their advancement. At that point, many choose to give up. Learning what they should have mastered previously consumes the time they realistically need to deal with adult issues, such as work and family. Had the truth been communicated earlier, intervention may have prevented the problems these adult learners had to face.

We can restore integrity to grading by making sure our assessment is revealed by our teaching and our teaching is based on learning. Architecture of Learning, with its critical intersections, can inform both the form and content of our assessment. Such congruence brings healthy alignment and integrity to all of our instruction. We should practice nothing less.

Questions

1. Why is congruence between learning, teaching, and assessment important? Explain the following statement: Assessment is revealed by our teaching and our teaching is based on learning.

2. Explain the difference between formative and summative assessment.

3. What is the relationship of formative assessment to student learning and achievement?

4. List and briefly describe each stage of the instructive feedback cycle (**FIGURE 6.3**).

5. What is the significance of Architecture of Learning's critical intersections? What is their relationship to assessment?

6. Identify an upcoming unit of instruction and list any of the following that relate: knowledge components, understanding components, utilization components, and integration components. How will you assess each component?

Chapter 7

MINDING THE INTERIOR

Engaging Thought to Construct Understanding

On the hottest day of the year, a bailiff locks twelve men in a room with no air-conditioning or even a working fan. He then stands outside the door and awaits their verdict. Thus opens Reginald Rose's drama *Twelve Angry Men*. The twelve men—jurors charged with deciding the fate of a young man charged with first-degree murder and facing the electric chair—must reach a unanimous decision. Eager to escape the heat and return to their normal lives, the jurors call for an immediate vote—all but one.

Juror 8 stands alone in his desire to deliberate. As he raises important questions, the jury's interaction reveals both the successes and the stumbling blocks of human thinking. Writer David Mamet conveys the gravity of the jury's role:

> Once empanelled on the jury, however, one is subsumed by what one realizes is the essential component of American Democracy... In the courtroom we see a poor man or woman—perhaps a criminal, perhaps a victim—caught in the awesome engine of the State, and we are told that, for the period of our service, we *are* the State...The lawyers can and will lie, elaborate, attempt to distract, embellish, and confuse; and nothing stands between the person in the box and the horror of an unchecked government except twelve diverse, reasonably intelligent people...Sitting in

> the jury box we console ourselves for the loss of time and income thinking, "Before God, that could be me on trial. If that were so, God forbid, I would want those in the jury to be as responsible as I pledge to be and as terrified of error as I am."[1]

Although *Twelve Angry Men* is a work of fiction, we recognize similar situations—times when groupthink or bias threatened to overwhelm sound reasoning—and we know our students will face similar challenges of integrity versus conformity.

How, then, can we develop Juror 8s, students who stand courageously and confidently when the majority is wrong? Do we need to teach critical thinking as a separate subject? Can we perhaps teach our current subject matter in ways that foster critical thinking skills? What is the relationship of thinking to learning?

Thinking to Learn; Learning to Think

What we know results from *what* and *how* we think. Researcher and critical thinking expert Diane F. Halpern explains:

> Knowledge is not something static that gets transferred from one person to another like pouring water from one glass to another. It is dynamic. Information becomes knowledge when we make our own meaning out of it…[We] create knowledge every time we learn a new concept.[2]

Educator Laura Erlauer agrees, explaining that thinking processes "allow the brain to thoroughly understand the new concepts and internalize them into meaningful memories."[3] Learning is a product of thinking.

But this only tells part of the story. By learning more about a subject, we increase our capacity to think about it. We deepen our thinking as we expand our understanding to include newly learned details. As the revised understanding emerges, we increase our potential to think about the subject from various perspectives and to seek out new knowledge regarding it.

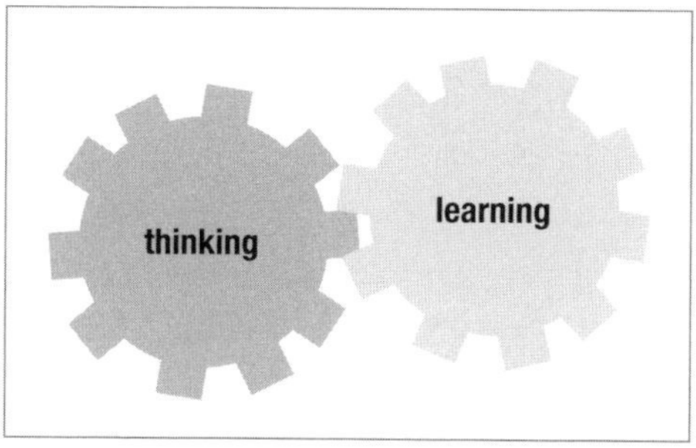

FIGURE 7.1 Complementary Processes

For example, I recently took up cycling as a hobby and fitness regimen. When I was growing up, I rode my bike to the county park near our home, to friends' homes in neighboring towns, and even behind fire trucks in the town Memorial Day parade. Since you never forget how to ride a bike, taking up the hobby as an adult seemed like a simple pursuit. Yet I took my naive childhood knowledge of cycling to a bike store and quickly realized the limits of my understanding! What kind of bike—road or mountain? What material: aluminum? a composite? What size bike? What type of shifting: Italian? Chinese? American? I had to learn so many new details! The patient salesman walked me through all of the options, and I finally chose a bike. Then I had to learn about cyclist gear—shorts, shoes, bibs, jerseys, gloves, saddles, clipless pedals…What happened to banana seats and simply pedaling?

Fast-forward a few weeks. I've added to my understanding and can talk, at least at a novice level, about cycling. Even my current low level of "expertise" required deepening my understanding, adding new details while constructing an expanded knowledge base of cycling. Now I'm pursuing new details. My reading material includes books on cycling, and I'm attending classes on bike maintenance and tune-ups. I better understand cycling, and this enables me to think more widely about it. I can strategically select my garb and gear based on my cycling habits, weather conditions, and preferences. I can strategically shift my bike's gears depending on terrain, fatigue, and desired speed. I can ask new questions about aspects I did not even know existed previously. Thinking empowers my learning, and my learning enables increased and improved thinking.

The relationship is mutually reinforcing. Thinking and learning are so intervolved that attempting to separate one from the other implies a misunderstanding of both. Educator John Barell views the relationship as so influential that he advocates critical thinking as "one of our most important curricular goals."[4]

Critical Thinking and Education

Many researchers find a dearth of thinking in today's classrooms. Richard Paul claims this is a "fundamental" problem and describes current teaching as characterized by "fragmentation and lower order reasoning," producing learning characterized by "superficial fragments" that lack "coherence, connection, and depth of understanding."[5] John Mighton relates an example of such all-too-common teaching gaps:

> Several weeks ago, I found an exercise in a Grade 3 book that asked students, in each question, to shade a given fraction of an

> array of boxes. In most of the questions the number of boxes in the array matched the denominator of the fraction, so the student simply had to look at the numerator of the fraction and shade that many boxes. But halfway through the exercise there was an array of 20 boxes with the instruction "Shade one-fifth of the boxes." Up to that point students had not been taught anything about equivalent fractions or even how to divide a number into equal parts.[6]

Because the students learned to solve the problems with minimal thinking, they were at a loss when complex context made finding the solution more thought-intensive. How would these students be able to transfer this knowledge to the real world, where contexts require thought beyond what they were taught?

This deficit of thinking is not limited to grade-school instruction. Diane Halpern and Milton Hakel claim "it would be difficult to design an educational model that is more at odds with current research on human cognition than the one that is used in most colleges and universities."[7] Researchers Arthur Graesser, Natalie Person, and Xiangen Hu concur, stating that college-level instruction fails to "fortify learners for generating inferences, solving problems, reasoning, and applying their knowledge to practical situations."[8]

Jerome Groopman, medical doctor and author of *How Doctors Think*, recalls an experience that illustrates this separation of thinking from learning. After making his rounds with a group of interns in tow, Dr. Groopman attempted to ignite a Socratic discussion. The interns' lack of response, of give-and-take, alarmed him. Upon reflection, Groopman recalled that clinical algorithms, flowcharts that direct diagnosis, had become a mainstay of current medical instruction. While helpful, such an approach can also be dangerously limiting. "Clinical algorithms can be useful for run-of-the-mill diagnosis...," claims Groopman. "But they quickly fall apart when a doctor needs to think outside their boxes, when symptoms are vague, or multiple and confusing, or when test results are inexact. In such cases—the kind of cases where we most need a discerning doctor—algorithms discourage physicians from thinking independently and creatively. Instead of expanding a doctor's thinking, they constrain it."[9] The interns' education had actually restricted, not expanded, their thinking capacities.

We learn by thinking, and we think about what we learn, but only by combining these processes can the learner thrive. Instructional expert James H. Stronge reaches a similar conclusion:

> Effective teachers emphasize meaning. They encourage students to respond to questions and activities that require them to discover and assimilate their own understanding, rather than to simply memorize material (Marzano et al., 1993). A study of 3rd and 8th graders found that students who received instruction that emphasized analytical, creative, and practical thinking performed better on assessments than students who received instruction that emphasized memorization or analytical thinking only (Sternberg, 2003). Eisner (2003/2004) explained that effective schools, and thus, effective teachers emphasize critical thinking, and they cultivate a propensity for applying critical thinking in order to make good judgments.[10]

Why isn't instruction characterized by increased thinking? In part, because many educators possess a deeply flawed understanding of critical thinking. Many educators have been "miseducated," resulting in poor reasoning, a tendency to "confuse issues and questions," and to be diverted from "the relevant to the irrelevant."[11] Researchers found widespread examples of such such thinking flaws in teachers' assessments of student writing.

Unfortunately, schools provide little help. Most professional development programs for teachers, claims Richard Paul, are "episodic, intellectually unchallenging, and fragmented" with "very little discussion on or about serious educational issues, and when there is such discussion it is often simplistic."[12]

Our past experiences as students also can work against our capacity to increase our students' thinking. Many teachers view knowledge as a bank deposit—put this fact in your brain until I ask you to withdraw it on the test. That is how many of us were taught, and since we tend to model our teaching on our past teachers, we may lack an understanding of critical thinking and its role in learning. And if we lack a fundamental understanding of what constitutes critical thinking, we may lack the capacity to engage in it ourselves and to teach it to students. What, then, constitutes critical thinking?

Critical Thinking's Building Blocks

Critical thinking is:

- *an intentional mode of thinking involving*
- *monitoring and assessing one's own thinking (metacognition) or that of others*
- *in relation to established standards.*
- It *considers relevant contextual elements* and
- *employs specific skills.*

The final element unifies thinker and thinking. Critical thinkers:

- possess *certain dispositions* that enable the effective application of critical thinking skills.

Let's examine these building blocks more closely.

Intentional Mode of Thinking

First, critical thinking is a purposely engaged manner of reasoning. Human thinking tends to be self-centered and arrogant, making one's own preferences and prejudices the basis of evaluation and decision-making. Richard Paul and Linda Elder identify five types of such thinking.[13]

Egocentrism holds a notion to be true because the individual believes it is true. It claims, "It is true *because I believe it*." He will resist, ignore, or defensively avoid evidence contrary to the belief.

Sociocentrism holds an idea to be true because the group believes it is true. It claims, "It is true *because we believe it*," and like egocentrism, defensively avoids or ignores contrary evidence.

Wish fulfillment holds something to be true because the individual wants it to be true. It claims, "It is true *because I want to believe it*." Like the other fallacies, it avoids contrary evidence.

Self-validation holds a belief to be true because the individual has always thought it was true. It claims, "It is true *because I have always believed it*," and it also avoids contrary evidence. This arrogant thought pattern often manifests itself in long-held prejudices.

Finally, selfishness holds a maxim to be true because the individual profits from it being true. It claims, "It is true *because it is in my interest to believe it.*" The personal investment makes this a difficult fallacy to overcome.

Through intentional critical thinking, the thinker overcomes, at least partially and temporarily, these hindrances to objectivity. Juror 8, who most closely personifies critical thinking in *Twelve Angry Men*, asks frequent questions, such as, "What does that prove?", "Could they be wrong?", and "Am I right so far?" He overcomes the self-centered, arrogant thinking that trips up his fellow jurors. He intentionally engages a manner of thinking that searches for verifiable truth. As Paul and Elder would say, he resists "the influence of both the conformist thinkers around [him] and the egocentric thinker within [him]."[14]

Metacognition

Second, critical thinking involves *monitoring and assessing one's own thinking or that of others.* Daniel J. Siegal describes this as "an engaged process of observation in which the contents of the mind are placed not only in awareness, but are approached with a sense of investigative interest."[15] The critical thinker places thinking under a microscope to retrace the thoughts that lead to conclusions or decisions so that faulty thinking can be identified and corrected.

Such activity requires thinking about thinking, a process known as metacognition. Metacognition is the "sine qua non of general intelligence," claims Kathleen Stein. It is "selective attention plus self-reflection...the innermost feedback loops of currents of information and memory in judgments of learning... or feelings of future knowing...."[16] Michael Scriven and Richard Paul describe metacognition as "that mode of thinking—about any subject, content, or problem—in which the thinker improves the quality of his or her thinking by skillfully taking charge of the structures inherent in thinking and imposing intellectual standards upon them."[17]

Metacognition is an evaluation of one's past or current thinking for appropriate future action. For example, if I engage my "innermost loops of currents of information" regarding the purchase of a new car, I trace my thinking, attempting to detect any illogical elements influencing my decision-making (e.g., Am I attracted to Car X merely because I like its stereo? Am I ignoring evidence about the car's quality because its speakers make the interior sound like a rolling concert hall?). I evaluate my thinking, refocusing on the critical factors so that I can revise my standards and reconsider evidence. Paul and Elder stress that self-assessment enables an individual to recognize thinking's "structure, observe its implications, and recognize its basis and vantage point."[18]

Questioning guides this reflective evaluation. Gerald M. Nosich suggests that questions initiate a three-step process. First, the thinker asks questions related to problems. Second, the thinker attempts to answer those questions, "drawing conclusions on the basis of reasons and giving due weight to all relevant factors."[19] Finally, the thinker responds with belief in and action based on the results. In metacognition, the thinker asks questions about previous or current thinking, answers those questions in relation to standards, and revises, rejects, or accepts the thinking. This enables confident action.

For example, I recently attended a conference where one of the main presenters failed to sustain my attention. It was late in the day and the gentleman read much of his presentation from a paper he'd had published. I considered walking out, but I began to ask myself questions. Does this presenter have expertise in this topic? Yes. Is his content well supported and beneficial. Again, yes. Would I be leaving simply because I'm not being entertained? Perhaps. If I worked harder to focus, could I potentially garner ideas worth consideration? Yes. My impulse was to leave, but by using questions to guide my thinking, I chose to stay. Exploring my own thinking resulted in a beneficial change in my thinking, my focus, and my behavior.

Standards

Third, critical thinking involves *evaluation in relation to established standards*. This does not imply that critical thinking is mean-spirited. Critical thinking analyzes ideas in an attempt to establish correctness and confidence. It evaluates within a search for better reasoning. For example, when teaching middle school social studies, my students approached a unit on New World exploration believing that Columbus "discovered" America. When I asked them exactly what that meant they explained that no one knew the continent was there before Columbus. But weren't people living there when Columbus arrived? I asked. The discussion that followed focused on this seeming contradiction: Columbus "discovered" a place that other people obviously knew existed because they lived there.

I challenged the students to examine the statement they had accepted for years. Is it true? Is it authentic? Where did the idea come from? Is this a reputable source? Critical thinkers ask such questions about their own reasoning and that of others. My students examined their own thinking by using such questions as a guide, and the results yielded a great discussion of how perspectives can slant what we believe about historic people and events. From that point, the students constantly evaluated the perspective and its influence on the textbook's presentation of history. They were no longer passive recipients of knowledge. They were engaged in a search for truth and validity.

Since critical thinking involves evaluating thought, potential errors must exist. When self-assessing via metacognition or assessing the thinking of others, what standards guide recognition of sound or faulty thinking? In *Why Good Arguments Often Fail*, James W. Sire identifies eight fallacies traditionally considered downfalls of sound reasoning[20]. This traditional list provides valuable initial benchmarks for evaluating thinking (**FIGURE 7.2**).

GENERAL FALLACY	FALLACY EXAMPLE
unsupported generalizations	firefighters know more about the dangers of smoking than anyone else
hasty generalizations	that firefighter is strong so all firefighters must be strong
post hoc or wrongly attributing correlation	red trucks are always at fires, so if you see a red truck there must be a fire
contradictory premises	firefighters are so smart they can create a written test on fire safety that they themselves cannot pass
emotionally potent but irrelevant reasoning	that firefighter has eight starving children at home so her income should be increased
false analogizing	since firefighters can use water to put out fires, people should be able to use guns to put out arguments
untrue premises	if the firefighters do not put out that house fire the entire state will be in cinders
discrediting the messenger rather than evaluating the message (ad hominem)	this firefighter attends Church X so you should ignore his fire safety suggestions

FIGURE 7.2 Traditional Thought Fallacies and Examples

Context

Fourth, critical thinking *considers relevant contextual elements.* Does the context influence the types of potential thinking errors? Or are thinking errors common across multiple contexts with the details differing? Do we need to teach potential errors for every context?

Jerome Groopman identifies thinking fallacies evident within the process of making a medical diagnosis. His experience *as a patient* highlighted three such errors. With pain in his wrist, Groopman sought the assistance of reputable hand surgeons. The first doctor, unable to reach a conclusion about the source of the pain, fabricated a diagnosis and recommended surgery. Experts rejected this fictional diagnosis and treatment, and Groopman labels the doctor's error a "commission bias," a tendency toward action—to "do something"—even though an effective treatment has not been identified. The second surgeon Groopman consulted perceived a hairline fracture on an MRI scan. Seeming to fixate on the fracture, the doctor recommended a series of surgeries. Though not wholly made up, experts also rejected this diagnosis and treatment. Groopman labels this second doctor's error, a "satisfaction of search" error and describes it as the tendency to "stop searching for a diagnosis once you find something." A third hand surgeon, of world renown, fell prey to the same error as the first doctor, though with a different fictional diagnosis.[21]

Groopman eventually found a young expert who accurately diagnosed the source of his discomfort and recommended an effective treatment. It is worth noting how Groopman and Dr. Terry Light, former president of the American Society for Surgery of the Hand, describe this young expert's approach to thinking:

> The key, Dr. Light continued, is for "everything to add up—the patient's symptoms, the findings on physical examination, what appears meaningful on the MRI or other x-rays. It has to come together to form a coherent picture." In effect he was describing pattern recognition, and saying that if a clear pattern is not apparent, the surgeon is in a quandary…The surgeon's brain is more important than his hands.[22]

The doctor who gave the correct diagnosis gathered and organized data from disparate sources (comprehension) and recognized a pattern formed by their connections (elaboration). However, the relevant point here is that the doctor-patient context is prone to various errors. Are such errors specific to their professional contexts?

Rather than taking action when inaction would be wiser (Groopman's "commission bias"), writers can err by directing energy a step ahead of where they actually are in the writing process. "Content problems are almost always process problems," claims Jack Hart, managing editor of *The Oregonian*. "A problem visible at any one stage of the writing process usually results from something that happened at the immediately preceding stage."[23] For example, a writer bogged down with too much information has likely failed to develop a focus. This failure sends the writer digging for any seemingly related information, no matter how remote the connection may be. The writer's premature action fosters confusion. We might term this a "dash to draft" error. Both doctors and writers err by taking action when more research or reflection would be beneficial. The error can be influential in both these contexts and in several others. The error is similar, but the context-based details differ.

Context appears to play a lesser role in the type of errors that are made, but a significant role in the specific content misinterpreted through faulty thinking and the implications of that flawed thinking. When writers move to action too soon, chaos generates inefficiency and distraction; when doctors err similarly, the consequences can be far more grave.

Since thinking errors are not context-specific, methods of recognizing and avoiding them may be applied to multiple contexts. An example of such application occurred recently in a fifth-grade class taught by a friend of mine. One group of students had been reading a the classic children's book *The Gammage Cup* by Carol Kendall, in which three unusual friends are cast out of their town when they begin warning of an impending attack by old enemies. During the group discussions of the novel, the students constantly pointed out that the townspeople discredited the messengers rather than evaluating the evidence that showed the message was true. A few weeks after the unit had ended, a student came to class eager to share an experience. The previous evening, she had been watching a cable news show with her parents. After several back-and-forth interactions between the interviewer and his guest, the student turned to her parents and said, "That was like watching the townspeople interview Muggles, Gummy, and Walter the Earl." Of course, she had to explain that the three were characters in the book and that the interviewer had acted just like the townspeople, ignoring the message and attacking the messenger. The original context, a classic fantasy novel for children, highlighted a thinking error that the student was able to relate to her current world. Her parents were surprised. Her teacher was delighted. Since it can be transferred to every area of life, critical thinking may be the most powerful and practical subject matter we can engage students in learning.

Skills

Fifth, critical thinking *employs specific skills*. Master critical thinkers may automatically apply those skills, but most of us have to deliberately apply them—i.e., to think our way through critical thinking. By knowing the skills and how to use them, we can strategically engage these abilities.

For example, to evaluate an argument, one must be able to identify conclusions and their supporting rationale. Another teacher friend of mine teaches high school math classes. In her geometry classes, she relates conditional statements and their proof to other areas in which similar reasoning is required. For example, she brings editorials expressed in blogs to class and engages the students in identifying the if-then argument and the author's chain of support. Just as the proofs in geometry must present complete and valid evidence, so, she explains, should a convincing argument. The students have gone so far as to structure a writer's argument in the same way they would a proof and have identified places where the writer lacks connections between supporting ideas. When the specific skill is deliberately engaged, the students can strategically apply it in new contexts.

Dispositions

Finally, character complements critical thinking. Thinking and attitude are so closely connected that it is difficult, perhaps impossible, to think critically without the accompanying *disposition* to do so. Let's look at the relationship of general critical thinking abilities to specific skills and associated dispositions.

Abilities, Skills, and Dispositions

Critical thinking requires focus and sustained attention to important details. Specifically, critical thinkers can identify and phrase questions, goals, and challenges. This enables the thinker to direct mental energies to details that matter. The general ability to focus enables the thinker to develop criteria for evaluating responses and results. This in turn enables the successful critical thinker to recognize potential solutions, which leads to a third specific: knowledge of how to devise a strategy for thinking. What are the right questions to ask? Which elements should be considered first? The effective critical thinker can plan thinking and focus mental energies on accomplishing the plan. Asking questions, establishing criteria, and planning thinking lead to one more specific skill related to focus: researching to identify relevant ideas from diverse fields and sources. Accumulating and recognizing applicable information provides the data needed to continue thinking and possibly reach a decision or solve a problem. Initiative and perseverance characterize individuals with these skills.

These may seem like abstract abilities, but watch them in action. Andrea, a high school student, faces a major research project for a biology class. She selects the anatomy of the human brain as her topic. As she does some preliminary research, she begins to identify important questions she needs to address:

1. What are the brain's basic "building blocks"?
2. What are the brain's major divisions?
3. What major functions are associated with each division?
4. Within each division, what are the major structures?
5. What important functions are associated with each structure?

6. How do the various structures and divisions communicate?
7. What results when these communications are disrupted?
8. What shapes the brain? Why does each individual have a brain that is different from anyone else's?

As Andrea reviews her preliminary questions, she begins to note criteria that will define when her thinking becomes successful: the results of her research will yield answers to the questions. Additionally, the results will connect the answers in such a way that others will be able to understand both the important details and the relationships between them. Others will be able to understand the human brain as she does. With a focus established and criteria for success recognized, Andrea directs her energy to planning her work. In what order should she seek information? Where should she seek information? How will she take notes on what she finds? More than managing her time, Andrea develops a flexible strategy to guide her own learning and ultimately produce the presentation required by her teacher. She then begins working her plan, finding resources that can provide data that is relevant to her focus.

As Andrea finds such data, she'll need additional thinking skills, including those of analysis. We often equate thinking with general analytical skills, but critical thinking uses specific skills of analysis, including identifying:

1. main ideas and their supporting details
2. conclusions and their supporting rationale, both stated and implied
3. irrelevant ideas or details and assumptions
4. the structure of an argument or presentation
5. all the critical details that contribute to the total situation

Possessing these skills fuels the complementary dispositions of curiosity and healthy skepticism.

Abilities of evaluation interact with those of analysis. Specific evaluation skills include:

1. assessing the credibility of a source
2. identifying needed information in collected data
3. contrasting potential solutions or actions
4. assessing potential solutions or actions in relation to goals

As the critical thinker engages in analysis, evaluation naturally arises. Conclusions and their supporting rationale are identified and assessed for credibility and relevance. Individuals with evaluation abilities display loyalty to the truth and commitment to optimal results.

As Andrea continues working on her research project, she gleans material from her resource materials. She identifies main ideas, conclusions, and their supporting details. As she does, she assesses the credibility of the source and the strength of the conclusions. She monitors her collected data in relation to the data she needs to complete the research. She cross-checks her sources and hunts down answers for discrepancies she discovers. She collects data that she is confident will provide her with accurate, supportable, and necessary information. She displays a mix of curiosity and skepticism and a drive to find the information that will enable her to prepare an excellent presentation.

As the critical thinker begins to process collected data, the need to make sense of it becomes evident. The general ability of clarification includes the specific skills of defining frequently used terms, identifying examples and/or non-examples, and accurately summarizing thoughts presented by others. As the thinker applies these skills, he demonstrates a commitment to being precise.

Andrea recognizes that she has accumulated a tremendous amount of reliable information on the brain's anatomy. Though she has proceeded with direction and focus, she recognizes that to communicate clearly, she needs greater precision in choosing relevant and important data. She needs to clarify what is important and deepen her understanding of it. As she examines the functions associated with various brain structures, she begins to develop examples that others will recognize. She checks the accuracy of her quotes and the clarity of her summaries. She identifies the terms that show up frequently (e.g., *lobe*) and defines them accurately and clearly. Where necessary, she adds examples. She acts to make her understanding and ability to communicate the information more precise.

With a clearer, more focused understanding, the critical thinker searches the emerging body of knowledge, the collected information, for patterns. This deduction or induction, depending on the structure of the information, leads the thinker to begin interpreting the information. How is the understanding of the information relevant to the questions or goals? How does the understanding address the questions or goals? What are the implications of the developing understanding? Who or what would be affected by acting on the understanding? This thinking, this act of intellectual independence, enables the thinker to own the information.

As Andrea continues to work with the information she's collected, she begins to notice certain relationships and patterns. For example, it becomes evident that sensory data generally moves from the back of the brain forward. She also notes patterns of brain activity associated with specific tasks, such as speech production. As these patterns become evident, Andrea begins to think about how to explain the brain. She begins to interpret the information, devising associations that help her continue to build an understanding and that will help others construct a similar understanding. She decides that computer keystrokes provide one such reference. When you want a computer to carry out a specific function, you hit a combination of keys to produce the desired result. Similarly, when someone wants to speak, the brain activates a combination, a network of connections, which enable speech to be produced. Through interpretation (i.e., elaboration), Andrea makes the information her own.

To benefit others, the results of critical thinking must be communicated. Developing a means of sharing the results involves two general abilities: perspective and communication. As a thinker prepares to present what his mind has processed, he considers how his audience may receive it. He assumes alternate points of view, searches his thinking for any personal bias, and adjusts his thinking and communication accordingly. He demonstrates humility and communicates a valuing of others through these actions. Additionally, the critical thinker considers how to communicate with the greatest clarity and efficacy. If supportive media would be helpful, he seeks it out and prepares to use it. He demonstrates a commitment to excellence in both content and its presentation.

As Andrea writes her report, she monitors her thinking and its communication. If she notes her personal bias creeping in, she adjusts her wording to reflect a fairer interpretation. She also considers how to best convey the information. Since she understood much from images taken through fMRI scans, she decides to include a few to support her ideas. If multimedia use is an option, Andrea considers the possibility of adding 3-D graphics of the brain with various structures highlighted to correspond with her presentation. *She constructs her communication with the same care and excellence she used to think through the material.*

At this point, you may be thinking that Andrea is an exemplary student. I agree. You may also think that such students must live on another planet, but before you settle on that conclusion, let me pose a question: Where and when are students taught to process new information and proceed through the steps that lead to excellence in self-directed learning and communication? I've observed many units that involved research projects where the teacher seemed more concerned about structure (e.g., citations and reference lists) than teaching the students how to think critically about their topic. While proper documentation is important, without instruction and guidance in using critical thinking as an approach to learning, we can't expect to have many students like Andrea. We can't expect students to know how to learn on their own.

Implications for Learning

We have reviewed what makes up critical thinking. The next question is: What does this mean for learning?

First, critical thinking cannot occur without content. The argument over teaching critical thinking as a separate subject or integrating critical thinking into current subjects is best resolved through a combined approach. This features direct instruction on prerequisite skills *and* applied critical thinking within established subject areas. To be critical thinkers, "we need background knowledge and familiarity with concepts within a particular area, as well as effective heuristics and habits of mind."[24]

We need to equip students with thinking skills, give them content worth thinking about, and engage them in critical thinking about it (**FIGURE 7.3**). For example, students taught to identify related ideas from diverse fields can use this ability to deepen their understanding of major historical eras, such as the Renaissance. From exploring da Vinci's approach to art, Brunelleschi's approach to architecture, Luther's approach to religion and Machiavelli's view of political life, students may understand that the period is characterized, in part, by an examination of what was and is to create something new. Ideas from art, religion, politics, and literature combine to build a more complete understanding of the era.

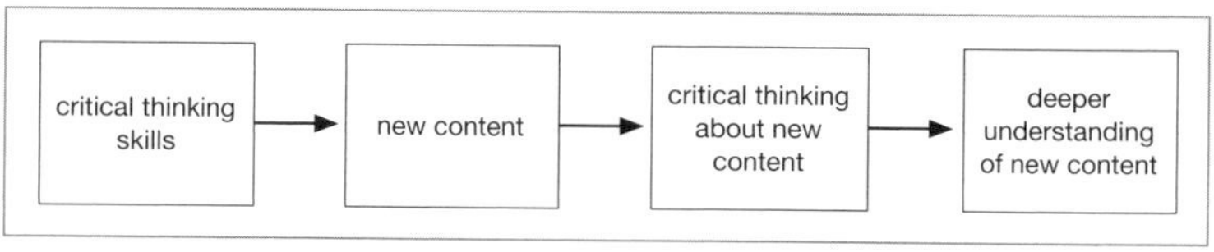

FIGURE 7.3 Sequence Leading to Increased Learning through Critical Thinking

Second, teaching critical thinking's specific skills exceeds most typical instruction. If a teacher emphasizes critical thinking, it's often through the use of a taxonomy or hierarchy of thinking forms, such as knowledge, analysis, and synthesis. Relying on a taxonomy may provide some instructional benefits, such as enhancing questioning variety, but on its own it fails to develop student critical thinking abilities. For example, skills of effectively communicating one's thinking and considering varying perspectives do not appear in many taxonomies. While one may engage in these processes, they are, at best, implied within most hierarchies of thinking and may, therefore, not be taught directly.

Third, instructional activities should engage students in

critical thinking to provide practice in this skill and to deepen learning. Because critical thinking does not occur automatically, a student must learn how to think critically. Developing individuals like Juror 8 requires us to teach students how to overcome the self-absorbed tendencies of their thinking and apply sound reasoning to their lives.

Students are often quick to judge individuals and cultures different from their own as inferior. This limits their ability to understand anything associated with such cultures. For example, students can resist trying to understand the narrative significance of mudra (hand gestures) in India's dance forms. As a result, they lose any benefit and enrichment such an understanding could add to their lives. Before introducing such material, a teacher can engage students in identifying and evaluating their general beliefs about India's culture and about dance, not judging but helping students recognize how their negative perceptions may prevent their learning and encouraging an adjustment in viewpoint.

When students think critically, their understanding of new material deepens. Their critical thinking abilities improve their learning capacity. However, *the teacher's instruction must integrate learning and critical thinking*. The Architecture of Learning Blueprints enable at least four levels of such integration.

Level 1: Guiding Critical Thinking with Questions

In *Twelve Angry Men*, Juror 8 uses questions to engage his own critical thinking and to encourage his fellow jurors to do likewise. Questions, according to John Barell, engage "our minds in complex processes of analysis—posing problems and resolving them, uncovering unstated assumptions, and searching for evidence that will lead us to logical, reasonable conclusions."[25] Expert Vincent

Ruggiero claims, "...critical thinking is a search for answers, a *quest.* Not surprisingly, one of the most important techniques used in critical thinking is asking probing questions."[26]

Questions can spur "investigative intent" as students review their own thinking and/or that of others. But what questions direct the "quest" for supportable answers? By converting Sire's list of traditional fallacies[27] into guiding questions, we create prompts for such investigating (**FIGURE 7.4**). For example, false analogies attempt to make a point based on a comparison of things that are essentially too different to support the conclusion—e.g., since firefighters can use water to put out fires, people should be able to use guns to put out arguments. When students encounter an analogy, they can ask, "Are the connections appropriate? relevant? accurate?" Their answers guide their response, enabling them to think critically about the analogy and its credibility as support for an argument.

GENERAL FALLACY	FALLACY EXAMPLE	GUIDING QUESTIONS
		• What claims are being made?
unsupported generalizations	firefighters know more about the dangers of smoking than anyone else	• What support is given for each claim? • Do any claims lack support? Does independent support for such claims exist? • Are any claims based on support that is impossible to prove or verify?
hasty generalizations	that firefighter is strong so all firefighters must be strong	• Are any claims based on single examples or limited support? • Do any claims exceed their verifiable support?
post hoc or wrongly attributing correlation	red trucks are always at fires, so if you see a red truck there must be a fire	• What relationships are stated or implied? • Do the facts support recognition of the relationship as valid? • Does the identified relationship exceed the facts?
contradictory premises	firefighters are so smart they can create a written test on fire safety that they themselves cannot pass	• Do any claims depend on themselves for support? • Do any claims suggest circumstances that cannot be tested for verification?
emotionally potent but irrelevant reasoning	that firefighter has eight starving children at home so her income should be increased	• Do any claims depend only on emotion (e.g., fear, pity) for support? • If emotional support exists, is it relevant to the issue?
false analogizing	since firefighters can use water to put out fires, people should be able to use guns to put out arguments	• Do any claims use other claims to illustrate their support? (Look for If…then or Since…then relationships.) • Are the connections appropriate? relevant? accurate?
untrue premises	if the firefighters do not put out that house fire the entire state will be in cinders	• Do any claims seem to exaggerate reality? • Is the support offered for any claims unverifiable? overstated?
discrediting the messenger rather than evaluating the message (ad hominem)	this firefighter attends Church X so you should ignore his fire safety suggestions	• Does any claim or support draw attention to a characteristic of the idea's presenter or originator rather than the idea? • Does the characteristic apply to the presenter's expertise of the idea (and is, therefore, appropriate) or some other aspect (and is, therefore, irrelevant)?

FIGURE 7.4 Questions for Guiding Recognition of General Thought Fallacies

A student's skill level suggests how such questions can effectively promote critical thinking. In early grades, the teacher guides such activity. For example, while reading a story featuring an illustration of a fire truck, Marie, an early elementary teacher, may ask her students what kind of truck the picture shows. When they respond, she asks the students how they know the truck is a fire truck. A child responds that the truck is red, and Marie follows up by asking, "Are all fire trucks red?" The children respond that yes, all fire trucks are red. Marie asks them why they think that is true, and the students respond with their experiences of seeing red fire trucks. Marie then shows a picture of a yellow fire truck and tells the students about seeing one at a parade. She then asks the students if they can say with certainty that all fire trucks are red or that all red trucks are fire trucks. She uses questioning to help the students accept that all fire trucks are not red, and that because a truck is red does not make it a fire truck.

Marie then shows students the illustration again and asks them to identify other, more reliable support for the claim that the pictured vehicle is a fire truck—i.e., to list a few other details that indicate the truck is a fire truck. She uses questions to guide students to recognize possible fallacies, assumptions influencing their thinking, and unsupportable generalizations. Though they may not be able to engage in such processing on their own, guided critical thinking provides students with the experience that aids later skill learning.

Similar discussions are appropriate at every grade level, but students in late elementary grades and beyond also benefit from direct critical thinking skill instruction followed by guided/supported and independent practice. Such instruction takes us to a second level of integration.

Level 2: Designing Direct Critical Thinking Instruction

Critical thinking employs specific skills—mental action sequences that are initiated to achieve some end. Instruction in these specific skills can be designed using the Architecture of Learning Skill Blueprint.

For example, consider a potential middle school unit on unsupported generalizations (**FIGURE 7.5**). In examining the skill, Ben, the teacher, notes a pattern: identify the content and structure of thinking; assess the thinking according to established standards; and accept, reject, or revise the thinking accordingly. Condensed, the pattern states, "Identify, assess, and act."

Critical Thinking: UNSUPPORTED GENERALIZATIONS					
		CORE PROCESSES			
FOCUS		experience	comprehension	elaboration	application
	EX	Equipment malfunction	Analysis and discussion of equipment experience	Pattern recognition: identify, assess, act	Other illustrations of the pattern
	CO	Skill instruction & modeling: unsupported generalizations	Process restatement, example, and symbolic steps	Pattern and process similarities	Guided, supported, whole group practice
	AP	Brief passages with unsupported generalizations	Student identification of generalizations	Pattern-process comparison	Rejection or revision and justification
	IN	Passages, think-alouds, media-based materials	Student identification of generalizations	Pattern-process comparison	Rejection or revision and justification

FIGURE 7.5 Sample Critical Thinking Direct Instruction Unit

For the **EX-ex** activity, Ben divides the class into small groups and gives each one some malfunctioning equipment, such as a pump and playground ball with a tiny hole in either the pump's hose or the ball. Ben tells the students not to touch the equipment, but to identify the task it is supposed to complete and to list each piece of it. With these two elements established, Ben instructs the students to try the equipment. Afterward, he asks the students to describe what happened, and to identify, if they can, the source of the malfunction. Ben then makes a few materials available (e.g., duct tape) and encourages the students to fix the equipment.

Moving to **EX-co**, Ben asks questions, guiding the students to recognize three steps:

1. They identified the equipment, its task, and its components.
2. They assessed whether the equipment would function.
3. They took action (attempting repairs, rejecting the equipment as unusable) based on that assessment.

This leads to **EX-el**, where Ben guides recognition of the pattern: identify, assess, act. **EX-ap** naturally follows as he asks the students to identify examples of the pattern from their own experiences. At first, students may share examples in which an overt problem led to assessment and action, such as a car making a strange noise leading to the identification of a flat tire. Ben then asks the students to think of times when they would illustrate this pattern prior to knowing a problem existed. For example, a doctor may perform a physical exam to identify unknown health problems a patient may have, or an auto mechanic may give a car a full inspection, diagnosing potential problems before they become obvious to the driver.

With the pattern and some illustrative experiences identified, Ben presents the skill sequence—identify the content and structure of thinking, assess the thinking according to established standards, and accept, reject, or revise the thinking according to the assessment. He describes the fallacy of an unsupported generalization (a broad statement that lacks factual support), illustrating with several examples. Ben demonstrates the skill several times, thinking aloud while identifying, assessing, and acting on a statement or series of statements (**CO-ex**). He then gives the students these instructions:

1. Restate and reorganize the process by writing each step on an index card and placing the index cards in order.
2. Create an example of an unsupported generalization, write it on an index card, and place it next to the index card that features the step in the process where such a statement would be discovered.
3. Brainstorm a possible symbol for each step of the process.

During this activity, Ben provides instructive feedback and support, redirecting student thinking and offering encouragement as necessary (**CO-co**). With the knowledge component established, Ben asks the students to identify similarities between the critical thinking process and the equipment experience (**CO-el**). Then he presents a series of statements on the chalkboard and guides students through the initial stages of applying the skill, prompting and supporting as necessary (**CO-ap**).

Instruction then moves into the APplication strand. Ben presents the students with a brief passage to read (**AP-ex**). Students use the skill's steps to identify the author's thinking, to assess the passage by noting unsupportable generalizations, and to suggest action—either rejection of the argument or ways to revise it (**AP-co**). The students then pause to consider their own thinking and skill use (**AP-el**), comparing it to the pattern: Have I identified? assessed? planned action? Finally, the students either explain why the argument is rejected or propose a revision that makes the passage's ideas well-founded (**AP-ap**). Ben repeats this series of activities with several other passages. He then thinks out loud, providing data input for the **AP-ex** cell. The students complete the same process for his thinking, identifying, assessing, and acting. Again, Ben repeats this process with the unsupportable generalizations becoming more and more subtle. As with the **CO-co** activity, Ben remains active, engaging in instructive feedback and supporting student practice of the skill. It should be noted that students will be on the alert for unsupportable generalizations in his comments from this point forward. This is a good development, though some teachers may initially view it as a challenge. The students are doing exactly what they've been taught to do: transferring their learning to a widened context. It's evidence of effective teaching.

The INtention strand makes this unit endlessly interesting and practical. Throughout the coming days and weeks, Ben presents passages, think-alouds, and any other materials in which students may find unsupportable generalizations. A newspaper's letters to the editor are good sources, as are an author's comments about a biographical subject. Ben also asks individual students to create think-alouds in which they include unqualified generalizations. These are presented to the class (**IN-ex**) as the basis for identification and assessment (**IN-co**), the process is checked to make sure the pattern is complete (**IN-el**), and appropriate action is taken (**IN-ap**). Such activity continues throughout the school year as Ben remains attentive to "teachable moments" since unsupportable generalizations will likely appear in unexpected places, such as textbook passages and Web site comments.

Identifying and addressing other general fallacies could

be taught similarly. As students learn to recognize each fallacy, their capacity to evaluate thinking increases. As a result, it can be tempting to expect students to find all the fallacies on an initial review of thinking. However, such a comprehensive evaluation is unlikely in a single review. In *A Writer's Coach*, editor Jack Hart models an approach that fosters successful revision. In each chapter, he identifies one significant element of writing to examine. For example, one chapter focuses on elements of brevity that contribute to writing quality. The chapter ends with a "Cheat Sheet"—a summarized list of revision methods based on the chapter's main points. As a writer reviews a manuscript with the "Cheat Sheet" nearby, unnecessary elements become evident and can be revised.[28] Reviewing material to identify fallacies can follow this successful approach—one type of fallacy per review. As students become increasingly proficient, they may be able to recognize multiple fallacies during a review, but initially, a one-at-a-time approach increases the likelihood of success.

Teaching critical thinking directly need not be limited to general fallacies. Instruction addressing the specific skills listed in **FIGURE 7.2** can also be designed on Architecture of Learning Blueprints. To do so, a teacher would analyze the skill to identify its specific action steps, establish the skill's action sequence, identify the general pattern the steps illustrate, and use the results to design instruction on the Architecture of Learning Skill Blueprint. Such instruction fosters the development of critical thinking skills, but other methods of merging critical thinking and instruction exist. The Architecture of Learning Blueprints are well-suited for such integration.

Level 3: Critical Thinking Through the Strands

By designing a unit that engages students in comprehension and elaboration, teachers can spark critical thinking throughout the course of instruction. For example, consider a science unit on the flow of energy through food chains. Faith, a fifth-grade teacher, presents new material (**CO-ex**), and the students restate and reorganize the essential ideas and trace energy flow by structuring food-chain examples that show who eats what and who eats whom (**CO-co**).

Faith then engages the students in connecting the flow of energy through food chains with the experience from the **EX-ex** activity. (She used jelly beans and arranged a system of bartering in which the jelly beans were used repeatedly—enclosed in plastic bags! Students then tracked each bag to illustrate the "flow" of something that enabled one person and then another.) In the **CO-el** activity, the students explore how food chains are like that initial experience, identifying connections between new information and the known experience.

Students then consider various implications of food chains (**CO-ap**). Faith encourages students to pose questions worth exploring. For example, she directs the students to the food chains they have reorganized and asks them to identify potential influences on the food chains (e.g., the loss of a specific element within the chain). Then she asks the students to consider potential sources of that influence and to identify the questions an individual or group should consider before taking action that could influence the food chain. For example, if proposed development of a forested region destroys the habitat of local chipmunk populations, what questions should be asked and answered or what actions could be taken prior to the start of construction?

Teachers can develop such activities by consulting the list of skills (**FIGURE 7.3**) and identifying points within the Blueprint where a critical thinking skill and the content effectively combine to address both the needed learning process (e.g., elaboration) and the desired critical thinking.

Level 4: Critical Thinking as the INtention Strand

The INtention strands of Content and Combination Blueprints create opportunities for even greater integration. **FIGURE 7.6** creates an effective process by sequencing the critical thinking skills. This process aligns with Architecture of Learning's core processes—experience, comprehension, elaboration, and application—which intersect each Blueprint strand. Overlaying this critical thinking process with the INtention strand of a Content or Combination Blueprint creates a sequence of critical thinking activities that promotes deep learning.

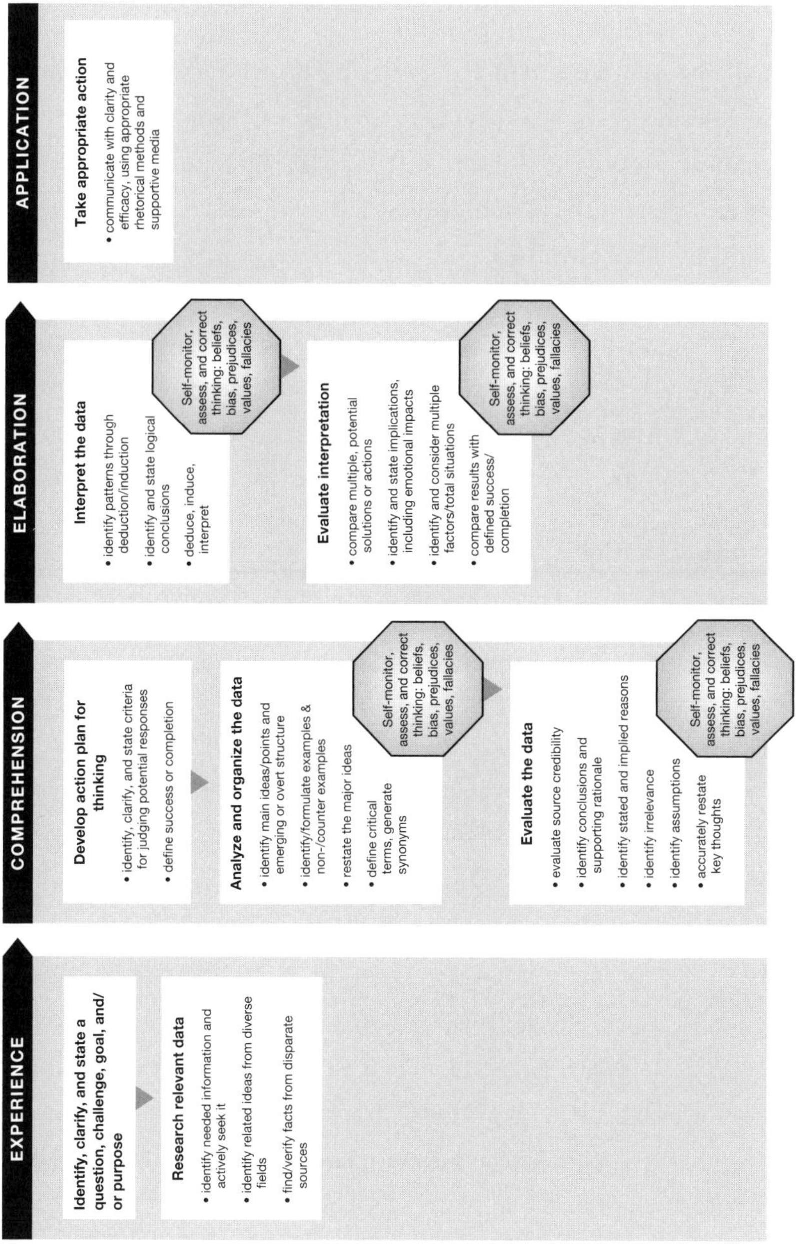

FIGURE 7.6 Overlay of Critical Thinking Process with the INtention Strand

For example, consider a high school or college-level unit on colonial America and the rising conflict preceding the American Revolution. A pattern statement for this unit might read, "Desire influences perspective," and instruction may focus on various groups present in colonial America, their desires regarding how they should be governed, their perspectives, and the results when these perspectives clashed.

The Sons of Liberty, a group with a significant role in the unit's events, stirred up controversy. Were they patriots? Were they terrorists?

Helen, a high school teacher, begins (**IN-ex**) by presenting students with an essay arguing one view or the other, or explaining the basis for each of the competing views: *the Sons of Liberty were patriots* versus *the Sons of Liberty were terrorists* (see "Talk: Sons of Liberty,"[29] for example). Such an article raises the question: How should the Sons of Liberty be perceived? The **IN-ex** activity continues as students, working in small groups, research relevant data to identify the information they need to make an informed judgment. They should seek such information from various sources, including primary sources, such as those cited in Milton Meltzer's *The American Revolutionaries: A History in Their Own Words 1750-1800.*[30] They can also use the various sources to establish and verify facts. Helen aids and guides students in their collection of data, suggesting sources and directing students to pursue a balance of viewpoints.

Once the students have accumulated the data, they enter the strand's comprehension phase (**IN-co**). They develop an action plan that includes criteria for documentation and supporting ideas, and a definition of *completion* (i.e., a description of sufficient evidence related to the judgment to be made). Comprehension continues as students sort the accumulated data, recognize potential main points, identify illustrative examples, and define critical terms, such as *patriot* and *terrorist*. Students use their criteria to evaluate the credibility of their sources, eliminate irrelevant data, identify their own assumptions (e.g., possible pro-patriot opinions based on their own national identity), and formulate statements of key and supporting ideas. Helen guides and supports as needed.

As indicated on **FIGURE 7.6**, each of these steps includes a pause for evaluation. Students should examine their recent thinking to identify and address fallacies. Helen guides these sessions as necessary. Based on the results, activity resumes, either returning students to the prior step to correct identified fallacies or enabling them to proceed confidently into the next step.

In the elaboration phase (**IN-el**), students engage in deep thinking about the data they have discovered. Advancing beyond merely identifying key ideas, the students interpret the results, noting relevant and supportive patterns (e.g., typical responses of the Sons of Liberty), and develop grounded conclusions. In other words, the students state a judgment that responds to the initial question and evaluate this judgment by comparing the results with the characteristics of completion they defined back in the **IN-co** step. Students also explore the judgment's significance (e.g., Does this judgment possess implications for how the Revolution is viewed? Does this judgment have any implications for how specific historic individuals should be viewed?).

Finally, students enter the application phase (**IN-ap**) and develop an effective presentation of the resulting judgment and, possibly, a reasoned dissension. The students may also present implications related to their judgment, such as how the Sons of

Liberty should be presented in history textbooks. A presentation by each group would naturally conclude the process and extend the process of application. Such presentations provide new data for all students to evaluate via critical thinking.

While such an approach to the INtention strand may consume significant instructional time, the resulting learning is rich, meaningful, and long-lasting. Not only do students explore the instructional topic in greater depth, they also engage in critical thinking's essential skills, including multiple periods when they review and assess their own work. Students also practice and develop research, organization, and communication skills. James H. Stronge explains the long-term benefits of such learning:

> In addition to applying basic principles in their lessons, effective teachers stress the importance of higher mental processes, such as problem-solving techniques, analytical thinking skills, and creativity. They use longer and more complex assignments in order to challenge students and engage them in learning (Allington, 2002). These skills enable students to *relate their learning to real-life situations and incorporate concepts into their long-term memory*... [italics added].[31]

Neurologist and educator Judy Willis agrees: "The best learning occurs when students are given opportunities to develop their capacities to think, interpret, and become engaged in subject matter."[32]

Conclusion

We are not merely educating students in the details of Columbus, magnetism, and predicate adjectives. We are teaching future judgment makers. Whether our students assess the validity of legal arguments, the wisdom of purchasing a new home, or the ethics of using new methods, their success depends, in large part, on how well they learn to think. That in turn depends on how well they are taught. By combining thinking and teaching, we create opportunities to foster independent thinking—the capacity and courage to ask questions that will overcome self-centered and conformist thinking to pursue truth. We equip and empower future Juror 8s:

> I only know as much as you do. According to the testimony the boy looks guilty. Maybe he is. I sat there in court for three days listening while the evidence built up...I had questions I would have liked to ask...It's very hard to keep personal prejudice out of a thing like this. And no matter where you run into it, prejudice obscures the truth....[33]

Questions

1. What is the relationship of critical thinking and learning? What does each contribute to the other?

2. Why do you think researchers tend to find a dearth of critical thinking in classrooms?

3. If critical thinking comprises specific skills, what are the implications for teaching?

4. What is the relationship between critical thinking skills and dispositions? How might teachers foster the development of these dispositions in students?

5. What role can teacher questioning play in fostering student critical thinking? Identify a classroom scenario in which teacher questioning could be used to ignite critical thinking and identify some of the questions the teacher could use.

6. Select one of the critical thinking skills (**FIGURE 7.1**). If you were to design a unit to teach students this skill, what would some of your instructional activities be? For an extra challenge, place your activities on an Architecture of Learning Skill Blueprint and identify the cells lacking activity. Brainstorm effective activities for the blank cells.

7. Explain how each level of integrating critical thinking and instruction contributes to student learning. Which level(s) could you use with your students? How will you incorporate these approaches into your instruction?

Chapter

8

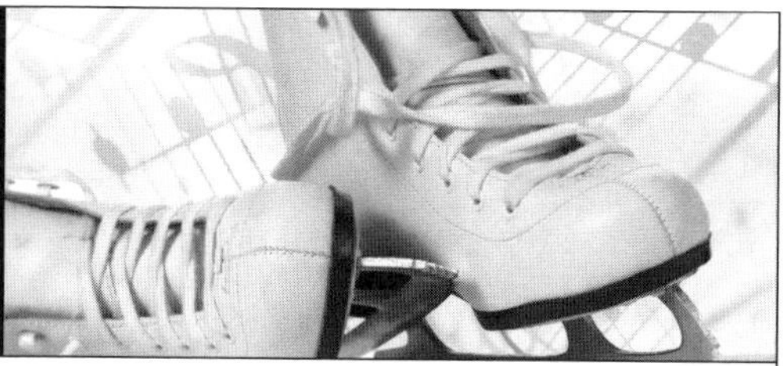

EXPANDING THE VIEW

Using Creativity to Complement Learning

"Do you think you could come up with something?" I was asked. After I had slaved away on the brochure's informative text, developing some new creative zinger didn't initially excite me. Yet my graphic designer felt the brochure lacked a spark, a bold stroke to grab a reader's interest and introduce the brochure's big ideas. "You know, something that contrasts designing and planning in an interesting way."

"I'll think about it," I promised. After a few days of what I call "percolating," the following story emerged:

"Music o'er a Frozen Moat"

> A king had a problem. His daughter, the princess, had reached the age when young women normally married, and suitable suitors had not been selected. After discussing the situation with the princess, the king sent his three wisest counselors to find three suitable suitors.
>
> The counselors began their search, exiting the castle and sliding across its moat. Because the kingdom was so far north, the castle's moat was frozen solid all year long. Though the counselors cursed as they struggled to stay upright while coming and going, the princess loved the frozen moat. For her the ice was a canvas and, when wearing her skates, she was an artist. She spent hours every day gliding around the castle, performing all kinds of jumps, spins, and fancy footwork.

After several days, the three counselors returned, each with an appropriate suitor. The king and princess conferred with the counselors, interviewed the suitors, and agreed that the three suitors were among the kingdom's finest young men.

The king announced a plan. In two weeks, each suitor would make a presentation to the princess. The suitor whose presentation won the princess's heart would become her husband and the future king. The suitors left the castle, aware of the challenge, the competition, and the opportunity.

On the appointed day, the suitors returned to the castle, sliding across the frozen moat, where one of them noticed the graceful skate markings in the ice and smiled.

The first suitor stepped confidently forward, bowed to the king and princess, and then sat on the castle floor to strap on a pair of ice skates. The king, princess, counselors, and other suitors hurried to the castle windows and watched as the first suitor glided over the frozen moat. For the past two weeks he had practiced skating, even taking lessons from Scooter Flemington, a skater known throughout the kingdom. Seeking to impress the princess, the suitor attempted a jump or two and then spun clumsily back into the castle's meeting room.

"Wow," said the princess, "that sure was, um, impressive. Next!"

The second suitor was a scholar, known far and wide as the kingdom's record holder for most hours spent in the library. He stepped confidently forward, cleared his throat, and began to speak.

"Your Highnesses, I have spent the last two weeks becoming an expert on the history of figure skating and have prepared a brief presentation on its highlights."

He began to wax eloquent—he had indeed become an expert. However, by the time he reached Betty Hemming's amazing accomplishments, the princess was struggling to pay attention. The ice on the moat was so smooth and perfect (except for the scars left by the first suitor's attempts) that she began to daydream about going on the ice herself.

The king sensed this, and just as the second suitor began to talk about Marthy Camel, the king raised his hand to stop the onslaught of words. "Sir," the king said, "you are indeed most knowledgeable. Thank you for such a thorough presentation."

"Next!" yelled the princess, hoping the final presentation would be more exciting.

The third suitor stepped forward. "Your Highnesses," he began, "I am a musician who has always longed for a partner who could create images of captivating beauty to accompany my compositions. I believe the princess possesses such talent. It would please me if the princess would retrieve her skates and meet me on the castle moat."

The princess thought this a most exciting development. Immediately, she raced for her skates, strapped them to her dainty princess feet, and glided out the castle door onto the moat, where the musician had a small orchestra waiting.

"Your Highness," the final suitor said, bowing to the princess, "I have watched you skate on the moat every day for the past fourteen days. Each time you skate, new music fills my mind. I have compiled this music into a composition. Your composition. It would be an honor if you would now skate to this music."

The princess was speechless but nodded in agreement. The final suitor raised his conductor's baton and the orchestra began to play. The music seemed magical, carrying the princess across the ice with more grace and beauty than ever before. As the final notes echoed through the castle, the first two suitors slipped silently across the moat and disappeared. There was no doubt who had won the princess's heart.

As the princess and the new prince danced at their wedding reception, the king's counselors gathered in a corner to talk. "I don't understand it," said the first counselor. "My selected suitor was such a great athlete. He set out to win the princess's heart by impressing her with his performance."

"Yes," said the second counselor, "my selected suitor had brains. That man set out to prove his intelligence by developing expertise in just fourteen days!"

> "Your selected suitors had plans," said the third counselor, "but the objective was to win the princess's heart. Designing the presentation with that purpose and princess in mind made the difference. And the princess skater and her prince musician sure look happy!" The other counselors nodded silently in agreement.

This tale of suitors and symphonies represents my attempt to provide what the brochure needed. My development of it illustrates the *general* sequence of creative processing. Before any creative work is produced, creative thinking takes place. And before creative thinking takes place, the individual gathers data via experience. Experience prompts thinking that creates expression. Since the experience and expression are observable and familiar to us, let's explore creativity's intermediate stage: thinking.

Creativity's Mysterious Middle Stage

Creativity comprises thinking (process) and doing (ability), moving from imagination to invention, from the conceptual to the concrete, from idea to realization. *How* one *thinks* and *how* one *does* influence the result. How, then, does a creative person think?

In the landmark book *The Creative Brain: The Science of Genius*, Dr. Nancy C. Andreasen hypothesizes:

> ...that during the creative process the brain begins by *disorganizing*, making links between shadowy forms of objects or symbols or words or remembered experiences that have not been previously linked. Out of this disorganization, self-organization eventually emerges and takes over in the brain. The result is a completely new and original thing: a mathematical function, a symphony, or a poem.[1]

A significant amount of evidence supports this hypothesis. The journals of creative individuals such as Mozart, Poincaré, and Tchaikovsky reveal a period of disorganization prior to creation.[2] Even the book of Genesis suggests such a period:

> In the beginning God created the heavens and the earth. The earth was *formless and void*, and darkness was over the surface of the deep, and the Spirit of God was moving over the surface of the waters.[3] [emphasis added]

Theologian Matthew Henry said of this passage, "Observe, that at first there was nothing desirable to be seen, for the world was without form, and void; it was confusion, and emptiness."[4] Pre-organized forms, it seems, play an initial role even in divine creation.

Comments of contemporary creative people also confirm such an initial period of disorganization. Architect Steven Holl, for example, describes the following:

> When we are at the beginning of a journey we, like Odysseus, contemplate a character (or concept) that does not yet exist. Absence and loss precede the appearance of an abstract driving force. Chaos, confusion, and implosion of information bound up in rules, constraints, and limited means precede every architectural challenge.[5]

Holl reinforces this idea, stating:

> In each project, we begin with information and disorder, confusion of purpose, program ambiguity, an infinity of materials and forms. All of these elements, like obfuscating smoke, swirl in a nervous atmosphere. Architecture is the result of acting on this indeterminacy.[6]

Before writing "Music o'er a Frozen Moat," I let ideas "swirl in a nervous atmosphere." The brochure's purpose was *informative.* The significant, unifying idea emphasized a contrast of *design* and *planning.* The graphic designer wanted something different, something *non-informative* in style, something that would *gain interest* and *lead readers* into the brochure's informative sections. These concepts formed an "implosion of information" that intermittently gained my attention over several days. The chaos cleared gradually as ideas began to take shape. But how do ideas emerge from the muddled ambiguity?

Within the "obfuscating smoke," cognitive processes are taking place. Identifying those processes became the focus of researchers Robert and Michèle Root-Bernstein. From their penetrating study, the Root-Bernsteins identify "thinking tools" employed by creative individuals.[7] These tools cross disciplines, showing creative breakthroughs in multiple professional fields.

As I reflect on developing "Music o'er a Frozen Moat," I can see a few of these tools contributing to the results. For example, I used the tool of *abstracting.* "What," I thought on several morning runs, "could illustrate or represent these contrasting concepts?" I considered the essence of the ideas—that design attended to audience and featured clear intent whereas planning tends to focus solely on the teacher's actions. Then I began to *analogize*:

"What could resemble these ideas in a concrete way?" Competing individuals came to mind, and from that idea, potential conflict began to emerge. The classic plot line of royalty choosing a spouse provided an organizing structure, a pattern, for developing these ideas into a coherent expression.

My period of disorganization gave way to a period of defining and organizing, which was followed by a period of associating data with known concepts and allowing a pattern to emerge. Sound familiar? Neuroscientists are discovering overlaps of creativity and learning. As *Science* writer Greg Miller explains, researchers at University College London found that the hippocampus, a brain structure critical for forming new memories, is also essential for *imagining* scenes. Such findings "provide experimental evidence that memory and imagination may share neural circuitry."[8] Learning forms memories. Creativity produces novelty. These constructive processes affect each other, but their mutual influence surpasses shared brain geography.

Creativity's Connection to Learning

As we saw previously, content learning engages four processes: experience, comprehension, *elaboration*, and intention. Skill learning also engages four processes: experience, comprehension, *application*, and intention. These processes form the focus—the strands—of the Content and Skill Blueprints. Creativity emerges from a modified combination of these processes. It begins by mirroring content learning. The creative encounters new data (experience), sorts and labels the new data (comprehension), and constructs understanding via conceptual blending (elaboration) of it.

The resulting understanding prompts a creative curve. The

mind says, "Wait a minute! Let's explore that again, but this time from a different perspective, or with a different reference point, or in multiple dimensions, or by combining it with ______." Neuroscientist and writer Gregory Berns describes this as "reverse perception." Creative thinking, claims Berns, "comes from using the same neural circuits used to perceive natural objects," but in reverse.[9] Instead of perceiving what is and acting on it, the mind seeks *what else could be*. The individual reexplores the new data, returning to comprehension to disorganize, relabel, and re-sort the data in a different way (**FIGURE 8.1**). This difference may be in perspective, in scale, in dimension, or in any ways that alter initial thinking about the data. For example, the creative individual may engage a creative tool (e.g., drawing an analogy) or explore representational variety (e.g., a multiple intelligences approach, such as representing verbal data in a musical or spatial form).

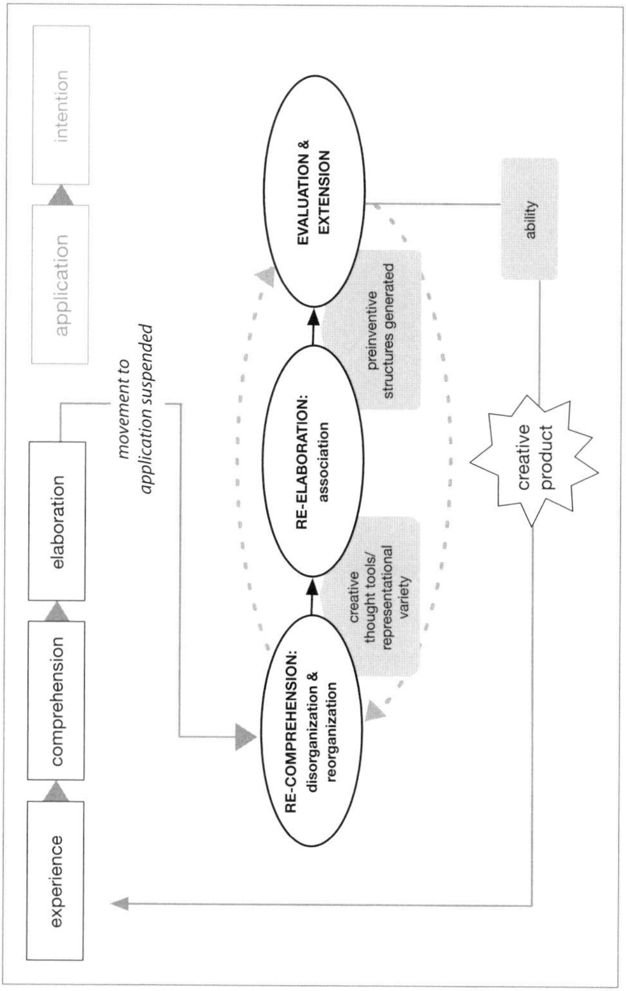

FIGURE 8.1 Creativity's Curve to Re-comprehension and Re-elaboration

The new organization of the data leads to exploring new associations. The creative mind engages in re-elaboration, identifying new associations between the reorganized data and past experiences. As the individual conceptually blends the new association with the reorganized data, a "preinventive structure" develops.[10] This is an idea with possibilities. The individual evaluates and perhaps expands the preinventive structure. One that seems worthwhile sparks action. The individual applies previously developed creative skills to form an expression of the idea. The re-comprehension and re-elaboration of the original data sparks application of creative or artistic skills to produce results.

The outcome can become new sensory input for both the creator and others. The expression can deepen understanding and inspire other creative ideas, as if it were "another person, with whom we converse."[11] Following a trip to the theater, I frequently experience the power of a creative endeavor to deepen understanding. My wife and I attend several dramatic performances each year. While I thoroughly enjoy the plays, our postshow discussion over dinner is often equally rewarding. As we revisit and discuss the play's characters, setting, plot, and themes, we engage in comprehension and elaboration, reorganizing and connecting specifics that construct new insights. We interact with the play as if it were "another person."

Similarly, creative works can deepen learning in the classroom. For example, Erica, a middle school teacher, has her students develop a series of symbols to summarize a work of literature. For example, one student summarizes Charles Dickens's *A Christmas Carol* in a series of three symbols: a tightly clenched hand, that same hand with three different colored streaks of light surrounding it and a large timepiece in the background, and finally an open hand extending forward. The results become new data for the other students. As they examine the symbols, the students reprocess the details of the literature, consider the connection between the story and the symbol, and make a decision regarding the symbol's effectiveness. This reprocessing—interacting with the symbols as if they were "another person"—mirrors learning's core processes, engaging recall and thought about the original stimulus. This rethinking fosters deeper learning of the subject matter.

Creativity possesses the potential to energize and increase learning. Why, then, is it not applied more commonly in our classrooms?

Education and Creativity

"Thank goodness I was never sent to school;" Beatrix Potter wrote, "it would have rubbed off some of the originality." Education and creativity are often portrayed as adversaries. Creativity expert Ken Robinson claims, "We are educating people out of their creativity,"[12] and Patrick F. Bassett suggests creativity's separation from school may exist because "we've found it easier to teach knowledge than creativity, partly perhaps because the former is easier to calibrate and measure than the latter."[13] Robinson adds that schools avoid creativity due to flawed perceptions, equating creativity with "children running wild and knocking down the furniture…"[14] As a result, explains educator Kieran Egan, imagination is "too often seen as something peripheral to the core of education, something taken care of by allowing students time to 'express themselves' in 'the arts,' while the proper work of educating goes on in the sciences and math and in developing conventionally efficient literacy."[15]

This separation places education at odds with corporate America. Findings from the study "Are They Really Ready to Work?" reveal that 81 percent of American corporate leaders consider creativity "an essential skill for the 21st-century workforce, yet only 21 percent reported excellence in this area among recent college graduates seeking employment with their companies."[16] Students exiting our schools and entering their adult lives often lack the creative capacities that could empower their success.

Teachers and schools face a daunting challenge. Society layers expectations on education, rarely exchanging one demand for another. While calls for instruction in creativity continue to rise, the public does not want other topics and skills to be removed from the curriculum. Teachers are expected to increase student creativity while still teaching all the traditional content. How can we meet this challenge?

Creative Learning

Creativity requires suspending straightforward movement into application, allowing the mind to re-comprehend, re-elaborate, and evaluate or expand ideas. In the Architecture of Learning Content and Combination Blueprints, the ELaboration strand offers a rich opportunity to creatively engage students in constructing understanding. The key lies in the strand's experience cell (**EL-ex**). If new or recalled data sparks creative thinking, the entire strand can possess a creative bent that increases learning.

For example, consider a social studies unit on the American Civil War. In designing the ELaboration strand, Henry, a high school teacher, recognizes that creativity often involves recognizing patterns and connecting ideas that initially seem unrelated. As he considers the unit's major individuals presented in the COmprehension strand, specific verbs naturally associate with each. For example, while considering Abraham Lincoln, Henry knows that his leadership will be emphasized. So *Lincoln* becomes associated with *lead*. Stonewall Jackson, a brilliant military leader in the war's early battles, becomes associated with *dies* because of his unusual death and its impact on subsequent battles. Harriet Tubman associates naturally with *frees* because of her prodigious Underground Railroad accomplishments.

However, Henry does not want to repeat the COmprehension strand. So, in developing the input for the experience cell (**EL-ex**), he mixes the individuals and verbs, developing combinations like, "Lincoln rebels," "Stonewall lives," and "Tubman surrenders." Index cards containing these unlikely, or seemingly unrelated, combinations are distributed to the students. They sort out both the subject (the person) and the verb, identifying and organizing the details of each. For the verb, students identify and detail definitions, including potential figurative meanings (**EL-co**). Next, the students identify connections between the subject and the verb answering the question, "In what way could it be said that the subject did what the verb indicates?" (e.g., "In what way could it be said that *Tubman surrenders*?") The students explore possible connections, relating their ideas to the unit's reference point (**EL-el**). Finally, the students write their explanation as if they were writing a newspaper account to accompany a headline composed of the subject and its unlikely verb (**EL-ap**).

Note what takes place through this process. The students review the unit's major individuals *in depth*, exploring ways the individuals could be associated with the unlikely verbs. They formulate preinventive structures—possible explanations that are evaluated and/or expanded. They compare these new associations with the established reference point, constructing deepened understanding of the topics. And they generate novel products, newspaper articles, which serve to prompt further thought in their fellow students. The results may not end up displayed in a museum, but the creative thinking put into them and the thinking they prompt through expression ignite deeper learning.

Similar approaches may incorporate other creative thinking

processes. For example, in the same unit Henry could give the students a list of the unit's important individuals (**EL-ex**). The students could reorganize the details associated with each individual (**EL-co**) and then combine each individual with another idea to form an analogy. Students may, for example, develop an analogy between Harriet Tubman and a cougar, an animal often associated with courage and leadership. Students would then relate the analogies to the reference point (pattern) established in the EXperience strand (**EL-el**), and explain their results, either verbally or in writing. Again, creative thinking ignites deeper learning.

Stimulating creative thinking to promote the learning of skills poses a greater challenge. First, the very nature of skills—sequenced steps that students replicate—limits the variability a teacher should emphasize during instruction. Second, because elaboration plays a lesser role in skill learning, fewer opportunities to sustain movement into application exist. Once skills are mastered, however, creative thinking can enrich review activities.

San Jose State University professor Scott Rice provides an example. The Bulwer-Lytton Fiction Contest recognizes and awards the best worst opening lines for potential works of fiction. To compete, contestants take their skills of formulating great opening lines, and "break all the rules" to produce the worst opening lines imaginable. The results must still be interesting enough to catch the judges' attention. Thus, while breaking the rules, the writers must still adhere to literary principles that make submissions interesting while still being terrible. For example, one winning entry reads, "The thing that goes back and forth inside the old grandfather clock swung back and forth like a pendulum."[17]

Notice the literary elements remain intact (e.g., simile, description) while the line itself is absurd. Such winning entries are published in Scott Rice's series of books, *It Was a Dark and Stormy Night*. By straying from the rules, creativity results; however, in this case, "high quality" describes the worst writing.

The Bulwer-Lytton Fiction Contest illustrates how twisting a skill's individual steps can engage creative thinking. It inquires, "What if we changed/eliminated/reordered this?" While not recommended during initial learning, such highly motivating play can engage students in reviewing and practicing skills with a creative twist that imbues the familiar with freshness.

So, we see that creative thinking can deepen student learning, but what about teaching? Can teachers be more creative in designing instruction?

Creative Teaching

Stories can be an effective option for Architecture of Learning EXperience strand activities. That's because a story can illustrate a unit's pattern and serve as a potent reference point for new learning.

Stories frame experience. Mark Turner suggests stories are actually fundamental, organizing structures: "Parable is the root of the human mind—of thinking, knowing, acting, creating, and plausibly even of speaking."[18] Neurologist and author Alice W. Flaherty agrees, suggesting metaphors, such as stories, contribute to memory formation and understanding:

> ...metaphors are cognitively useful because they rephrase an abstract concept in more physical terms. This engages the cortex with its visual, auditory, tactile, and olfactory maps, and the

> limbic system with its emotional charge...[Metaphors] create a sense of understanding by an analogous mechanism. By giving abstract concepts tastes, colors, smells, and emotional resonance, metaphors fix them in our minds and make us feel like we understand them.[19]

The human mind frequently thinks in terms of stories, communicates in stories, and converts new learning into stories. By framing experience, stories provide a structure for exploring and making sense of experience.

Stories also replicate experience. Chip and Dan Heath, authors of *Made to Stick: Why Some Ideas Survive and Others Die*, claim stories provide "simulation" of experience by establishing memorable connections between characters and concepts.[20] Egan agrees, explaining stories are "very effective at communicating information in a memorable form" and are able to "orient the hearer's feelings about the information being communicated."[21] When we share a story—our own, others', or fictional—we experience or reexperience events, emotions, themes, and other significant elements within a familiar structure. Stories create "a sequential intellectual and emotional experience..."[22] By combining the intellectual with the emotional, stories bridge the worlds of content and creativity.

Telling a story often works well as a unit opener (**EX-ex**). The remaining EXperience strand activities take their cues from the story. Students sort out and restructure the important details (**EX-co**), examine the tale for a pattern (**EX-el**), and share examples from their own lives that illustrate the same pattern (**EX-ap**). How can such a story be developed? Much of what we understand about creativity can assist us!

First, to be more creative in designing instruction, resist moving to application too soon. In instructional design, this means allowing time between identifying the unit to be taught and actually developing the unit. This may seem simple, but it is probably a teacher's greatest challenge to increasing instructional creativity. Creativity, which entails re-comprehension and re-elaboration, requires time, a scarce resource. However, a memorable story illustrating the unit's pattern provides such a powerful reference point that the time commitment can pay off in more effective teaching, and the thinking during this pause does not need to be concentrated, sit-still-and-cogitate thinking. Some of the best ideas develop while we are actively living out other parts of our lives. Running, for example, helps me cultivate and develop ideas. Sleep is another fruitful activity. Awakening with ideas in the dead of night is an occasionally welcome interruption of a night's sleep. Both these activities provide a change of scenery, a change that can spark creative thinking:

> Sometimes a simple change of environment is enough to jog the perceptual system out of familiar categories. This may be one reason why restaurants figure so prominently as sites of perceptual breakthroughs...When confronted with places never seen before, the brain must create new categories. It is in this process that the brain jumbles around old ideas with new images to create new syntheses.[23]

Giving the brain time to "percolate" increases the likelihood of creative ideas. To stimulate critical thinking about teaching, get out of the school building and go for a walk, visit a local coffeehouse, go somewhere that changes what your senses commonly experience.

Second, review the unit's pattern statement. It holds the unit's critical concepts, which you will want to emphasize within the unfolding story.

Third, find the "binary opposites" of the unit's critical concepts.[24] For example, the binary opposite for Byzantine history (see Chapter 4) might be *hoarding*, the tendency to grasp and keep rather than give and influence. By identifying the binary opposites, a framework emerges on which to establish conflict and construct plot. Kieran Egan provides another illustrative example: "If the quality identified as important is ingenuity, then you might build your unit on the opposition between ingenuity and cluelessness, or you could frame it as between imaginativeness and unimaginativeness."[25] The Byzantine history unit could be framed as *contributing vs. hoarding.*

Once opposing concepts are identified, plot ideas often begin to form. I find it useful to consider what kind of character might personify each trait. For example, what type of character might *hoard*? A greedy squirrel? A selfish monarch? An insecure child? The same process can be used for the opposite idea. What type of character might *contribute*? A grateful mouse? A kind servant? An understanding uncle? Personifying opposite concepts creates memorable characters and aids plot construction.

Finally, organize the elements into a cohesive narrative featuring a conflict that highlights the opposite concepts. Write down as much of the story as needed to enable its confident retelling. For example, with the Byzantine history unit, a story about a generous monarch and a selfish servant might work well. The monarch generously gives of himself for the betterment of the kingdom (present and future), meaningfully highlighting the idea of contribution, but must deal with a servant who steals from the king's coffers. The story may feature several examples of the king's generosity and the servant's selfish, secret hoarding, climaxing with the king catching the servant stealing. The conclusion could drive home the idea—the selfish servant dies a lonely death and is subsequently buried in an unmarked tomb while the king's generosity earns accolades from future generations who trace current conditions to his contributions.

Steps for Instructional Narrative Development
1. Pause before planning activities, allowing the mind to "percolate" in a different setting, if possible
2. Review the unit's pattern statement
3. Identify the binary opposites implicit in the pattern
4. Develop plot ideas
5. Weave the ideas into a coherent story

FIGURE 8.2 Steps for Developing Instruction-focused Stories

Conclusion

Creativity and learning complement each other. Deeply understanding a subject increases the ability to think creatively about it. In turn, thinking creatively about a subject deepens understanding of it. Teachers can infuse teaching with creativity by using creative thinking while designing instruction. Story development, for example, provides an outlet for teacher creativity and can provide a powerful reference point for constructing understanding. Teachers can also stimulate students' creative thinking by designing activities that invite and ignite use of creative thinking tools. When students use new learning as a basis for creativity, they take steps toward moving material from working memory to long-term memory. As James E. Zull puts it, "...we have done the work and we can remember what that work produced. We remember because we made it!"[26]

Questions

1. Why are learning and creativity often viewed as incompatible? Is such a perspective supportable? What problems does this perception create?

2. What role does dis-/re-organization play in creativity? Explain the creative curve into re-comprehension and re-elaboration (**FIGURE 8.1**).

3. What are preinventive structures? What is their role in creativity?

4. How can creative thinking improve learning and ignite additional thinking that continues to deepen learning?

5. How does the ELaboration strand in Architecture of Learning Content and Combination Blueprints create opportunities for students to think creatively?

6. How can teachers engage student creative thinking when reviewing previously mastered skills?

7. Why are stories effective within Blueprint EXperience strands?

8. What are the suggested steps for story development? Try using these to develop a story for an upcoming unit's EXperience strand.

Chapter 9

ASSESSING THE STRUCTURE

Evaluating and Revising Instruction

Tools matter. At a recent training event I asked the participants to imagine a well-stocked toolbox and list the tools it would include. They asked, but I did not specify, what task would need to be accomplished. I instructed them to be as thorough as possible so their toolbox would have what they needed for a variety of tasks. They brainstormed and shared ideas between groups. Only then did I reveal the task: changing the pedals on a bicycle. To do this right, you need a tool called a pedal wrench. Not surprisingly, no one had put one in their toolbox. Without a pedal wrench, other tools could be tried but would likely fail or require so much compromise that the results would be less than optimal.

Many teachers want tools to improve instruction, tools they can use in self-assessing and revising instructional design and practice. But not just any tool will work. We need instruments that align with our approach to instructional design and teaching.

Revision Tools

Optimal instruction requires excellent instructional design, and excellence often develops through revision. A series of prompts, or a "coach on paper," provides a proven process for assessing and improving instructional design developed on Architecture of Learning Blueprints. Four focus areas—critical intersections, assessment, strands, and transitions—provide a starting point for assessment, feedback, and revision.

Critical Intersections

The critical intersections of an Architecture of Learning Blueprint are the points where a focus process (strand) meets itself in the core processes (column) (see Chapter 6). These points can guide a teacher's choice of testing material and how the test asks a student for the material. Because of this, the critical intersections often reveal a unit's essence, the critical knowledge, understanding, application, and integration of the material a teacher hopes to achieve.

A series of questions focused on assessing and revising the critical intersections can help a teacher improve a unit or proceed to teach it with confidence:

1. Does the **EX-ex** activity (reference point) illustrate a pattern to which the new material readily relates?
2. Does the **CO-co** activity (knowledge component) engage students in reorganizing the material's critical details, all of them, in a meaningful way?
3. Does the **EL-el** activity (understanding component) engage students in relating the new material to the illustrative experience in such a way that deepened connections are recognized and understanding is constructed?
4. Does the **AP-ap** (utilization component) activity engage students in utilizing the skill to produce evidence of its mastery?
5. Does the **IN-ap** activity (integration component) engage students in utilizing the new material to understand or address contemporary contexts?

Assessment

The Architecture of Learning Blueprints help teachers develop assessments based on learning and revealed through teaching. By engaging in formative assessment and developing tests based on a unit's critical intersections, a teacher imbues educational practice with integrity. Alignment between the content and methods of instruction and content and methods of testing should be the focus for reviewing and revising any summative assessments:

1. Does a clear correlation exist between the content and methods of assessment and the content and methods of instruction?
2. Do students engage in all the thinking required on the test while they are learning the material?

If such alignment is missing, the instruction and assessment will lack integrity. How the students will be assessed needs to be reflected in how the students will be taught.

Strands

Each strand within an Architecture of Learning Blueprint serves an important instructional purpose. Each strand builds on those that precede it to take students through a thorough learning experience. Again, questions provide guidance for assessing and revising a unit's strands:

1. Does the EXperience Strand engage students in processing the initial experience to the point of pattern recognition and establishment of a meaningful reference point for new learning?
2. Does the COmprehension Strand present new material and engage students in processing it?
3. Does the ELaboration Strand engage students in deepened thought about the new material and its relationship to the reference point established in the EXperience Strand? As a result of the activities, will students construct richer and/or more meaningful understandings of the new material?

4. Does the APplication Strand provide sufficient practice to promote proficiency? Is the practice sufficient to witness students' increasing correctness and efficiency?
5. Is the INtention Strand designed? Will it enlarge the context in which students will apply the skill or consider the content in relation to current conditions?

Transitions

Effective instruction shares many characteristics with good writing, including coherence and flow. Notice how Mark Tredinnick describes these elements:

> *Unity* (making every stone suggestive of, and of a piece with, the whole wall) and *flow* (making each stone distinct and sequential) characterize good writing; and they stand in tension. The one is about sameness; the other is about change. Linkage is how you resolve them: you keep saying new things, you keep carrying the story forward, but you never stop helping your reader understand how each new development...is related, and how all are related, to the whole. *Transition* is how you make your writing both hang and flow.[1]

An effective unit will both "hang and flow" with a unity supported by the transitions between activities. Rather than distinct cells or even distinct strands, optimal instructional design moves smoothly from the initial experience (**EX-ex**) through the use of new learning in widened contexts (**IN-ap**). Questions that guide assessment and revision of a unit's transitions include:

1. Does the Experience Strand flow naturally into the COmprehension Strand by preparing students to explore how their experience relates to new material?

2. For Content and Combination Blueprints, does the COmprehension Strand flow naturally into the ELaboration Strand by encouraging students to reorganize critical details in such a way that patterns and connections to their experience begin to emerge?
3. For Skill Blueprints, does the COmprehension Strand flow naturally into the APplication Strand by providing thorough instruction (step-by-step description and modeling) and initial, guided, supportive practice with instructive feedback?
4. For Content Blueprints, does the ELaboration Strand flow naturally into the INtention Strand by deepening students' processing of new material and its relation to students' experiences? Do students process the pattern deeply enough to recognize it in new contexts?
5. For Skill and Combination Blueprints, does the APplication Strand flow naturally into the INtention Strand by engaging students in enough practice to increase transfer capacity? Do students know when and where to use the skill well enough to transfer it to new contexts?

FIGURE 9.1 groups the questions for revising each major element of a unit designed on an Architecture of Learning Blueprint.

FOCUS	REVISION PROMPTS
critical intersections	• Does the EX-ex activity (reference point) illustrate a pattern to which the new material readily relates? • Does the CO-co activity (knowledge component) engage students in reorganizing the material's critical details, all of them, in a meaningful way? • Does the EL-el activity (understanding component) engage students in relating the new material to the illustrative experience in such a way that deepened connections are recognized and great understanding is constructed? • Does the AP-ap (utilization component) activity engage students in utilizing the skill to produce evidence of its mastery? • Does the IN-ap activity (integration component) engage students in utilizing the new material to understand or address contemporary contexts?
assessment	• Is there clear correlation between the content and methods of assessment and the content and methods of instruction? Are the critical intersections and assessment forms and constructs in alignment? • Do students engage in all the thinking required on the test while they are learning the material?
strands	• Does the EXperience Strand engage students in processing the initial experience to the point of pattern recognition and establishment of a meaningful reference point for new learning? • Does the COmprehension Strand present new material and engage students in processing it? • Does the ELaboration Strand engage students in deepened thought about the new material and its relationship to the reference point established in the EXperience Strand? As a result of the activities, will students construct richer and/or more meaningful understandings of the new material? • Does the APplication Strand provide sufficient practice to promote proficiency? Is the practice sufficient to witness increasing student correctness and efficiency? • Is the INtention Strand designed? Will it enlarge the context in which students will apply the skill or consider the content in relation to current conditions?

FIGURE 9.1 Blueprint Assessment Foci and Prompts

FOCUS	REVISION PROMPTS
transitions (eg., EX-ap→ CO-ex)	• Does the Experience Strand flow naturally into the COmprehension Strand by preparing students to explore how their experience relates to new material? • For Content and Combination Blueprints, does the COmprehension Strand flow naturally into the ELaboration Strand by encouraging students to reorganize critical details in such a way that patterns and connections to their experience begin to emerge? • For Skill Blueprints, does the COmprehension Strand flow naturally into the APplication Strand by providing thorough instruction (step-by-step description and modeling) and initial, guided, supportive practice with instructive feedback? • For Content Blueprints, does the ELaboration Strand flow naturally into the INtention Strand by deepening students' processing of new material and its relation to student experience? Do students process the pattern deeply enough to recognize it in new contexts? • For Skill and Combination Blueprints, does the APplication Strand flow naturally into the INtention Strand by engaging students in enough practice to increase transfer capacity? Do students know when and where to use the skill well enough to transfer it to new contexts?

FIGURE 9.1 [continued] Blueprint Assessment Foci and Prompts

The third focus area, strands, can also be assessed and revised using the Architecture of Learning Strands Rubric (**FIGURE 9.2**). In using the rubric, the goal should be to "move" a Blueprint as close to "exemplary" as possible; however, some aspects may not be possible at all grade levels. For example, the emphasis on critical thinking described as exemplary within the INtention strand may be possible only at upper grade levels.

	EXEMPLARY	EXCELLENT	EFFECTIVE
EX	All Excellent descriptors, plus… • strand features obvious coherence between its individual cells and the remaining strands in the unit; the strand serves more than an introductory purpose, actually centering the unit's remaining strands and their individual activities	All Effective descriptors, plus… • experience strongly relates to pattern statement, providing an illustration of it and a reference point for learning • experience includes sufficient creativity (e.g., teacher-developed narrative, engrossing activity for students) to be memorable • pattern statement recognition enables recall of application (skill, combination) or recall of important details (content); the pattern statement emerges from the subject matter and is not thematic in nature	Strand includes: • an experience that illustrates a pattern related to the material to be learned • an activity that engages students in sorting out and labeling the experience • an activity that results in the identification/stating of a pattern statement • an activity that explores other examples of the pattern
CO	All Excellent descriptors, plus… • strand features obvious coherence between its individual cells and the other strands in the unit; the strand presents and has students process new materials in ways that link to the reference point and to the forthcoming activities in future strands	All Effective descriptors, plus… • "sorting out" activity requires students to do more than repeat information—e.g., students have to organize information in a way that reveals relationships, such as sequence (e.g., steps in a skill) • connection between the pattern statement and the new material is more than cursory, serving to deepen understanding of the new material	Strand includes: • instruction in new, appropriate material (e.g., skill instruction and modeling for skill Blueprint) • a "sorting out" of the new material • a connection between the unit's pattern statement and the new material • an activity that explores examples, demonstrates student comprehension of new material, or provides initial practice of the new material

FIGURE 9.2 Architecture of Learning Strands Rubric

	EXEMPLARY	EXCELLENT	EFFECTIVE
EL	All Excellent descriptors, plus... • strand features obvious coherence between its individual cells and the other strands in the unit, resulting in a unit with an easy flow • strand includes activities that engage creative thinking tools (e.g., imaging, abstracting, analogizing)	All Effective descriptors, plus... • the EL-el activity fosters deepened understanding through greater connectedness of the new material, pattern statement, and new illustration (the EL-ex activity)—i.e., the student is engaged in thought that fosters connection identification and understanding beyond surface or superficial elements	Strand includes: • experience that fosters deepened understanding of the new material and its relation to the unit's pattern statement • a "sorting out" of the experience with an emphasis on identifying those characteristics that relate to the new material and pattern statement • a connection between the unit's pattern statement, the new material, and the experiential reference point and production of evidence showing a deepening understanding of the new material
AP	All Excellent descriptors, plus... • strand features obvious coherence between its individual cells and the other strands in the unit, resulting in a unit with an easy flow and student mastery of new material	All Effective descriptors, plus... • the AP-ap activity produces evidence of pre-action thought (e.g., a statement of justification for the application) and evidence of successful application	Strand includes: • activities that engage students in thoughtful use of new understandings; careful thought, possibly including recognition of the pattern statement within a scenario, precedes application of new knowledge
IN	All Excellent descriptors, plus... • strand engages students in critical thinking, using the individual cells as stages in a thorough thought process	All Effective descriptors, plus... • the widened context is current and relevant to students—more natural than manufactured • the activities prompt development and use of prescriptive knowledge (wisdom)	Strand is planned so that integration is not left to chance, presenting activities similar to those of the AP strand but with an emphasis on a wider or different (i.e., more "real world") sphere of use

FIGURE 9.2 [continued] Architecture of Learning Strands Rubric

The Blueprint Revision Prompts (**FIGURE 9.1**) and Strands Rubric (**FIGURE 9.2**) effectively guide group Blueprint revision sessions. Such group interaction, or collaboration, is one of the most effective yet little-used professional development practices. Research from a variety of areas validates how much collaboration can contribute to improving performance.

Surgeon and author Dr. Atul Gawande details conclusions of a Harvard Business School study on the learning curve surgeons experience when learning new surgical techniques. Practice in itself proved an unreliable predictor of learning rate and success, but *how* surgeons practiced made a significant difference. A surgeon leading one of the quickest-learning teams picked "team members with whom he had worked well before" and kept "them together through the first fifteen cases before allowing any new members. He had the team go through a dry run the day before the first case, then deliberately scheduled six operations in the first week, so little would be forgotten in between. He convened the team before each case to discuss it in detail and afterward to debrief." In contrast, a surgeon who had significantly more experience led one of the slowest-learning teams. He involved different personnel in each surgery, "which is to say that it was no team at all," and led no pre- or post-operation discussions. Increased collaboration quickened learning rate and improved performance. Most important, patients benefitted from the surgeon's collaborative approach.[2]

Educational research reaches a similar conclusion: collaboration improves teacher performance. In *Qualities of Effective Teachers*, James H. Stronge cites collaboration as a hallmark of effective teachers, claiming such teachers "are willing to share their ideas and assist other teachers with difficulties."[3]

Educator and author Thomas J. Sergiovanni links collaboration and school culture. Exemplary teachers, claims Sergiovanni, are "committed and generous…open to change and eager to learn… [able] to see beyond their own private successes and failures." However, according to Sergiovanni, most schools possess cultures of "privatism and isolation" and administrators who encourage competition rather than collaboration.[4] Our learning institutions may impede professional growth by inhibiting collaboration. As a result, we can actually hinder student learning by *our* approach to learning, including how we practice and master new instructional design methods.

Schools with teachers who commit to learning the instructional design model and commit to collaboration, especially in the beginning phase of implementation, experience success with Architecture of Learning. To achieve your best instruction, remember that *how* you practice influences the outcome. Teacher collaboration enables deeper and quicker teacher learning, and teacher learning influences student learning.

Accepting Responsibility

In my undergraduate days, an influential professor reminded us almost daily that becoming a *professional* meant committing ourselves to continual growth. We alone were responsible for this, she exhorted. Schools may offer us opportunities for additional training and education, but whether we grew as educators or not would be our choice and responsibility.

I have yet to meet a teacher who even implied that mediocrity was a professional goal. Yet, as mentioned earlier, school-sponsored professional development programs can lack meaningful content and cohesiveness. For instance, I once spent an entire session brainstorming alternate ways of making a living! Exceptions definitely exist, but they are too rare to meet the development needs of most teachers. So, as my college professor emphasized, we must take responsibility for our professional growth and aggressively pursue it.

In such a pursuit, understanding how students learn should be a priority. Though it often becomes obscured by other school-related pressures, learning represents our profession's true aspiration. A greater grasp of the process of learning aids our instructional design. If we know how to make our pupils think, we can design instruction that makes our hope a reality.

This book reiterates several significant learning-related premises:

1. A teacher who understands learning designs instruction that intentionally aligns his methods and students' cognitive processes to produce learning. For teachers, knowledge of learning is critical to instructional design; teaching processes should be based on learning processes.
2. The quality of a teacher's instructional design often determines the quality of her instruction. As a blueprint guides new home construction, instructional design guides teaching. In both cases, a flawed blueprint cripples reliable construction.
3. Learning results from engaging five interacting processes: experience, comprehension, elaboration, application, and intention.
4. Effective instruction includes all five processes, but not in equal measure. Subject matter type—skill, content, combination—influences how much focus is placed on each process. Alignment of subject matter and focus produces the strongest learning.
5. A *skill* comprises a sequence of steps used to accomplish a task automatically and efficiently. *Content* comprises ideas and their relationships that students should understand

for analyzing current conditions, guiding evaluative thinking, and making decisions. *Combination* subject matter comprises both, emphasizing contextual recognition and associated skill application.

6. Assessment gains integrity by aligning with what is taught.
7. Thinking produces learning, and learning increases thinking capacity. In other words, the more one thinks, the more one knows, and the more one knows, the more one can think. Critical thinking—an intentional mode of thinking, involving evaluation in relation to established standards, empowered by specific skills and accompanying dispositions—can deepen learning. Creative thinking—thinking that produces quality, novel, and appropriate ideas and/or work—can improve teaching and deepen learning.

Architecture of Learning Blueprints provide an instructional design tool based on these premises.

Conclusion

In *Better: A Surgeon's Notes on Performance*, Dr. Atul Gawande discusses the bell curve, suggesting that most doctors are average practitioners. He then offers the following insight:

> There is no shame in being one of [the average doctors], right?
>
> Except, of course, there is. What is troubling is not just being average but settling for it. Everyone knows that averageness is, for most of us, our fate. And in certain matters—looks, money, tennis—we would do well to accept this. But in your surgeon, your child's pediatrician, your police department, your local high school? When the stakes are our lives and lives of our children, we want no one to settle for average.[5]

Settling for average means accepting mediocrity. Most teachers I know reject this as antithetical to being an educator. Learning, our profession's aspiration, must be *our* passion. We must be the learners we want to see our students become. We must take the initiative to grow in knowledge, understanding, and wisdom. As exemplary learners, we can teach in ways that produce lasting learning, the proof of our instructional effectiveness. At that point, we can follow the advice of shipbuilder Henry J. Kaiser: "When your work speaks for itself, don't interrupt."[6]

May our teaching ignite learning that validates our committed, daily, and intentional instructional efforts.

Questions

1. Review the Blueprint Revision Prompts **(FIGURE 9.1)** and Strands Rubric **(FIGURE 9.2)**. Try using one to self-assess and self-coach an Architecture of Learning Blueprint you developed.

2. Try using the Blueprint Revision Prompts **(FIGURE 9.1)** and Strands Rubric **(FIGURE 9.2)** in a collaborative revision session. What advantages does collaboration offer?

3. Who is responsible for a teacher's professional growth? What are you doing to fulfill this responsibility?

4. In your teaching, what would work that "speaks for itself" look like? What would its results be? What would you need to generate such work?

Afterword

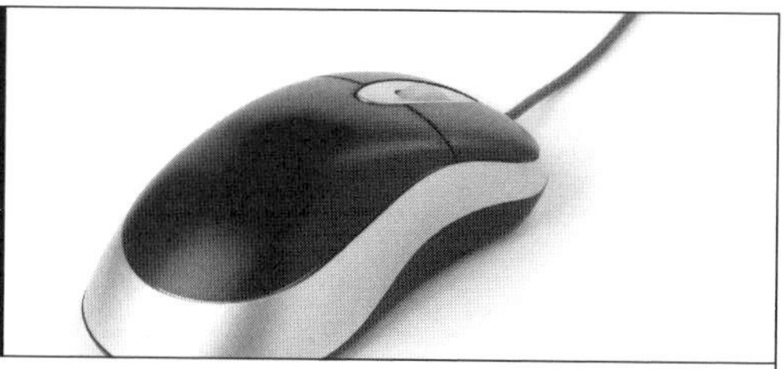

WHAT ABOUT TECHNOLOGY?

"The need to know the capital of Florida died when my phone learned the answer. Rather, the students of tomorrow need to be able to think creatively: they will need to learn on their own, adapt to new challenges and innovate on-the-fly."[1] This high school student's insight reveals a significant tension among educators. With technology so widely available, how should teachers and schools adapt? What role should technology have in teaching and learning?

To complicate the issue, not all teachers have access to the same type and quality of technology. Add in teachers who have access but lack the know-how, and the current confusion and heated conversations about integrating technology result.

This is unfortunate because technology can be a powerful tool. However, like any other tool, its effectiveness relates directly to its use. Even a simple hammer can build up or destroy, depending on how the craftsperson uses it. The same is true of computers, cell phones, and every other technology-based tool. Effectiveness is found in how it's used, not in the tool itself.

How, then, can we use technology effectively to aid student learning? A few guiding principles may help.

First, having a tool does not mean its use will produce the most effective or efficient results. On a recent Saturday morning run through a local park, I was stopped by a young man dressed in his high school track uniform. He had a confused look on his face and a gadget in his hand. His satellite-based navigation system was telling him he had reached his destination, but not a single member of his track team was there. As we talked, I realized he wanted to be in a different town's Veterans Park. For the next ten minutes, I tried to give him simple driving directions to the site, but he insisted on typing the park into his gadget over and over again. Not surprisingly, the results were the same: according to the technology, he had reached his destination. I finally suggested he try inputting a community college near the site of his track meet. That apparently produced a different result because he thanked me and drove off. If he'd been willing to follow my directions, he would have arrived at the site in the same amount of time it took him to get the navigation system to point his way.

Obviously, this young man was not teaching a class, but I've seen teachers act in similar ways. Ideas that could be conveyed simply and efficiently through clear explanation combined with simple diagrams become confusing and time-consuming displays of electronic chaos. The tools, while potentially powerfully, get poorly used and are therefore ineffective.

Second, what the technology actually contributes to student learning is important. A few guiding questions may clarify this principle:

1. What is the technology actually engaging the user or observer in doing?
2. Is the technology providing the user/observer new data (experience)? or is it aiding the user/observer in organizing ideas (comprehension)? or is it assisting the user/observer in merging new data with previous experiences (elaboration)? or is it engaging the user/observer in utilizing some process

to achieve a result or generate evidence of new knowledge or understanding (application)? or is it engaging the user/observer in two or more of these processes?

3. What thought processes does the user/observer engage while working with the tool?

Whether it's hardware or software, examining a technological tool with these questions in mind enables a teacher to identify roles the tools could play in learning. This enables the teacher to use them effectively.

Knowing when in the teaching process to use technological tools for optimal learning is one advantage of working with a framework such as an Architecture of Learning Blueprint to design instruction. Once a teacher identifies how the tool engages the user/observer's thinking, it can be used in the sequence of instructional activities so that it contributes to authentic learning.

For example, in designing a science unit on mammals, Kate finds several video clips online that show mammals interacting within their natural environments. She decides to use these as part of her **CO-ex** activities to introduce the defining characteristics of mammals and point out how these traits influence the animal's behavior and choice of habitat. She also finds an online application that allows the user to develop concept webs that can include multimedia elements, such as photos and video clips. She decides to have students use the application as one of her **CO-co** activities. Developing the concept webs will engage the students in sorting out important details of the content and the results will enable Kate to determine the students' knowledge of the content. Kate also knows the students have the know-how to use a simple design program to develop Web pages. She plans to use this as part of her **CO-ap** activities. Students will develop interactive and informative Web pages on mammals, using one self-selected mammal to illustrate the general characteristics of all mammals.

While relatively simple, Kate's use of these tools reveals that she understands student learning well enough to integrate technology in ways that contribute to it.

Similarly, as Calvin prepares a social studies unit on World War II, he finds an electronic game that draws its players into simulations of several major events without directly engaging them or exposing them to acts of violence. In reviewing the game, Calvin identifies all the core learning processes with an overall significant emphasis on merging the player's past experiences with the people and events of the historical era. With some follow-up discussions added, Calvin makes the game the central focus of his ELaboration strand. Like Kate, he understands student learning well enough to integrate technology in ways that contribute to it.

So, what can we conclude about technology? It is a tool. One that we should be using to optimize student learning. However, *it does not eliminate our responsibility to design effective instruction.* Whether it be a sheet of paper and a pencil or a handheld device with access to cloud applications, the tool that fosters the thinking needed to promote student learning is the teacher's best choice.

NOTES

Introduction

image ©iStockphoto.com/zoom-zoom

1. Williams, R., *The Non-designer's Design Book* (Berkeley, CA: Peachpit Press, Inc., 1994), 14.
2. Marzano, R.J., *What Works in Schools: Translating Research into Action* (Alexandria, VA: Association for Supervision and Curriculum Development, 2003), 106, 78.
3. Bransford, J.D., Brown, A.L., & Cocking, R.R., eds., *How People Learn: Brain, Mind, Experience, and School* (Washington, DC: National Academy Press, 1999), xviii.
4. Marzano, 78.
5. Halpern, D.F., & Hakel, M.D., eds., *Applying the Science of Learning to University and Beyond* (San Francisco: Jossey-Bass, 2002), 4.

Chapter 1

image ©iStockphoto.com/purelook

1. Thompson, R.F., & Madigan, S.A., *Memory: The Key to Consciousness.* (Washington, DC: Joseph Henry Press, 2005), 27.
2. Visscher, K.M., Kaplan, E., Kahana, M.J., & Sekuler, R., "Auditory Short-term Memory Behaves Like Visual Short-term Memory," *PLoS Biology,* 5, no. 3 (2007).
3. Paul, R. The State of Critical Thinking Today: The Need for a Substantive Concept of Critical Thinking. http://www.criticalthinking.org/resources/articles/the-state-ct-today.shtml.
4. Blair, C., Knipe, H., & Gamson, D., "Is There a Role for Executive Function in the Development of Mathematics Ability?" *Mind, Brain, and Education,* 2, no. 2 (2008): 80-89.
5. Levitin, Daniel J., *This is Your Brain on Music: The Science of a Human Obsession* (New York: Penguin Group, 2006), 103.
6. Halpern, D., *Thought and Knowledge: An Introduction to Critical Thinking* (Mahwah, NJ: Lawrence Erlbaum Associates, 2003), 106.
7. Paul, R. & Elder, L., *Critical Thinking: Tools for Taking Charge of Your Learning and Your Life* (Upper Saddle River, NJ: Prentice Hall, 2001), 62.
8. Montagne, R. (Interviewer), "One Man, One Year, One Mission: Read the OED" [Radio Broadcast Episode], in B. Gordemer (Producer), *Morning Edition* (Washington, D.C.: National Public Radio, August 8, 2008).
9. Burton, R.A., *On Being Certain: Believing You are Right Even When You're Not* (New York: St. Martin's Press, 2008), 85.
10. Ibid., 85.

11. Baddeley, A., "Working Memory: An Overview," in S.J. Pickering (Ed.), *Working Memory and Education* (Burlington, MA: Academic Press, 2006) 6, 24.

12. Fauconnier, G., & Turner, M., *The Way We Think: Conceptual Blending and the Mind's Hidden Complexities* (New York: Basic Books, 2002).

13. Levitin, 130-131.

14. Fauconnier.

15. Mamet, D., *Three Uses of the Knife: On the Nature and Purpose of Drama* (New York: Columbia University Press, 1998), 70-71.

16. Pinker, S., *The Stuff of Thought: Language as a Window into Human Nature* (New York: Viking, 2007), 238.

17. Ibid., 241.

18. deWinstanley, P.A., & Bjork, R.A., "Successful Lecturing: Presenting Information in Ways that Engage Effective Processing," in Halpern, D.F., & Hakel, M.D. (Eds.), *Applying the science of learning to university and beyond,* vol. 89 (San Francisco: Jossey-Bass, 2002).

19. Gardner, H., *Changing Minds: The Art and Science of Changing Our Own and Other People's Minds* (Boston: Harvard Business School Press, 2006).

20. Willis, J., *Research-based Strategies to Ignite Student Learning* (Alexandria, VA: Association for Supervision and Curriculum Development, 2006), 6.

21. Nouwen, H., *The Return of the Prodigal Son* (New York: Image Books, 1992), 3.

22. Jensen, E., *Enriching the Brain: How to Maximize Every Learner's Potential* (San Francisco: Jossey-Bass, 2006), 20.

23. Bransford, J.D., Brown, A.L., & Cocking, R.R. (Eds.), *How People Learn: Brain, Mind, Experience, and School* (Washington, DC: National Academy Press, 1999), 41, 43.

24. Ibid.,44.

Chapter 2

image ©iStockphoto.com/moustyk

1. Gardner, H., *Changing Minds: The Art and Science of Changing Our Own and Other People's Minds* (Boston: Harvard Business School Press, 2006).

2. Zull, J.E., *The Art of Changing the Brain: Enriching the Practice of Teaching by Exploring the Biology of Learning* (Sterling, VA: Stylus Publishing, 2002), 128.

3. Immordino-Yang, M.H. & Damasio, A., "We Feel, Therefore We Learn: The Relevance of Affective and Social Neuroscience to Education." In Jossey-Bass Publishers (Ed.), *The Jossey-Bass Reader on the Brain and Learning* (San Francisco: Jossey-Bass, 2008), 196.

4. LeDoux, J., "Remembrance of Emotions Past." In Jossey-Bass Publishers (Ed.), *The Jossey-Bass reader on the Brain and Learning* (San Francisco: Jossey-Bass, 2008), 170.

5. Ibid., 170-173.
6. Medina, J., *Brain Rules: 12 Principles for Surviving and Thriving at Work, Home, and School.* (Seattle: Pear Press, 2008), 83.
7. Ibid.
8. Willis, J., *Research-based Strategies to Ignite Student Learning* (Alexandria, VA: Association for Supervision and Curriculum Development, 2006), 24, 26.
9. Medina, 81.
10. Ibid., 84.
11. McManus, E.R., *Wide Awake* (Nashville: Thomas Nelson, 2008), 42.
12. Willis (2006), 26.
13. Willis, J., "Brain-research Based Strategies to Help Students Turn Sensory Data into Long-term Memories," (presentation at Learning & the Brain: How to Shape the Developing Brain for Learning & Achievement, Cambridge, MA, November 16-18, 2007).
14. Ratey, J.J., *A User's Guide to the Brain: Perception, Attention, and the Four Theaters of the Brain* (New York: Pantheon Books, 2001), 247.
15. Wolfe, P., *Brain Matters: Translating Research into Classroom Practice* (Alexandria, VA: Association for Supervision and Curriculum Development, 2001), 103.
16. Medina, 204-205.
17. Immordino-Yang, 187, 190-191.

Chapter 3

1. Restak, R., *The Naked Brain: How the Emerging Neurosociety is Changing How We Live, Work, and Love* (New York: Harmony Books, 2006), 59-60.
2. Karpicke, J.D. & Roediger, H.L. III., "The Critical Importance of Retrieval for Learning," *Science,* 319, no. 5865 (2008): 966-968.

Chapter 4

image ©iStockphoto.com/deliormanli

1. Wolfe, P., *Brain Matters: Translating Research into Classroom Practice* (Alexandria, VA: Association for Supervision and Curriculum Development, 2001), 84.
2. Root-Bernstein, R. & Root-Bernstein, M., *Sparks of Genius: The 13 Thinking Tools of the World's Most Creative People* (Boston: Mariner Books, 2001), 118.
3. Sousa, D., *How the Brain Learns*, 2nd ed., (Thousand Oaks, CA: Corwin Press, Inc., 2001).
4. Wiggins, G. & McTighe, J., "Examining the Teaching Life," *Educational Leadership,* 63, no. 6 (2006): 26-29.

5. Zull, J.E., *The Art of Changing the Brain: Exploring the Practice of Teaching by Exploring the Biology of Learning* (Sterling, VA: Stylus Publishing, 2002), 185.

Chapter 5

image ©iStockphoto.com/sjlocke

1. Tredinnick, M., *Writing Well: The Essential Guide* (New York: Cambridge University Press, 2008), 44-45.

Chapter 6

image ©iStockphoto.com/traveler1116

1. O'Connor, K., "Foreword," in Butler, S.M. & McMunn, N.D., *A Teacher's Guide to Classroom Assessment: Understanding and Using Assessment to Improve Student Learning* (San Francisco: Jossey-Bass, 2006), xiii.
2. Mentkowsi, M., & Associates, *Learning That Lasts: Integrating Learning, Development, and Performance in College and Beyond* (San Francisco: Jossey-Bass, 2000), 229.
3. Black, P. & Wiliam, D., "Inside the Black Box: Raising Standards Through Classroom Assessment," *Phi Delta Kappa,* 80, no. 2 (October 1998), 139-148.
4. Wiggins, G. & McTighe, J., "Examining the Teaching Life," *Educational Leadership* 63, no. 6 (March 2006), 26-29.
5. Leahy, S., Lyon, C., Thompson, M., & Wiliam, D. (2005). "Classroom Assessment Minute by Minute, Day by Day," *Educational Leadership,* 63, no. 3 (November 2005), 18-24.
6. Wiggins, G., "Healthier Testing Made Easy," *Edutopia* (April-May 2006). http://www.edutopia.org/healthier-testing-made-easy
7. Butler, S.M. & McMunn, N.D., *A Teacher's Guide to Classroom Assessment: Understanding and Using Assessment to Improve Student Learning* (San Francisco: Jossey-Bass, 2006), xxv.
8. Washburn, K.D., *Analysis of Reading Comprehension and Thinking Process Achievement Based on Neurocognitive Research* (Lynchburg, VA: Doctoral Dissertation, Liberty University, 2006).
9. Hattie, J., quoted in Marzano, R.J., *What Works in Schools: Translating Research into Action* (Alexandria, VA: Association for Supervision and Curriculum Development, 2003), 37.
10. Black, 139.
11. Zull, J.E., *The Art of Changing the Brain: Exploring the Practice of Teaching by Exploring the Biology of Learning* (Sterling, VA: Stylus Publishing, 2002), 63.
12. Marzano, 37.
13. Willis, J., *Research-based Strategies to Ignite Student Learning* (Alexandria, VA: Association for Supervision and Curriculum Development, 2006), 82.

14. Mentkowski, 227.
15. Reeder, E., "Measuring What Counts: Memorization Versus Understanding," *Edutopia.* (Feb-March 2002). http://www.edutopia.org/measuring-what-counts-memorization-versus-understanding
16. Willis, 77.
17. Washburn.

Chapter 7

image ©iStockphoto.com/ftwitty

1. Mamet. D., "Introduction," in Rose, R., *Twelve Angry Men* (New York: Penguin Books, 2006), viii-ix.
2. Halpern, D., *Thought and Knowledge: An Introduction to Critical Thinking* (Mahwah, NJ: Lawrence Erlbaum Associates, 2003), 6.
3. Erlauer, L.,*The Brain-compatible Classroom* (Alexandria, VA: Association for Supervision and Curriculum Development, 2003), 83.
4. Barell, J., *Developing More Curious Minds* (Alexandria, VA: Association for Supervision and Curriculum Development, 2003), 22.
5. Paul, R., *Critical Thinking: How to Prepare Students for a Rapidly Changing World* (Santa Rosa, CA: The Foundation for Critical Thinking, 1995).
6. Mighton, J., *The Myth of Ability: Nurturing Mathematical Ability in Every Child* (New York: Walker & Co., 2003), 26.
7. Halpern, D., & Hakel, M.D., "Learning That Lasts a Lifetime: Teaching for Long-term Retention and Transfer," in Halpern, D.F., & Hakel, M.D. (Eds.), *Applying the Science of Learning to University and Beyond*, Vol. 89 (San Francisco: Jossey-Bass, 2002), 4.
8. Graesser, A.C., Person, N.K., & Hu, X., "Improving Comprehension Through Discourse Processing," in Halpern, D.F., & Hakel, M.D. (Eds.), *Applying the Science of Learning to University and Beyond*, Vol. 89 (San Francisco: Jossey-Bass, 2002), 33.
9. Groopman, J., *How Doctors Think* (Boston: Houghton Mifflin, 2007), 5.
10. Stronge, J.H., *Qualities of Effective Teachers,* 2nd ed. (Alexandria, VA: Association for Supervision and Curriculum Development, 2007), 74.
11. Paul, R., Why Students and Teachers Don't Reason Well. http://criticalthinking.org/page.cfm?PageID=603&CategoryID=69.
12. Ibid.
13. Paul, R. & Elder, L., *The Miniature Guide to Critical Thinking Concepts and Tools* (Santa Rosa, CA: The Foundation for Critical Thinking, 2006), 9.
14. Paul, R., & Elder, L., *Critical Thinking: Tools for Taking Charge of Your Learning and Your Life* (Upper Saddle River, NJ: Prentice Hall, 2002), 35.
15. Siegal, D.J., *The Mindful Brain: Reflection and Attunement in the Cultivation of Well-being* (New York: W. W. Norton and Co., 2007), 128.

16. Stein, K., *The Genius Engine: Where Memory, Reason, Passion, Violence, and Creativity Intersect in the Human Brain* (Hoboken, NJ: John Wiley & Sons, Inc., 2007), 95.

17. Scriven, M. & Paul, R., Defining Critical Thinking. http://www.criticalthinking.org/page.cfm?PageID=410&CategoryID=51.

18. Paul & Elder (2002), xviii.

19. Nosich, G.M., *Learning to Think Things Through: A Guide to Critical Thinking Across the Curriculum* (Upper Saddle River, NJ: Prentice Hall, 2001), 10.

20. Sire, J., *Why Good Arguments Often Fail* (Downers Grove, IL: InterVarsity Press, 2006).

21. Groopman, 157-165.

22. Ibid., 167-169.

23. Hart, J., *A Writer's Coach: An Editor's Guide to Words that Work* (New York: Pantheon Books, 2006), 7.

24. Stout, M., "Critical Thinking, Imagination, and New Knowledge in Education Research," in Egan, K., Stout, M., & Takaya, K. (Eds.), *Teaching and Learning Outside the Box: Inspiring Imagination Across the Curriculum* (New York: Teachers College Press, 2007), 45.

25. Barell, 80.

26. Ruggiero, V. R., *Beyond Feelings: A Guide to Critical Thinking*, 7th ed. (New York: McGraw-Hill, 2003), 17.

27. Sire.

28. Hart.

29. Wikipedia, Talk: Sons of Liberty. http://en.wikipedia.org/wiki/Talk:Sons_of_Liberty.

30. Meltzer, M., *The American Revolutionaries: A History in Their Own Words 1750-1800* (New York: HaperTrophy, 1993).

31. Stronge, 69.

32. Willis, J., *Research-based Strategies to Ignite Student Learning* (Alexandria, VA: Association for Supervision and Curriculum Development, 2006), 19.

33. Rose, R., *Twelve Angry Men* (New York: Penguin Books, 2006), 19, 66.

Chapter 8

images ©iStockphoto.com/perkmeux & stocksnapper

1. Andreasen, N.C., *The Creative Brain: The Science of Genius* (New York: Penguin Group, 2005), 77-78.

2. Ibid.

3. Lockman Foundation, *New American Standard Bible* (La Habra, CA: The Lockman Foundation, 1995), Genesis 1:1-2.

4. Henry, M., *Matthew Henry's Commentary* (Vol. 1), (McLean, VA: Mac Donald Pub. Co., 1985), 3.

5. Holl, S., *Parallax* (New York: Princeton Architectural Press, 2001), 346.

6. Holl, S., Phenomena and Idea. http://www.stevenholl.com/writings/phenomena.html

7. Root-Bernstein, R. & Root-Bernstein, M., *Sparks of Genius: The 13 Thinking Tools of the World's Most Creative People* (Boston: Mariner Books, 2001).

8. Miller, G., "A Surprising Connection Between Memory and Imagination," *Science*, 315, (2007), 312.

9. Berns, G., *Iconoclast: A Neuroscientist Reveals How to Think Differently* (Boston: Harvard Business School Publishing, 2008), 54.

10. Ward, T.B., Smith, S.M. & Finke, R.A., "Creativity, the Self, and the Environment," in Sternberg, R. (Ed.), *Handbook of Creativity* (New York: Cambridge University Press, 1999), 192.

11. Holl, S., Pallasmaa, J. & Pérez-Gómez, A., *Questions of Perception: Phenomenology of Architecture* (San Francisco: William Stout Publishers, 2006), 36.

12. Robinson, K., We are Educating People out of Their Creativity. http://www.inter-actions.biz/blog/2007/05/we_are_educating_people_out_of.html.

13. Bassett, P.F., Independent Thinking: Creativity in Schools. http://www.nais.org/publications/ismagazinearticle.cfm?Itemnumber=475&sn.ItemNumber=145956&tn.ItemNumber=145958.

14. Robinson, K., *Out of Our Minds: Learning to be Creative* (Chichester, West Sussex, UK: Capstone Publishing Limited, 2001), 113.

15. Egan, K., *An Imaginative Approach to Teaching* (San Francisco: Jossey-Bass, 2005), xii.

16. Rappaport, J., Arts Skills are Life Skills.http://www.boston.com/news/education/k_12/articles/2007/06/12/arts_skills_are_life_skills/.

17. Malesky, R. (Senior Producer), "Honoring the Very Best of the Worst in Fiction," Radio broadcast, (Washington, D.C.: National Public Radio, July 1, 2007).

18. Turner, M., *The Literary Mind: The Origins of Thought and Language* (New York: Oxford University Press, 1996), i.

19. Flaherty, A.W., *The Midnight Disease: The Drive to Write, Writer's Block, and the Creative Brain* (Boston: Houghton Mifflin, 2004), 230.

20. Heath, C. & Heath, D., *Made to Stick: Why Some Ideas Survive and Others Die* (New York: Random House, 2007), 205-206.

21. Egan, 10.

22. Kramer, M., "Reporting for Narrative: Ten Overlapping Rules," in Kramer, M. & Call, W. (Eds.), *Telling True Stories: A Nonfiction Writers' Guide from the Nieman Foundation at Harvard University* (New York: Penguin Group, 2007), 24.

23. Berns, 33.
24. Egan, 42.
25. Ibid.
26. Zull, J.E., *The Art of Changing the Brain: Exploring the Practice of Teaching by Exploring the Biology of Learning* (Sterling, VA: Stylus Publishing, 2002), 182.

Chapter 9

image ©iStockphoto.com/ClaudiaKnieling

1. Tredinnick, M., *Writing Well: The Essential Guide* (New York: Cambridge University Press, 2008), 226.
2. Gawande, A., *Complications: A Surgeon's Notes on an Imperfect Science* (New York: Picador, 2002), 29-30.
3. Stronge, J.H., *Qualities of Effective Teachers,* 2nd Edition (Alexandria, VA: Association for Supervision and Curriculum Development, 2007), 29.
4. Sergiovanni, T.J., *Moral Leadership: Getting to the Heart of School Improvement* (San Francisco: Jossey-Bass, 1992), 88.
5. Gawande, A., *Better: A Surgeon's Notes on Performance* (New York: Henry Holt, 2007), 230.
6. Kaiser, H.J., Henry J. Kaiser Quotes. http://thinkexist.com/quotes henry_j._kaiser/.

Afterword

image ©iStockphoto.com/Devonyu

1. Trevor M., "My Favorite Quotes about Education (part one)," 2009. Available at http://www.blogcatalog.com/blog/edutechnophobia/894af54 96c8e557d970d5197c346d847.

INDEX

U

W

Z